Mutiny!

T0097025

Drawn & Etched by   Lieut? Col? Batty

George Young, & his Wife (Hannah Adams),
of Pitcairns Island.

From Sketches by Lieut? Smith, of H. M. S. Blofsom.

Published by John Murray, Albemarle Street, 1831

Mutiny!

•THE REAL HISTORY OF THE *H.M.S. BOUNTY* •

Sir John Barrow

New Introduction by **Edward E. Leslie**

Cooper Square Press

First Cooper Square Press edition 2003

This Cooper Square Press paperback edition of *Mutiny!: The Real History of the H.M.S. Bounty* is an unabridged republication of the edition first published in London in 1831 and originally titled *The Eventful History of the Mutiny and Piratical Seizure of H.M.S. Bounty: Its Causes and Consequences.* It is supplemented with a new introduction by Edward E. Leslie.

New introduction copyright © 2003 by Edward E. Leslie

All rights reserved. No part of this book may be reproduced in any form or by any electronic or mechanical means, including information storage and retrieval systems, without written permission from the publisher, except by a reviewer who may quote passages in a review.

Published by Cooper Square Press
A Member of the Rowman & Littlefield Publishing Group
200 Park Avenue South, Suite 1109
New York, New York 10003-1503
www.coopersquarepress.com

Distributed by National Book Network

Library of Congress Control Number: 2002116074

ISBN 0-8154-1251-7 (pbk : alk. paper)

♻™ The paper used in this publication meets the minimum requirements of American National Standard for Information Sciences—Permanence of Paper for Printed Library Materials, ANSI/NISO Z39.48-1992.

Manufactured in the United States of America.

CONTENTS.

LIST OF PLATES.

INTRODUCTION TO THE
COOPER SQUARE PRESS
EDITION

SIR John Barrow has been called the "father of modern Arctic exploration." He was also the force behind the African expeditions to chart the course of the Niger River and to search for the legendary city of Timbuktu. But the Arctic remained an object of intense fascination for him from the time he was a young man, when he first sailed to Greenland. Furthermore, as a matter of patriotic pride, he wanted British sailors—not the Russians or, God forbid, the upstart Americans—to be the first to discover the fabled and long-sought Northwest Passage. As a result, he planned and dispatched a number of famous (though often-failed and sometimes disastrous) expeditions to the Arctic.

Although Barrow was the son of a struggling farmer, his diligence and hard work, administrative ability and determination, and charm and what today would be called networking skills, earned him the post of second secretary to the Admiralty, a position of immense—albeit behind-the-scenes—power that he held for forty years. There was a succession of first secretaries who

theoretically had greater authority, but they came
and went. His influence derived from his longevity
(one historian referred to Barrow as the "perma-
nent" secretary to the Admiralty), and he possessed the successful bureaucrat's gift for endearing
himself to those above him and, indeed, to anyone
who could do him good.

In addition to his duties at the Admiralty, Barrow, who left school at age thirteen, managed to
write twelve volumes of nonfiction, one hundred
ninety-five essays and reviews, and twelve articles
for the *Encyclopaedia Britannica*. His biograph-
ies of Lord Howe and Lord Anson continue to be
used as sources by historians and scholars, and
his account of the *Bounty* mutiny has been re-
printed in various editions since it was originally
published in 1831.

Having made voyages to China and what is now
South Africa in his youth, he became a leading
British authority on Chinese, Australasian, and
African affairs. He used his writings to make his
countrymen aware of what used to be called "the
wider world." As British historian Christopher
Lloyd put it in *Mr. Barrow of the Admiralty*, the
only full-scale biography of Sir John that has ever
been written:

> By the time of his death in the middle of the nine-
> teenth century, Britain, by virtue of her indus-
> trial and maritime superiority, was the centre of
> that wider world. The British Empire, a cause
> that lay close to his heart, was becoming the
> means by which European civilization was spread
> to distant lands unknown to previous genera-
> tions. The cultural expansion of Europe had been

gathering strength over the past three centuries, a tidal movement in history that has now been on the ebb for fifty years. In his own lifetime, Mr. Barrow of the Admiralty was undoubtedly one of those chiefly responsible for piloting his country into the age of her maritime and imperial supremacy.

Of course, Professor Lloyd wrote those words in 1970, a decade or so before the politically correct movement transformed the study of history into a morality play devoid of nuance and with simplistic, absolute notions of good and evil. The paragraph seems remarkably innocent today or at least antique given its lack of even a *pro forma* condemnation of British imperialism.

* * *

The Canadian historian, Pierre Berton, writing in *Arctic Grail*, described Barrow as "a moon-faced man with short-cropped hair, bristling black brows, and the tenacious temperament of a bull terrier." Berton added:

> In his job he took all the latitude allowed. He was responsible for the internal operations of the Admiralty, but in that role he could be highly selective. If you wanted to get on in the Navy it was useful to be on the right side of the second secretary—and it helped if you were a member of the upper crust. Barrow, the dirt farmer's son, had some of the snobbery of the British working class.

As for his being the father of modern Arctic exploration:

He wasn't imaginative, but he was curious. He shared with his contemporaries that passion for charts and statistics that was the mark of the English adventurer. The "most honourable and useful" employment for the Navy in peacetime, Barrow felt, was to complete the geographical and hydrographical surveys that had been launched in the previous century by such seamen as Cook and Vancouver.

The last expedition that Barrow planned before his retirement was the Franklin Expedition of 1845, which became the greatest tragedy of polar exploration—perhaps the greatest tragedy in the history of exploration—resulting in the loss of 129 men, most notably the leader, Sir John Franklin, a British hero. Over the next ten years, fifty search expeditions were dispatched in the futile effort to find survivors. Some searchers died, several ships were lost, and great sums of money were expended, until at last it became known that all were dead, some, shockingly, having committed survival cannibalism on their death march south.

Barrow's name appears in a footnote to another famous historical event. In 1815, when British authorities were arguing over where to imprison the defeated but still immensely dangerous Napoleon, Barrow forcefully advocated a bleak and remote island he had visited on one of his youthful voyages: St. Helena. Barrow was the only Admiralty official who had ever been to the island, but he nevertheless won the debate. As Prime Minister Robert Banks Jenkinson expressed it subsequently, "Mr. Barrow . . . decidedly recommended St. Helena as the place in the world the best calcu-

lated for the confinement for such a person. . . .
At such a distance and in such a place, all intrigue
would be impossible, and being withdrawn so far
from the European world, he would very soon be
forgotten." Napoleon knew of the island, and
when, while still confined on a British warship, he
was informed that he would be exiled there, he
cried, "No, no, not St. Helena. I will not leave
here. I will not go to St. Helena. I prefer death
here."

* * *

Berton is not the only historian to describe
Barrow's father, Roger, as a "dirt farmer." It is
an old phrase, but an odd one, especially in this
case since, rice not being an English crop and the
agricultural science of hydroponics being an invention of the twentieth century, one wonders
what else Roger might be expected to have farmed
in besides dirt. Surely the phrase is meant to convey an approximation to poverty. Roger and his
wife Mary (*née* Dawson) lived in a small cottage
adjacent to several fields. Roger and various relatives worked the fields, meaning that he was just
one or two steps above being a farm hand.

In Sir John's *An Auto-biographical Memoir*,
published in 1847 when he was eighty-three, he
reported that the cottage had been passed down
through his mother's ancestors for 200 years—a
remarkable length of time, the more so because
the cottage still exists today. The nearest hamlet
was Dragleybeck* and the nearest town Ul-

* The modern rendering of the town's name is Dragley Beck, and
since Barrow's time the final "e" has been dropped from Ulver-
stone. In 1895, Sir John's son, John Barrow, Jr., gave the cottage

verstone—two wonderful, Dickensian English
names—situated in north Lancashire. Barrow was
born in the cottage on June 19, 1764. The only
formal education he ever received was at the
Town Bank Grammar School where he studied:
Greek, Latin, mathematics, and Shakespeare. As
noted before, he left school at age thirteen, having
been hired to survey a local estate and to tutor a
midshipman older than himself. From his pupil he
learned navigation. Continuing to read and study,
Sir John also pursued astronomy. "If ever there
was a self-educated man who made a success of
life by the industrious cultivation of his talents, it
was John Barrow," observed Professor Lloyd.

His father pressured him to become a priest,
but, lacking the vocation, he found work as an ap-
prentice, keeping the accounts of an iron foundry
instead. When the owner died, a friend offered
Barrow a berth on a whaler. Over the course of a
summer the ship visited Spitzbergen Island, Nor-
way, and Greenland, killing six whales near the
ice pack.

After a few months Barrow was back on land,
teaching school in Greenwich. He supplemented
his meager salary by privately tutoring pupils.
One was Thomas Staunton, who became his life-
long friend. Thomas's father, Sir George Staunton, also befriended Barrow and became his first
patron. When the skilled and shrewd diplomat
George, Earl of Macartney, was appointed the
first British ambassador to China in 1792, Sir

to the town of Ulverston. Today it is a museum devoted to the life
and work of Sir John and to the Barrow family.

George Staunton was part of the embassy, and he arranged for his son and Barrow to go along, too. As the principal purpose of dispatching Lord Macartney to the Celestial Empire was to negotiate a treaty of commerce, British manufacturers sent a wide variety of goods as presents to the emperor: among other things, there were many crates of machinery and a dissembled planetarium, as well as a hot-air balloon, a diving bell, and even a coach and four horses. Barrow, who was now twenty-eight years old and who had learned Chinese from missionaries just before setting sail, acted as quartermaster; his duties included safeguarding the presents. Also accompanying the delegation was an eccentric Scottish "professor of philosophy" named Dinwiddie (another one of those wonderful Dickensian names), whose assignment was to demonstrate the various machines, to assemble and operate the planetarium, to ascend in the balloon, and to descend in the diving bell. Since he was the inventor of what he called "philosophical fireworks," he would demonstrate the pyrotechnic devices—to the Chinese, who invented fireworks!—as well as perform, according to Lord Macartney's instructions, "experiments on air, electricity, mechanics, and other branches of experimental philosophy; astronomical and other calculations."

Poor Dinwiddie must have felt terribly deflated because, as it turned out, Emperor Chien Lung, who was eighty-three years old, declined to allow him to perform any experiments or to demonstrate any of the items. The emperor and his advisors regarded all these things as nothing more

than children's toys. The rest of the mission was a
failure, too: the Chinese refused to make a treaty
with the British, whom they considered their infe-
riors. In the long run, China would be forced to
trade by defeat in war, not by successful diplo-
macy.

But Barrow was able to look on the bright side
of things:

> By the mission to China we obtained a knowledge
> of the navigation of the Yellow Sea, hitherto un-
> visited by European ships, and of the wide gulph
> of Petchlee to the very mouth of the river leading
> to the capital [Beijing]; it furnished an opportu-
> nity to those who composed it of travelling more
> than a thousand miles through the heart of the
> Empire; and it has been the means of making us
> somewhat better informed of the real character
> of the Chinese nation, which has been most ex-
> travagantly misrepresented.

While journeying through China, Barrow had
been able to visit shrines, temples, and farms, and
he had conversed with mandarins and peasants
alike. He had sketched plants, people, buildings,
and landscapes, and he had collected various bo-
tanical samples. He had also developed an ap-
preciation for Chinese paintings and porcelain,
though not for the Chinese practice of using
human excrement as fertilizer. There was "not a
water-closet in all China," he lamented. Everywhere he went the smell appalled him. However,
he had developed the highest regard for the Chinese people and admired their friendliness and
industry.

From the intercourse I had with all ranks [he recalled twelve years later], I should say that the natural faculties of the Chinese mind are of the first order, but, misdirected in youth, and confined and confirmed to one fixed unalterable course through life, which no exuberance of talent can venture to turn into a new channel, no progressive improvement can therefore be looked for, in moral or physical knowledge—no discovery in arts or science. . . . I must say that the impression left on my mind, and mostly on the minds of my companions, was that in our estimation of the character of the Chinese, on leaving England, we were far from doing them that justice, which on a closer acquaintance we found them to deserve.

Arriving back home with the rest of the embassy in early September 1794, almost two full years after embarking from Portsmouth, he set about correcting the misimpression that his fellow Britons had of China by writing several books and articles and by making himself, as Christopher Lloyd put it, "the leading sinologist of the day." Lloyd added that "John Barrow did more than anyone else in his generation to bring China to the attention of the Western world."

Before long, he was offered another chance to travel, this time to a dramatically different, though no less exotic, locale: South Africa. His newfound patron, Lord Macartney, had been appointed governor of the "Cape Colony" and took Barrow along as his private secretary. According to Professor Lloyd:

It was Barrow's lively curiosity about every sort of subject, his industrious habits of taking notes,

collecting specimens, making observations, as
well as his training as a surveyor, which made
him such a suitable choice. Aged thirty-three, he
was healthy, hard working, honest, good at figures, a well-informed amateur botanist and geolo-
gist, and possessing a pleasant, sociable manner.
He was unmarried and unattached at home. . . .
The world was his oyster, so he jumped at the invitation to visit and record a part of the world,
which at that date was only known as a victualling
base on the road to India.

The governor's party departed from Portsmouth
in January 1797, and arrived at the Cape the following May. Lady Anne Barnard, wife of the colony's secretary, was immediately and favorably
impressed with Barrow. She characterized him in
a letter to a friend in London as "one of the plea-
santest, best-informed and most eager-minded
young men in the world about everything curious
or worth attention."

Barrow and his admirer had hardly gotten to
know each other before Lord Macartney sent him
to Graaf Reinet, deep in the interior of the country. There were no reliable maps, but Barrow resolutely set off on horseback, accompanied by a
couple of ox-drawn wagons, one other white man,
and several Hottentot drivers and servants. They
crossed mountains and deserts. At night Barrow
slept in a ship's hammock slung in a tent. During
the day the beauty of the country astonished him.
He collected specimens, made observations, and
expertly shot all manner of game with a double-
barreled rifle that he had inherited from a friend
who had committed suicide.

He was impressed with the "Koussie" (Zulus) he encountered, in contrast to the servile and, as he thought, ugly Hottentots whom he had observed on the coast. A few years later, he recalled that "[the Koussie were] the finest specimens of the human figure I ever beheld. They possessed a firmness of carriage and an open, manly demeanour, which, added to the good nature that illuminated their features, declared them at once to be equally unconscious of fear, suspicion, or treachery."

Having made the first census and drawn the first accurate map of the region, Barrow returned to Cape Town. He reported presciently to Lord Macartney on the ongoing, round-robin strife among the Boers, Hottentots, and Zulus, and on the dismaying propensity of both Bantus and Boers to exterminate the Bushmen. The Bushmen's vivid and richly colored rock paintings entranced Barrow, and although he found these "little people" to be physically unprepossessing, to say the least, they had qualities he admired:

These unfortunate beings are in every respect, I should suppose, the ugliest of all human nature: the flat nose, high cheek-bones, prominent chin, and concave visage partake much of the apish character, which their keen eyes, always in motion, does not tend to diminish. The upper lid of this organ, as in that of the Chinese and the Hottentots, is rounded into the lower on the side next to the nose. They are known in the colony, from this circumstance probably, by the name of Chinese Hottentots. The activity of this diminutive race is incredibly great. It is said that the klipspringing antelope can scarcely excel them in leaping from rock to rock, and that on rough ground and up the sides of mountains horsemen have no chance of keeping pace with them; yet the form of their bodies would not appear to indicate this. The great curvature of the spine inwards and the remarkable extended posteriors are characteristic of the whole Hottentot race; but in some of the little Bosjesmans they are carried to such an extravagant degree as to excite laughter. In most other respects, mentally at least, they differ very widely. In disposition the latter is lively and cheerful; in his person active; adverse from idleness, he seldom wants employment. Concealed by day in his hovel, for fear of the Boers, he will dance on moonlight nights from the setting to the rising of the sun. Yet every morsel the Bosjesman eats is earned with danger and fatigue— danger from their inveterate enemies the Boers, and fatigue in searching and laying out plans for capturing different kinds of game.

While in South Africa, he did every thing he could to stop the extermination of the Bushmen.

Barrow returned from his seven-month trip in December 1797. His map and his notes so impressed Lord Macartney that he soon dispatched him to survey what is now called South West Africa. Mapping the terrain and collecting specimens, he was gone three months and was back in Cape Town in June 1798. During the two trips he had traveled a total of 3,000 miles on foot, on horseback, and by wagon. Macartney appointed him Auditor General of Public Accounts at twice his previous salary.

The raise in pay enabled Barrow to marry

Anne Maria Trüter, whose father was a local
judge. The newlyweds bought a cottage at the base
of Table Mountain. Anne gave birth to a son,
George, who, sadly, lived only briefly. (Lady Anne
and Sir John would remain married for fifty years
until his death in 1848. In addition to the infant
who died in South Africa, they had six children,
all of whom reached adulthood, and one of whom,
the aforementioned John Barrow, Jr., became a
secretary in the Admiralty and, indeed, oversaw
the hunt for the Franklin party after his father's
retirement.)

Worsening gout forced Macartney to return to
England. He carried with him a manuscript that
Barrow had written, and arranged for its publication under the title *Travels into the Interior of
Southern Africa* (1801). Barrow and his wife returned to England in May 1803. The day after
they arrived, Barrow reported to the Admiralty,
where he was appointed second secretary at the
behest of Lord Macartney and Barrow's latest patron, General Francis Dundas, whom he had gotten to know during his stay in South Africa.

Barrow would spend nearly the rest of his life
at the Admiralty and deserves much of the credit
for its modernization. In 1835, as the result of appeals to King William IV by several friends and
still more patrons, Barrow was honored with a
baronet because of his stellar public service, his
literary achievements, and scientific accomplishments.

Today, of course, Barrow's life as a bureaucrat
is of interest to those who are close students of
British maritime history only because of the Afri-

can and Arctic expeditions that he planned and
promoted. Readers wishing to know more about
the expeditions are advised to read Fergus Flem-
ing's *Barrow's Boys.*

After retiring in 1845 at the age of eighty, Sir
John devoted the remaining three years of his life
to various writing projects, including his autobi-
ography. He died in his sleep on November 23,
1848. He was buried at the Pratt Street church in
Camden Town. A marble obelisk marks his tomb.

*   *   *

In writing *The Eventful History of the Mutiny
and Piratical Seizure of the H.M.S. Bounty,* as
this book was originally titled, Sir John had access
to both official and unofficial documents, as well
as to the journal of James Morrison and the papers of Captain Peter Heywood, R. N., who had
been a sixteen-year-old midshipman on the
Bounty. Thus, Barrow was able to correct errors
and misstatements in earlier accounts of the mutiny. "The fidelity of his own narrative is not to be
questioned," concluded British admiral and historian Sir Cyprian A. G. Bridge in an essay published in 1914. But Sir Cyprian added that "He
has sometimes blamed, and in vigorous terms,
persons whom fuller evidence has shown to be un-
deserving of his censure." As an Admiralty official
Barrow could not even appear to condone mutiny,
but his account shows some sympathy for the mutineers and champions at length the innocence of
Heywood.

William Bligh essentially blamed the "revolt"
on the crew's laziness and on their desire for Tahi-
tian women:

I can only conjecture that the mutineers had
flattered themselves with the hopes of a more
happy life among the Otaheiteans, than they
could possibly enjoy in England; and this, joined
to some female connections, most probably occasioned the whole transaction.

The women of Otaheite are handsome, mild,
and cheerful in their manners and conversation,
possessed of great sensibility, and have sufficient
delicacy to make them admired and beloved. The
chiefs were so attached to our people, that they
rather encouraged their stay among them than
otherwise, and even made them promises of large
possessions. Under these, and many other attendant circumstances, equally desirable, it is now
perhaps not so much to be wondered at, though
scarcely possible to have been foreseen, that a set
of sailors, most of them void of connections,
should be led away; especially when, in addition
to such powerful inducements, they imagined it in
their power to fix themselves in the midst of
plenty, on one of the finest islands in the world,
where they need not labour, and where the allurements of dissipation are beyond anything
that can be conceived.

However, Barrow, the dirt farmer's son who became a baronet and something of a snob, asserted
that the cause was Bligh's personality, especially
as it was expressed in the treatment of his subordinates. Although from a Cornish family that had
produced several distinguished Royal Navy officers, Bligh began his naval career in the merchant
service and entered the navy as a warrant officer
under Captain James Cook. "It was Bligh's misfortune not to have been educated in the cockpit

of a man-of-war among young gentlemen, which is
to the navy what a public school is to those who
are to move in civil society," wrote Barrow. "[He]
was a man of coarse habits, and entertained very
mistaken notions with regard to discipline. . . . His
temper was irritable in the extreme."

(Of course, the captain's tempestuous personality on the one hand, and the allurements of Tahi-
tian females and the prospect of a dissipated life
without the tiresome necessity of labor on the
other, are not mutually exclusive as explanations
for the mutiny.)

While acknowledging Bligh's virtues—his first-
rate abilities as a navigator, his "strong and imperious will," "indefatigable industry," and "great
physical powers of enduring long-continued hard-
ship," which served him and his loyal followers
well during the open boat journey—Sir Cyprian
was no less of a snob and no less judgmental than
Sir John had been:

> In fact he was not a gentleman either by bringing
> up or by nature. To speak plainly, he was a bully,
> and not a truthful one. He cursed and swore at
> his officers, called them vile names, and accused
> them without proof or reason of discreditable of-
> fenses. [He] could not confine himself to the
> truth. Sir John Barrow puts it very mildly when
> he says: 'The allegation that Bligh falsified his
> narrative it is to be feared is not without founda-
> tion.'
> In times of difficulty and danger Bligh was res-
> olute, self-possessed, and equal to emergencies. In
> the ordinary and unexciting or monotonous
> course of peace service he proved himself quite

unfitted for the command of men. He was a tyrant
whose mode of asserting his rights was brutal. It
is to the credit of the officers and men of the
Bounty that they recognised his good qualities,
whilst unable to tolerate his bad ones. If this had
not been the case he could not have kept his control of them as long as he did: and to it we may
attribute the wonderful success with which he
conducted his boatload of starving shipmates for
thousands of miles across the ocean.

Bligh's open boat journey is, in my opinion, one
of the great feats of seamanship and navigation in
the maritime history of Western civilization. It is
no small irony that the romantic aura of the mutineers and their escape to Pitcairn Island has
largely eclipsed Bligh's exploit in the popular
imagination.

Admiral Bridge offered another reason for the
mutiny: Bligh was purser as well as captain on the
Bounty, and, like other pursers, it was in his fi-
nancial interest to save money by either buying
inferior supplies or by short weighting the rations:

There is direct evidence that Bligh was determined not to be a loser in his victualling transactions, and there is strong presumptive evidence
that he at least tried to make a profit out of them.
If there is one thing that the British sailor hates
and despises in an officer more than any other
thing it is meanness: and if the meanness is practised at his expense, the sailor's hatred and contempt are greatly increased. He can tolerate a
bully, but a mean bully is more than 'lower deck'
flesh and blood can put up with. Bligh's mean-

ness, like his tyranny, was comprehensive. It embraced the officers as well as the 'foremast hands.'

Of course, shipboard conditions in the British navy in the days of sail were hardly ideal. Voyages lasted weeks or even months. The meals were monotonous and hardly digestible: salt beef and salt pork were issued on alternate days. A visit to a port allowed for the taking on of supplies of fresh vegetables, but these were depleted quickly. The fresh water allowance per man was dismayingly small. "Except in gales of wind, which do not occur so often as shore-going people think they do, the life on board was as monotonous as the food," observed Sir Cyprian.

Subordinates had little to think of except their own grievances, real or imagined, so that dissatisfaction with trifles was apt to grow into serious discontent. The life of the captain was nearly as monotonous as that of the crew; his, moreover, being largely solitary. As a result, he was inclined to magnify symptoms of disorder and make what were really trifling offences into serious delinquencies. Unsuitable food, the impossibility of taking sufficient bodily exercise, confined quarters, and—often enough—sultry climate, unfavourably affected men's livers, and made many peevish and some irritable to the verge of insanity. . . . A Captain Cook or a Commodore Anson, not to mention other South Sea navigators, would have conducted the breadfruit expedition without rendering those under their command dangerously discontented. To a man of Bligh's disposition and character, fine as we know that some of his qualities were, that was impossible in the circumstances of the voyage. Fletcher Christian's starting a mutiny was undoubtedly an act of madness, because it was the act of a man maddened by the conditions of life on board the ship combined with Bligh's brutal and intolerable tyranny.*

Given the levels of rage and frustration the mutineers must have felt, it is surprising that they did not kill Bligh and his loyal followers. Only by massacring them could the mutineers be certain they would not be able to alert British authorities to the mutiny. Yet, the mutineers provided Bligh and the rest with five days of food, enough to sustain them until they reached a nearby island, and also gave them a compass, the launch rather than the unseaworthy cutter, and four cutlasses. Christian gave Bligh his own sextant and a book of nautical tables. The mutineers' allowing Bligh and the others to live and providing them with food, navigational tools, and the best boat speaks well for their humanity, or perhaps for their conditioning as British sailors and, in the case of Fletcher

* Historians and aficionados have long debated the causes of the mutiny and Bligh's culpability in it. Indeed, in *The Life of Vice-Admiral William Bligh*, published in 1936, the Australian historian Dr. George Mackaness devoted more than forty pages to ruminations over these matters. At least one historian has even theorized—without any solid supporting evidence—that Bligh and Christian had had a homosexual relationship during the voyage to Tahiti and that after the *Bounty* arrived at the island and Christian turned his attention to the Polynesian females, Bligh became jealous and took his anger out on the crew. Clearly, there is not enough room in this introduction to make a comprehensive examination of the mutiny's causes. I have highlighted Sir Cyprian's observations as a way of introducing the subject and because as a British admiral and historian who was born just fifty-one years after the mutiny, I think his perspective is unique.

Christian and the other rebellious officers, English gentlemen. Whatever the motives, setting Bligh, a superior navigator, free ultimately meant the capture of fourteen mutineers who chose to remain behind on Tahiti rather than sail for Pitcairn Island. (Seven of these men died of drowning aboard the shipwrecked *Pandora* or were executed.)

Bligh first landed at Tofoa, where hostile inhabitants killed one of his men, John Norton. Thereafter, Bligh sailed 3,618 nautical miles in a small open boat over the course of forty-nine days. Daily rations were dishearteningly meager. Still, Bligh brought all the men through save Norton. Sir Cyprian calls this "that most marvellous of all voyages of shipwrecked mariners." And it certainly was. Give the devil his due: whatever Bligh's faults as a peacetime naval officer, he was a brave and resolute man and an extraordinary navigator. He was also one hell of a seaman.

EDWARD E. LESLIE

EDWARD E. LESLIE is the author of *Desperate Journeys, Abandoned Souls: The True Story of Castaways and Other Survivors*, and *The Devil Knows How to Ride: The True Story of William Clarke Quantrill and His Confederate Raiders*. He lives in Massillon, Ohio.

PREFACE.

THE Editor of this little volume (for he presumes not to write *Author*) has been induced to bring into one connected view what has hitherto appeared only in detached fragments, (and some of these not generally accessible)—the historical narrative of an event which deeply interested the public at the time of its occurrence, and from which the naval service in particular, in all its ranks, may still draw instructive and useful lessons.

The story in itself is replete with interest. We are taught by *The Book* of sacred history, that the disobedience of our first parents entailed on our globe of earth a sinful and a suffering race : in our time there has sprung up from the most abandoned of this sinful family—from pirates, mutineers, and murderers—a little society which, under the precepts of that sacred volume, is characterized by religion, morality, and innocence. The discovery of this happy people, as unexpected as it was accidental, and all that regards their condition and history, partake so much of the romantic, as to render the story not ill adapted for an epic poem. Lord Byron, indeed, has partially treated the subject ; but by blending two incongruous stories, and leaving both of them imperfect, and by mixing up fact with fiction, has been less felicitous than usual ; for, beautiful as many passages in his ' Island' are, in a region where every tree, and flower, and fountain breathe poetry, yet as a whole the poem is feeble and deficient in dramatic effect.

There still remains to us at least one Poet, who, if he could be prevailed on to undertake it, would do justice to the story. To his suggestion the publication of the present narrative owes its appearance. But a higher object at present is engaging his attention, which, when completed, judging from that portion already before the public, will have raised a splendid and lasting monument to the name of William Sotheby, in his translation of the Iliad and the Odyssey.

To the kindness of Mrs. Heywood, the relict of the late Captain Peter Heywood, the Editor is indebted for those beautiful and affectionate letters, written by a beloved sister to her unfortunate brother, while a prisoner and under sentence of death; as well as for some occasional poetry, which displays an intensity of feeling, a tenderness of expression, and a high tone of sentiment, that do honour to the head and heart of this amiable and accomplished lady. Those letters also from the brother to his deeply afflicted family will be read with peculiar interest.

THE

EVENTFUL HISTORY

OF THE

MUTINY OF THE BOUNTY,

CHAPTER I.

OTAHEITE.

'THE gentle Island, and the genial soil,
The friendly hearts, the feasts without a toil,
The courteous manners, but from nature caught,
The wealth unhoarded, and the love unbought,
    .   .   .   .   .   .
The bread-tree, which, without the ploughshare, yields
The unreap'd harvest of unfurrow'd fields,
And bakes its unadulterated loaves
Without a furnace in unpurchased groves,
And flings off famine from its fertile breast,—
A priceless market for the gathering guest;—
These,' &c. ——   BYRON.

THE reign of George III. will be distinguished
in history by the great extension and improvement which geographical knowledge received under
the immediate auspices of this sovereign. At a
very early period, after his accession to the throne
of these realms, expeditions of discovery were
undertaken, 'not (as Dr. Hawkesworth observes)
with a view to the acquisition of treasure, or the
extent of dominion, but for the improvement of
commerce, and the increase and diffusion of know-

ledge.' This excellent monarch was himself no
mean proficient in the science of geography; and
it may be doubted if any one of his subjects, at
the period alluded to, was in possession of so
extensive or so well-arranged a cabinet of maps
and charts as his was, or who understood their
merits or their defects so well as he did.

The first expeditions that were sent forth, after
the conclusion of the war, were those of Byron,
Wallis, and Carteret. In the instructions to the
first of these commanders it is said, 'there is
reason to believe that lands and islands of great
extent, hitherto unvisited by any European power,
may be found in the Atlantic Ocean, between the
Cape of Good Hope and the Magellanic Strait,
within the latitudes convenient for navigation, and
in climates adapted to the produce of commodities
useful in commerce.' It could not require much
knowledge or consideration to be assured that,
between the Cape and the Strait, climates producing commodities useful in commerce, with
the exception of whales and seals, were likely to
be found. The fact was that, among the real
objects of this and other subsequent voyages,
there was one which had engaged the attention of
certain philosophers, from the time of the Spanish
navigator, Quiros : this able navigator had main-
tained that a *Terra Australis incognita* must
necessarily exist, somewhere in the high latitudes
of the southern hemisphere, to counterbalance the
great masses of land in those of the northern one,
and thus maintain a just equipoise of the globe.

While these expeditions were in progress, the
Royal Society, in 1768, addressed an application

to the king, praying him to appoint a ship of war to convey to the South Seas Mr. Alexander Dalrymple (who had adopted the opinion of Quiros), and certain others, for the main purpose, however, of observing the transit of Venus over the sun's disc, which was to happen in the year 1769. By the king's command, a bark of three hundred and seventy tons was taken up by the Admiralty to perform this service, but, as Mr. Dalrymple was a civilian, he could not be entrusted with the command of the ship, and on that account declined going in her.

The command was therefore conferred on Lieutenant James Cook, an officer of undoubted ability, and well versed in astronomy and the theory and practice of navigation, with whom the Royal Society associated Mr. Charles Green, who had long been assistant to Dr. Bradley, the astronomer royal, to aid him in the observation of the transit. Mr. Banks, a private gentleman of good fortune, who afterwards became the valuable and distinguished President of the Royal Society, and Dr. Solander, a Swedish gentleman of great acquirements, particularly in natural history, accompanied Lieutenant Cook on this interesting voyage. The islands of Marquesas de Mendoza, or those of Rotterdam or Amsterdam, were proposed by the Royal Society as proper places for making the observation. While fitting out, however, Captain Wallis returned from his expedition, and strongly recommended, as most suitable for the purpose, Port Royal Harbour, on an island he had discovered, to which he had given the name of ' King George's

Island,' and which has since been known by its
native name, *Otaheite* or *Tahite**.

This lovely island is most intimately connected
with the mutiny which took place on board the
Bounty, and with the fate of the mutineers and
their innocent offspring. Its many seducing
temptations have been urged as one, if not the
main, cause of the mutiny, which was supposed,
at least by the commander of that ship, to have
been excited by

' Young hearts which languish'd for some sunny isle,
Where summer years, and summer women smile,
Men without country, who, too long estranged,
Had found no native home, or found it changed,
And, half uncivilized, preferr'd the cave
Of some soft savage to the uncertain wave.'

It may be proper, therefore, as introductory to
the present narrative, to give a general description
of the rich and spontaneous gifts which Nature
has lavished on this once ' happy island ; '—of the
simple and ingenuous manners of its natives;—and
of those allurements which were supposed, erroneously however, to have occasioned the unfortunate catastrophe alluded to ;—to glance at

' The nymphs' seducements and the magic bower,'

as they existed at the period of the first intercourse

---

* The discovery of this island is owing to Fernandez de
Quiros in 1606, which he named *La Sagittaria*. Some
doubts were at first entertained of its identity with Otaheite,
but the small difference of a few miles in latitude, and about.
two degrees of longitude, the description as to size, the low
isthmus, the distance from it of any other island at all
similar, and above all, the geographical position—all prove
its identity—although Quiros calls it, what it certainly is
not, a low island.

between the Otaheitans and the crews of those
ships, which carried to their shores, in succession,
Wallis, Bougainville, and Cook.

The first communication which Wallis had with
these people was unfortunately of a hostile nature.
Having approached with his ship close to the
shore, the usual symbol of peace and friendship, a
branch of the plantain tree, was held up by a
native in one of the numerous canoes that surrounded the ship.   Great numbers, on being
invited, crowded on board the stranger ship, but
one of them, being butted on the haunches by a
goat, and turning hastily round, perceived it rear-
ing on its hind legs, ready to repeat the blow, was
so terrified at the appearance of this strange animal, so different from any he had ever seen, that,
in the moment of terror, he jumped overboard, and
all the rest followed his example with the utmost
precipitation.

This little incident, however, produced no mischief; but as the boats were sounding in the bay,
and several canoes crowding round them, Wallis
suspected the islanders had a design to attack
them, and, on this mere suspicion, ordered the
boats by signal to come on board, ' and at the
same time,' he says, ' to intimidate the Indians, I
fired a nine-pounder over their heads.'   This, as
might have been imagined, startled the islanders,
but did not prevent them from attempting immediately to cut off the cutter, as she was standing
towards the ship.   Several stones were thrown
into this boat, on which the commanding officer
fired a musket, loaded with buck-shot, at the man
who threw the first stone, and wounded him in the
shoulder.

Finding no good anchorage at this place, the ship proceeded to another part of the island, where, on one of the boats being assailed by the Indians in two or three canoes, with their clubs and paddles in their hands, 'Our people,' says the commander, ' being much pressed, were obliged to fire, by which one of the assailants was killed, and another much wounded.' This unlucky rencontre did not, however, prevent, as soon as the ship was moored, a great number of canoes from coming off the next morning, with hogs, fowls, and fruit. A brisk traffic soon commenced, our people exchanging knives, nails, and trinkets, for more substantial articles of food, of which they were in want. Among the canoes that came out last were some double ones of very large size, with twelve or fifteen stout men in each, and it was observed that they had little on board except a quantity of round pebble stones. Other canoes came off along with them, having only women on board; and while these females were assiduously practising their allurements, by attitudes that could not be misunderstood, with the view, as it would seem, to distract the attention of the crew, the large double canoes closed round the ship; and as these advanced, some of the men began singing, some blowing conchs, and others playing on flutes. One of them, with a person sitting under a canopy, approached the ship so close, as to allow this person to hand up a bunch of red and yellow feathers, making signs it was for the captain. He then put off to a little distance, and, on holding up the branch of a cocoanut tree, there was an universal shout from all the

canoes, which. at the same. moment moved towards the ship, and a. shower of stones was,
poured into her on every side. The guard. was
now ordered to, fire,. and' two of the quarter-deck,
guns, loaded with small shot, were fired among'
them at the same time, which created great terror,
and confusion,. and caused them to retreat to a
short distance. In a few minutes,. however, they
renewed. the attack. The great guns were now
ordered to. be discharged among them, and also,
into a mass of canoes that were putting off from,
the shore. It. is stated. that, at this time, there,
could. not. be less than three hundred, canoes about
the ship, having on board at least two thousand,
men. Again they dispersed, but having soon collected into something like order, they hoisted,
white streamers, and pulled towards the ship's,
stern, when they again began to throw stones,
with great force and dexterity, by the help of
slings, each of the stones weighing about two.
pounds,. and many of them wounded the people on,
board. At length a shot. hit the canoe that apparently had the chief on board, and cut it asunder,,
This was no sooner observed by the rest, than,
they all dispersed in such haste, that in. half an,
hour there was not. a single canoe to be seen ; and.
all the people who had crowded the shore fled,
over the hills, with the utmost precipitation. What,
was to happen on the following day was matter of.
conjecture, but this point was soon decided.

'The white man landed ;—need the rest be told?
The new world stretch'd its dusk hand to the old.'

Lieutenant Furneaux, on the next morning,
landed, without opposition,, close to a fine river

that fell into the bay—stuck up a staff on which was hoisted a pendant,—turned a turf,—and by this process took possession of the island in the name of his Majesty, and called it *King George the Third's Island.* Just as he was embarking, an old man, to whom the Lieutenant had given a few trifles, brought some green boughs, which he threw down at the foot of the staff, then retiring, brought about a dozen of his countrymen, who approached the staff in a supplicating posture, then retired and brought two live hogs, which they laid down at the foot of the staff, and then began to dance. After this ceremony the hogs were put into a canoe and the old man carried them on board, handing up several green plantain leaves, and uttering a sentence on the delivery of each. Some presents were offered him in return, but he would accept of none.

Concluding that peace was now established, and that no further attack would be made, the boats were sent on shore the following day to get water. While the casks were filling, several natives were perceived coming from behind the hills and through the woods, and at the same time a multitude of canoes from behind a projecting point of the bay. As these were discovered to be laden with stones, and were making towards the ship, it was concluded their intention was to try their fortune in a second grand attack. ' As to shorten the contest would certainly lessen the mischief, I determined,' says Captain Wallis, ' to make this action decisive, and put an end to hostilities at once.' Accordingly a tremendous fire was opened at once on all the groupes of canoes, which had the effect of immediately dispersing them. The fire was then directed into the wood, to drive out the islanders, who had assembled in large numbers, on which they all fled to the hill, where the women and children had seated themselves. Here they collected to the amount of several thousands, imagining themselves at that distance to be perfectly safe. The captain, however, ordered four shot to be fired over them, but two of the balls, having fallen close to a tree where a number of them were sitting, they were so struck with terror and consternation, that, in less than two minutes, not a creature was to be seen. The coast being cleared, the boats were manned and armed, and all the carpenters with their axes were sent on shore, with directions to destroy every canoe they could find; and we are told this service was effectually performed, and that more than fifty canoes, many of which were sixty feet long, and three broad, and lashed together, were cut to pieces.

This act of severity must have been cruelly felt by these poor people, who, without iron or any kind of tools, but such as stones, shells, teeth, and bones supplied them with, must have spent months and probably years in the construction of one of these extraordinary double boats.

Such was the inauspicious commencement of our acquaintance with the natives of Otaheite. Their determined hostility and perseverance in an unequal combat could only have arisen from one of two motives—either from an opinion that a ship of such magnitude, as they had never before beheld, could only be come to their coast to take

their country from them; or an irresistible
temptation to endeavour, at all hazards, to possess themselves of so valuable a prize. Be that
as it may, the dread inspired by the effects of the
cannon, and perhaps a conviction of the truth of
what had been explained to them, that the 'strangers wanted only provisions and water,' had the
effect of allaying all jealousy; for from the day of
the last action, the most friendly and uninterrupted
intercourse was established, and continued to the
day of the Dolphin's departure; and provisions of
all kinds, hogs, dogs, fruit, and vegetables, were
supplied in the greatest abundance, in exchange
for pieces of iron, nails, and trinkets.

As a proof of the readiness of these simple
people to forgive injuries, a poor woman, accompanied by a young man bearing a branch of the
plantain tree, and another man with two hogs,
approached the gunner, whom Captain Wallis had
appointed to regulate the market, and looking
round on the strangers with great attention, fixing
her eyes sometimes on one and sometimes on
another, at length burst into tears. It appeared
that her husband and three of her sons had been
killed in the attack on the ship. While this was
under explanation, the poor creature was so affected, as to require the support of the two young
men, who from their weeping were probably two
more of her sons. When somewhat composed,
she ordered the two hogs to be delivered to the
gunner, and gave him her hand in token of friendship, but would accept nothing in return.

Captain Wallis was now so well satisfied that
there was nothing further to apprehend from the

hostility of the natives, that he sent a party up
the country to cut wood, who were treated with
great kindness and hospitality by all they met, and
the ship was visited by persons of both sexes, who
by their dress and behaviour appeared to be of a
superior rank.   Among others was a tall lady
about five and forty years of age, of a pleasing
countenance and majestic deportment. She was
under no restraint, either from diffidence or fear,
and conducted herself with that easy freedom
which generally distinguishes conscious superiority
and habitual command.   She accepted some small
present which the captain gave her, with a good
grace and much pleasure; and having observed
that he was weak and suffering from ill health, she
pointed to the shore, which he understood to be an
invitation, and made signs that he would go thither
the next morning.   His visit to this lady displays
so much character and good feeling, that it will
best be described in the captain's own words.

' The next morning I went on shore for the first
time, and my princess or rather queen, for such by
her authority she appeared to be, soon after came
to me, followed by many of her attendants.   As
she perceived that my disorder had left me very
weak, she ordered her people to take me in their
arms, and carry me not only over the river, but all
the way to her house; and observing that some
of the people who were with me, particularly the
first lieutenant and purser, had also been sick, she
caused them also to be carried in the same manner, and a guard, which I had ordered out upon
the occasion, followed.   In our way, a vast multitude crowded about us, but upon her waving her

hand, without speaking a word, they withdrew,
and left us a free passage. When we approached
near her house, a great number of both sexes came
out to meet her ; these she presented to me, after
having intimated by signs that they were her relations, and taking hold of my hand she made
them kiss it.

' We then entered the house, which covered a
piece of ground three hundred and twenty-seven
feet long, and forty-two feet broad. It consisted
of a roof thatched with palm leaves, and raised
upon thirty-nine pillars on each side, and fourteen
in the middle. The ridge of the thatch, on the
inside, was thirty feet high, and the sides of the
house, to the edge of the roof, were twelve feet
high ; all below the roof being open. As soon as
we entered the house, she made us sit down, and
then calling four young girls, she assisted them to
take off my shoes, draw down my stockings, and
pull off my coat, and then directed them to smooth
down the skin, and gently chafe it with their
hands. The same operation was also performed
on the first lieutenant and the purser, but upon
none of those who appeared to be in health.
While this was doing, our surgeon, who had
walked till he was very warm, took off his wig to
cool and refresh himself : a sudden exclamation of
one of the Indians, who saw it, drew the attention
of the rest, and in a moment every eye was fixed
upon the prodigy, and every operation was suspended. The whole assembly stood some time
motionless, in silent astonishment, which could not
have been more strongly expressed, if they had
discovered that our friend's limbs had been screwed

on to the trunk. In a short time, however, the
young women who were chafing us, resumed their
employment, and having continued for about half
an hour, they dressed us again, but in this they
were, as may easily be imagined, very awkward;
I found great benefit, however, from the chafing,
and so did the lieutenant and the purser.

' After a little time our generous benefactress
ordered some bales of Indian cloth to be brought
out, with which she clothed me, and all that were
with me, according to the fashion of the country.
At first I declined the acceptance of this favour, but
being unwilling not to seem pleased with what was
intended to please me, I acquiesced. When 'we
went away, she ordered a very large sow, big with
young, to be taken down to the boat, and accompanied us thither herself. She had given directions to her people to carry me, as they had done
when I came, but as I chose rather to walk, she
took me by the arm, and whenever we came to a
plash of water or dirt, she lifted me over with as
little trouble as it would have cost me to have
lifted over a child, if I had been well.'

The following morning Captain Wallis sent her
a present by the gunner, who found her in the
midst of an entertainment given to at least a thousand people. The messes were put into shells of
cocoa-nuts, and the shells into wooden trays, like
those used by our butchers, and she distributed them
with her own hands to the guests, who were seated
in rows in the open air, round the great house.
When this was done, she sat down herself upon
a place somewhat elevated above the rest, and
two women, placing themselves, one on each side

of her, fed her, she opening her mouth as they
brought their hands up with the food. From this
time, provisions were sent to market in the greatest
abundance. The queen frequently visited the captain on board, and always with a present, but she
never condescended to barter, nor would she
accept of any return.

One day, after visiting her at her house, the captain at parting made her comprehend by signs,
that he intended to quit the island in seven days:
she immediately understood his meaning, and by
similar signs, expressed her wish that he should
stay twenty days; that he should go with her a
couple of days' journey into the country, stay
there a few days, return with plenty of hogs and
poultry, and then go away; but on persisting in
his first intention, she burst into tears, and it was
not without great difficulty that she could be pacified. The next time that she went on board, Captain Wallis ordered a good dinner for her entertainment and those chiefs who were of her party;
but the queen would neither eat nor drink. As
she was going over the ship's side, she asked, by
signs, whether he still persisted in leaving the
island at the time he had fixed, and on receiving
an answer in the affirmative, she expressed her
regret by a flood of tears; and as soon as her
passion subsided, she told the captain that she
would come on board again the following day.

Accordingly, the next day she again visited the
ship twice, bringing each time large presents of
hogs, fowls, and fruits. The captain, after expressing his sense of her kindness and bounty,
announced his intention of sailing the following

morning. This, as usual, threw her into tears, and after recovering herself, she made anxious inquiry when he should return; he said in fifty days, with which she seemed to be satisfied. ' She stayed on board,' says Captain Wallis, ' till night, and it was then with the greatest difficulty that she could be prevailed upon to go on shore. When she was told that the boat was ready, she threw herself down upon the arm-chest, and wept a long time, with an excess of passion that could not be pacified; at last, however, with the greatest reluctance, she was prevailed upon to go into the boat, and was followed by her attendants.'

The next day, while the ship was unmooring, the whole beach was covered with the inhabitants. The queen came down, and having ordered a double canoe to be launched, was rowed off by her own people, followed by fifteen or sixteen other canoes. She soon made her appearance on board, but, not being able to speak, she sat down and gave vent to her passion by weeping. Shortly after a breeze springing up, the ship made sail; and finding it now necessary to return into her canoe, ' she embraced us all,' says Captain Wallis, ' in the most affectionate manner, and with many tears; all her attendants also expressed great sorrow at our departure. In a few minutes she came into the bow of her canoe, where she sat weeping with inconsolable sorrow. I gave her many things which I thought would be of great use to her, and some for ornament; she silently accepted of all, but took little notice of any thing. About ten o'clock we had got without the reef, and a fresh breeze springing up, our Indian friends, and par-

ticularly the queen, once more bade us farewell,
with such tenderness of affection and grief, as filled
both my heart and my eyes.'

The tender passion had certainly caught hold of
one or both of these worthies; and if her Majesty's
language had been as well understood by Captain
Wallis, as that of Dido was to Æneas, when
pressing him to stay with her, there is no doubt it
would have been found not less pathetic—

> Nec te noster amor, nec te data dextera quondam,
> Nec moritura teuet crudeli funere Dido?

This lady, however, did not sink, like the ' miser-
rima Dido,' under her griefs ; on the contrary, we
find her in full activity and animation, and equally
generous, to Lieut. Cook and his party, under the
name of *Oberea*, who, it now appeared, was no
queen, but whose husband they discovered was
uncle to the young king, then a minor, but from
whom she was separated.   She soon evinced a par-
tiality for Mr. Banks, though not quite so strong as
that for Wallis, but it appears to have been mutual,
until an unlucky discovery took place, that she had,
at her command, a stout strong-boned *cavaliere
servente;* added to which, a theft, rather of an
amusing nature, contributed for a time to create
a coolness, and somewhat to disturb the good
understanding that had subsisted between them.
It happened that a party, consisting of Cook,
Banks, Solander, and three or four others, were
benighted at a distance from the anchorage.   Mr.
Banks, says Lieut. Cook, thought himself fortunate in being offered a place by Oberea, in her
own canoe, and wishing his friends a good night,
took his leave.   He went to rest early, according

to the custom of the country; and taking off his clothes, as was his constant practice, the nights being hot, Oberea kindly insisted upon taking them into her own custody, for otherwise, she said, they would certainly be stolen. Mr. Banks having, as he thought, so good a safeguard, resigned himself to sleep with all imaginable tranquillity ; but awakening about eleven o'clock, and wanting to get up, he searched for his clothes where he had seen them carefully deposited by Oberea, when he lay down to sleep, and perceived, to his sorrow and surprise, that they were missing. He immediately awakened Oberea, who, starting up and hearing his complaint, ordered lights, and prepared in great haste to recover what had been lost. Tootahah (the regent) slept in the next canoe, and being soon alarmed, he came to them and set out with Oberea in search of the thief. Mr. Banks was not in a condition to go with them, as of his apparel scarcely any thing was left him but his breeches. In about half an hour his two noble friends returned, but without having obtained any intelligence of his clothes or of the thief. Where Cook and Solander had disposed of themselves he did not know ; but hearing music, which was sure to bring a crowd together, in which there was a chance of his associates being among them, he rose, and made the best of his way towards it, and joined his party, as Cook says, ' more than half naked, and told us his melancholy story.'

It was some consolation to find that his friends were fellow-sufferers, Cook having lost his stockings, that had been stolen from under his head, though he had never been asleep, and his asso-

ciates their jackets. At day-break Oberea brought
to Mr. Banks some of her country clothes; ' so
that when he came to us,' says Cook, ' he made a
most motley appearance, half Indian and half
English.' Such an adventure must have been
highly amusing to him who was the object of it,
when the inconvenience had been removed, as
every one will admit who knew the late venerable President of the Royal Society. He never
doubted, however, that Oberea was privy to the
theft, and there was strong suspicion of her
having some of the articles in her custody. Being
aware that this feeling existed, she absented
herself for some time, and when she again appeared, she said a favourite of hers had taken
them away, whom she had beaten and dismissed ;
' but she seemed conscious,' says Cook, ' that she
had no right to be believed ; she discovered the
strongest signs of fear, yet she surmounted it
with astonishing resolution, and was very pressing
to be allowed to sleep with her attendants in Mr.
Banks's tent; in this, however, she was not gratified.' Sir Joseph might have thought that, if he
complied with her request, his breeches might be
in danger of following the other articles of his
dress.

The Otaheitans cannot resist pilfering. ' I must
bear my testimony,' says Cook, ' that the people
of this country, of all ranks, men and women, are
the errantest thieves upon the face of the earth ;
but,' he adds, ' we must not hastily conclude that
theft is a testimony of the same depravity in them
that it is in us, in the instances in which our
people were sufferers by their dishonesty ; for their

temptation was such, as to surmount what would
be considered as a proof of uncommon integrity
among those who have more knowledge, better
principles, and stronger motives to resist the
temptations of illicit advantage ; an Indian among
penny knives and beads, and even nails and
broken glass, is in the same state of mind with
the meanest servant in Europe among unlocked
coffers of jewels and gold.' Captain Wallis has
illustrated the truth of this position by an experiment he made on some persons, whose dress and
behaviour indicated that they were of a superior
cast. ' To discover what present,' he says, ' would
most gratify them, I laid down before them a
Johannes, a guinea, a crown piece, a Spanish
dollar, a few shillings, some new halfpence, and
two large nails, making signs that they should
take what they liked best. The nails were first
seized with great eagerness, and then a few of the
halfpence, but the silver and gold lay neglected.'
Here then it might with truth be said was discovered

  ' The goldless age, where gold disturbs no dreams.'

But their thirst after iron was irresistible ; Wallis's
ship was stripped of all the nails in her by the
seamen to purchase the good graces of the women,
who assembled in crowds on the shore. The men
even drew out of different parts of the ship those
nails that fastened the cleats to her side. This
commerce established with the women rendered
the men, as might readily be expected, less obedient to command, and made it necessary to
punish some of them by flogging. The Otaheitans regarded this punishment with horror. One

of Cook's men having insulted a chief's wife, he
was ordered to be flogged in their presence. The
Indians saw him stripped and tied up to the
rigging with a fixed attention, waiting in silent
suspense for the event; but as soon as the first
stroke was given, they interfered with great agitation, earnestly entreating that the rest of the
punishment might be remitted; and when they
found they were unable to prevail, they gave vent
to their pity by tears. ' But their tears,' as Cook
observes, ' like those of children, were always
ready to express any passion that was strongly
excited, and like those of children, they also appeared to be forgotten as soon as shed.' And he
instances this by the following incident:—Mr.
Banks seeing a young woman in great affliction,
the tears streaming from her eyes, inquired earnestly the cause; but instead of answering, she
took from under her garment a shark's tooth, and
struck it six or seven times into her head with
great force; a profusion of blood followed, and
disregarding his inquiries, she continued to talk
loud in a melancholy tone, while those around
were laughing and talking without taking the
least notice of her distress. The bleeding having
ceased, she looked up with a smile, and collecting
the pieces of cloth which she had used to stanch
the blood, threw them into the sea; then plunging
into the river, and washing her whole body, she
returned to the tents with the same gaiety and
cheerfulness as if nothing had happened. The
same thing occurred in the case of a chief, who
had given great offence to Mr. Banks, when he
and all his followers were overwhelmed with grief

and dejection; but one of his women, having
struck a shark's tooth into her head several times,
till it was covered with blood, the scene was immediately changed, and laughing and good humour took place. Wallis witnessed the same
kind of conduct. This, therefore, and the tears,
are probably considered a sort of expiation or
doing penance for a fault.

But the sorrows of these simple and artless
people are transient. Cook justly observes, that
what they feel they have never been taught either
to disguise or suppress ; and having no habits of
thinking, which perpetually recall the past and
anticipate the future, they are affected by all the
changes of the passing hour, and reflect the colour
of the time, however frequently it may vary.
They grieve for the death of a relation, and place
the body on a stage erected on piles and covered
with a roof of thatch, for they never bury the
dead, and never approach one of these *morais*
without great solemnity; but theirs is no lasting
grief.

An old woman having died, Mr. Banks, whose
pursuit was knowledge of every kind, and to gain
it made himself one of the people, requested he
might attend the ceremony and witness all the
mysteries of the solemnity of depositing the body
in the morai. The request was complied with,
but on no other condition than his taking a part in
it. This was just what he wished. In the evening he repaired to the house of mourning, where he
was received by the daughter of the deceased and
several others, among whom was a boy about
fourteen years old. One of the chiefs of the dis-

trict was the principal mourner, wearing a fantastical dress. Mr. Banks was stripped entirely of his European clothes, and a small piece of cloth was tied round his middle. His face and body were then smeared with charcoal and water, as low as the shoulders, till they were as black as those of a negro: the same operation was performed on the rest, among whom were some women, who were reduced to a state as near to nakedness as himself; the boy was blacked all over, after which the procession set forward, the chief mourner having mumbled something like a prayer over the body. It is the custom of the Indians to fly from these processions with the utmost precipitation. On the present occasion several large bodies of the natives were put to flight, all the houses were deserted, and not a Otaheitan was to be seen. The body being deposited on the stage, the mourners were dismissed to wash themselves in the river, and to resume their customary dresses and their usual gaiety.

They are, however, so jealous of any one approaching these abodes of the dead, that one of Cook's party, happening one day to pull a flower from a tree which grew in one of these sepulchral inclosures, was struck by a native who saw it, and came suddenly behind him. The morai of Oberea was a pile of stone-work raised pyramidically, two hundred and sixty-seven feet long, eighty-seven feet wide, and forty-four feet high, terminating in a ridge like the roof of a house, and ascended by steps of white coral stone neatly squared and polished, some of them not less than three feet and a half by two feet and

a half. Such a structure, observes Cook, raised
without the assistance of iron tools, or mortar to
join them, struck us with astonishment, as a work
of considerable skill and incredible labour.

On the same principle of making himself acquainted with every novelty that presented itself,
Captain Cook states that ' Mr. Banks saw the
operation of *tattooing* performed upon the back
of a girl about thirteen years old. The instrument used upon this occasion had thirty teeth,
and every stroke, of which at least a hundred were
made in a minute, drew an ichor or serum a little
tinged with blood. The girl bore it with most
stoical resolution for about a quarter of an hour ;
but the pain of so many hundred punctures as she
had received in that time then became intolerable :
she first complained in murmurs, then wept, and
at last burst into loud lamentations, earnestly im-
ploring the operator to desist. He was however
inexorable ; and when she began to struggle, she
was held down by two women, who sometimes
soothed and sometimes chid her, and now and
then, when she was most unruly, gave her a
smart blow. Mr. Banks stayed in the neighbour-
ing house an hour, and the operation was not
over when he went away.'

The sufferings of this young lady did not however deter the late President of the Royal Society
from undergoing the operation on his own person.

The skill and labour which the Otaheitans bestow on their large double boats is not less wonderful than their stone morais, from the felling of
the tree and splitting it into plank, to the minutest
carved ornaments that decorate the head and the

stern. The whole operation is performed without the use of any metallic instrument. ' To fabricate one of their principal vessels with their tools is,' says Cook, ' as great a work as to build a British man of war with ours.' The fighting boats are sometimes more than seventy feet long, but not above three broad ; but they are fastened in pairs, side by side, at the distance of about three feet ; the head and stern rise in a semicircular form, the latter to the height of seventeen or eighteen feet. To build these boats, and the smaller kinds of canoes ;—to build their houses, and finish the slight furniture they contain ;—to fell, cleave, carve, and polish timber for various purposes ;— and, in short, for every conversion of wood— the tools they make use of are the following : an adze of stone ; a chissel or gouge of bone, generally that of a man's arm between the wrist and elbow ; a rasp of coral ; and the skin of a sting-ray, with coral sand as a file or polisher.

The persons of the Otaheitan men are in general tall, strong, well-limbed and finely shaped ; equal in size to the largest of Europeans. The women of superior rank are also above the middle stature of Europeans, but the inferior class are rather below it. The complexion of the former class is that which we call a brunette, and the skin is most delicately smooth and soft. The shape of the face is comely, the cheek bones are not high, neither are the eyes hollow, nor the brow prominent ; the nose is a little, but not much, flattened ; but their eyes, and more particularly those of the women, are full of expression, sometimes sparkling with fire, and some-

times melting with softness; their teeth also are,
almost without exception, most beautifully even
and white, and their breath perfectly without taint.
In their motions there is at once vigour as well
as ease; their walk is graceful, their deportment
liberal, and their behaviour to strangers and to
each other, affable and courteous. In their dis-
positions they appear to be brave, open and
candid, without suspicion or treachery, cruelty or
revenge. Mr. Banks had such confidence in
them, as to sleep frequently in their houses in
the woods, without a companion, and consequently
wholly in their power. They are delicate and
cleanly, almost wholly without example.

' The natives of Otaheite,' says Cook, ' both
men and women, constantly wash their whole
bodies in running water three times every day;
once as soon as they rise in the morning, once
at noon, and again before they sleep at night,
whether the sea or river be near them or at a distance. They wash not only the mouth, but the
hands at their meals, almost between every
morsel; and their clothes, as well as their persons,
are kept without spot or stain.'

If any one should think this picture somewhat
overcharged, he will find it fully confirmed in an
account of them made by a description of men
who are not much disposed to represent worldly
objects in the most favourable light. In the first
missionary voyage, in the year 1797, the natives
of Otaheite are thus described.

' Natural colour olive, inclining to copper;
the women, who carefully clothe themselves, and
avoid the sun-beams, are but a shade or two

darker than an European brunette; their eyes are
black and sparkling; their teeth white and even;
their skin soft and delicate; their limbs finely
turned; their hair jetty, perfumed and ornamented with flowers; they are in general large
and wide over the shoulders; we were therefore
disappointed in the judgment we had formed from
the report of preceding visiters; and though here
and there was to be seen a young person who
might be esteemed comely, we saw few who, in
fact, could be called beauties; yet they possess
eminent feminine graces: their faces are never
darkened with a scowl, or covered with a cloud of
sullenness or suspicion. Their manners are
affable and engaging; their step easy, firm and
graceful; their behaviour free and unguarded;
always boundless in generosity to each other, and
to strangers; their tempers mild, gentle, and
unaffected; slow to take offence, easily pacified,
and seldom retaining resentment or revenge,
whatever provocation they may have received.
Their arms and hands are very delicately formed;
and though they go barefoot, their feet are not
coarse and spreading.

'As wives in private life, they are affectionate,
tender and obedient to their husbands, and un-
commonly fond of their children: they nurse
them with the utmost care, and are particularly
attentive to keep the infant's limbs supple and
straight. A cripple is hardly ever seen among
them in early life. A rickety child is never
known; anything resembling it would reflect the
highest disgrace on the mother.

'The Otaheitans have no partitions in their

houses; but, it may be affirmed, they have in
many instances more refined ideas of decency
than ourselves; and one, long a resident, scruples
not to declare, that he never saw any appetite,
hunger and thirst excepted, gratified in public.
It is too true that, for the sake of gaining our
extraordinary curiosities, and to please our brutes,
they have appeared immodest in the extreme.
Yet they lay this charge wholly at our door,
and say that Englishmen are ashamed of nothing,
and that we have led them to public acts of in-
decency never before practised among themselves.
Iron here, more precious than gold, bears down
every barrier of restraint; honesty and modesty
yield to the force of temptation *.'

Such are the females and the mothers here described, whose interesting offspring are now
peopling Pitcairn's Island, and who, while they
inherit their mothers' virtues, have hitherto kept
themselves free from their vices.

The greater part of the food of Otaheitans is
vegetable. Hogs, dogs, and poultry are their only
animals, and all of them serve for food. ' We all
agreed,' says Cook, ' that a South-Sea dog was
little inferior to an English lamb,' which he ascribes
to its being kept up and fed wholly on vegetables.
Broiling and baking are the only two modes of
applying fire to their cookery. Captain Wallis
observes, that having no vessel in which water
could be subjected to the action of fire, they had
no more idea that it could be made *hot*, than that
it could be made *solid ;* and he mentions that one

* A Missionary Voyage to the Southern Pacific Ocean,
Appendix, pp. 336, 342.

of the attendants of the supposed queen, having observed the surgeon fill the tea-pot from an urn, turned the cock himself, and received the water in his hand; and that as soon as he felt himself scalded, he roared out and began to dance about the cabin with the most extravagant and ridiculous expressions of pain and astonishment; his companions, unable to conceive what was the matter, staring at him in amaze, and not without some mixture of terror.

One of Oberea's peace-offerings to Mr. Banks, for the robbery of his clothes committed in her boat, was a fine fat dog, and the way in which it was prepared and baked was as follows. Tupei, the high priest, undertook to perform the double office of butcher and cook. He first killed him by holding his hands close over his mouth and nose for the space of a quarter of an hour. A hole was then made in the ground about a foot deep, in which a fire was kindled, and some small stones placed in layers, alternately with the wood, to be heated. The dog was then singed, scraped with a shell, and the hair taken off as clean as if he had been scalded in hot water. He was then cut up with the same instrument, and his entrails carefully washed. When the hole was sufficiently heated, the fire was taken out, and some of the stones, being placed at the bottom, were covered with green leaves. The dog, with the entrails, was then placed upon the leaves, and other leaves being laid upon them, the whole was covered with the rest of the hot stones, and the mouth of the hole close stopped with mould. In somewhat less than four hours, it was again

Drawn & Etched by

Lieut. Col. Batty.

Neni, near Matavai Bay, Otaheite.

From an Original Drawing by Webber

Published by John Murray, Albemarle Street, 1831

opened, and the dog taken out excellently baked, and the party all agreed that he made a very good dish. These dogs it seems are bred to be eaten, and live wholly on bread-fruit, cocoa-nuts, yams and other vegetables of the like kind.

The food of the natives, being chiefly vegetable, consists of the various preparations of the bread-fruit, of cocoa-nuts, bananas, plantains, and a great variety of other fruit, the spontaneous products of a rich soil and genial climate. The bread-fruit, when baked in the same manner as the dog was, is rendered soft, and not unlike a boiled potatoe; not quite so farinaceous as a good one, but more so than those of the middling sort. Much of this fruit is gathered before it is ripe, and by a certain process is made to undergo the two states of fermentation, the saccharine and acetous, in the latter of which it is moulded into balls, and called *Mahie*. The natives seldom make a meal without this sour paste. Salt water is the universal sauce, without which no meal is eaten. Their drink in general consists of water, or the juice of the cocoa-nut; the art of producing liquors that intoxicate by fermentation being at this time happily unknown among them; neither did they make use of any narcotic, as the natives of some other countries do opium, beetel-nut, and tobacco. One day the wife of one of the chiefs came running to Mr. Banks, who was always applied to in every emergency and distress, and with a mixture of grief and terror in her countenance, made him understand that her husband was dying, in consequence of something the strangers had given him to eat. Mr. Banks found his friend leaning his head against a post, in an attitude of the utmost languor and despondency. His attendants brought out a leaf folded up with great care, containing part of the poison of the effects of which their master was now dying. On opening the leaf Mr. Banks found in it a chew of tobacco, which the chief had asked from some of the seamen, and imitating them, as he thought, he had rolled it about in his mouth, grinding it to powder with his teeth, and ultimately swallowing it. During the examination of the leaf he looked up at Mr. Banks with the most piteous countenance, and intimated that he had but a very short time to live. A copious draught of cocoa-nut milk, however, set all to rights, and the chief and his attendants were at once restored to that flow of cheerfulness and good-humour, which is the characteristic of these single-minded people.

There is, however, one plant from the root of which they extract a juice of an intoxicating quality, called *Ava,* but Cook's party saw nothing of its effects, probably owing to their considering drunkenness as a disgrace. This vice of drinking ava is said to be peculiar almost to the chiefs, who vie with each other in drinking the greatest number of draughts, each draught being about a pint. They keep this intoxicating juice with great care from the women.

As eating is one of the most important concerns of life, here as well as elsewhere, Captain Cook's description of a meal made by one of the chiefs of the island cannot be considered as uninteresting, and is here given in his own words.

' He sits down under the shade of the next

tree, or on the shady side of his house, and a large
quantity of leaves, either of the bread-fruit or
bananas, are neatly spread before him upon the
ground as a table-cloth ; a basket is then set by
him that contains his provision, which, if fish or
flesh, is ready dressed, and wrapped up in leaves,
and two cocoa-nut shells, one full of salt water
and one of fresh. His attendants, which are not
few, seat themselves round him, and when all is
ready, he begins by washing his hands and his
mouth thoroughly with the fresh water, and this
he repeats almost continually throughout the whole
meal. He then takes part of his provision out of
the basket, which generally consists of a small fish
or two, two or three bread-fruits, fourteen or fifteen
ripe bananas, or six or seven apples. He first
takes half a bread-fruit, peels off the rind, and
takes out the core with his nails ; of this he puts as
much into his mouth as it can hold, and while he
chews it, takes the fish out of the leaves and breaks
one of them into the salt water, placing the other,
and what remains of the bread-fruit, upon the
leaves that have been spread before him. When
this is done, he takes up a small piece of the fish
that has been broken into the salt-water, with all
the fingers of one hand, and sucks it into his
mouth, so as to get with it as much of the salt-
water as possible. In the same manner he takes
the rest by different morsels, and between each, at
least very frequently, takes a small sup of the
salt-water, either out of the cocoa-nut shell, or the
palm of his hand. In the meantime one of his
attendants has prepared a young cocoa-nut, by
peeling off the outer rind with his teeth, an opera-

tion which to an European appears very surprising; but it depends so much upon sleight, that
many of us were able to do it before we left the
island, and some that could scarcely crack a
filbert. The master when he chooses to drink
takes the cocoa-nut thus prepared, and boring a
hole through the shell with his fingers, or breaking it with a stone, he sucks out the liquor.
When he has eaten his bread-fruit and fish, he
begins with his plantains, one of which makes but
a mouthful, though it be as big as a black-pud-
ding; if instead of plantains he has apples, he
never tastes them till they have been pared; to
do this a shell is picked up from the ground,
where they are always in plenty, and tossed to
him by an attendant. He immediately begins to
cut or scrape off the rind, but so awkwardly that
great part of the fruit is wasted. If, instead of
fish, he has flesh, he must have some succedaneum
for a knife to divide it; and for this purpose a
piece of bamboo is tossed to him, of which he
makes the necessary implement by splitting it
transversely with his nail. While all this has
been doing, some of his attendants have been
employed in beating bread-fruit with a stone pestle
upon a block of wood; by being beaten in this
manner, and sprinkled from time to time with
water, it is reduced to the consistence of a soft
paste, and is then put into a vessel somewhat like
a butcher's tray, and either made up alone, or
mixed with banana or *mahie*, according to the
taste of the master, by pouring water upon it by
degrees and squeezing it often through the hand.
Under this operation it acquires the consistence of

a thick custard, and a large cocoa-nut shell full of
it being set before him, he sips it as we should do
a jelly if we had no spoon to take it from the
glass. The meal is then finished by again washing his hands and his mouth. After which the
cocoa-nut shells are cleaned, and everything that
is left is replaced in the basket.'

Captain Cook adds, 'the quantity of food which
these people eat at a meal is prodigious. I have
seen one man devour two or three fishes as big as
a perch; three bread-fruits, each bigger than two
fists ; fourteen or fifteen plantains or bananas, each
of them six or seven inches long, and four or five
round ; and near a quart of the pounded bread-
fruit, which is as substantial as the thickest un-
baked custard. This is so extraordinary that I
scarcely expect to be believed; and I would not
have related it upon my own single testimony, but
Mr. Banks, Dr. Solander, and most of the other
gentlemen have had ocular demonstration of its
truth, and know that I mention them on the occasion.'

The women, who, on other occasions, always
mix in the amusements of the men, who are particularly fond of their society, are wholly excluded
from their meals ; nor could the latter be prevailed
on to partake of anything when dining in company on board ship; they said it was not right:
even brothers and sisters have each their separate
baskets, and their provisions are separately prepared ; but the English officers and men, when visiting the young ones at their own houses, frequently
ate out of the same basket and drank out of the
same cup, to the horror and dismay of the older

D

ladies, who were always offended at this liberty ;
and if by chance any of the victuals were touched,
or even the basket that contained them, they
would throw them away.

In this fine climate houses are almost unnecessary. The minimum range of the thermometer is
about 63°, the maximum 85°, giving an average of
74°. Their sheds or houses consist generally of a
thatched roof raised on posts, the eaves reaching
to within three or four feet of the ground; the
floor is covered with soft hay, over which are laid
mats, so that the whole is one cushion, on which
they sit by day and sleep by night. They eat in
the open air, under the shade of the nearest tree.
In each district there is a house erected for general
use, much larger than common, some of them
exceeding two hundred feet in length, thirty
broad, and twenty high. The dwelling-houses all
stand in the woody belt which surrounds the
island, between the feet of the central mountains
and the sea, each having a very small piece of
ground cleared, just enough to keep the dropping
of the trees from the thatch. An Otaheitan wood
consists chiefly of groves of bread-fruit and cocoa-
nuts, without underwood, and intersected in all
directions by the paths that lead from one house
to another. ' Nothing,' says Cook, ' can be
more grateful than this shade, in so warm a climate, nor anything more beautiful than these
walks.'

With all the activity they are capable of displaying, and the sprightliness of their disposition,
they are fond of indulging in ease and indolence.
The trees that produce their food are mostly of

spontaneous growth—the bread-fruit, cocoa-nut, bananas of thirteen sorts, besides plantains; a fruit not unlike an apple, which, when ripe, is very pleasant; sweet potatoes, yams, and a species of *arum;* the pandanus, the jambu and the sugar-cane ; a variety of plants whose roots are esculent—these, with many others, are produced with so little culture, that, as Cook observes, they seem to be exempted from the first general curse that ' man should eat his bread in the sweat of his brow.' Then for clothing they have the bark of three different trees, the paper mulberry, the bread-fruit tree, and a tree which resembles the wild fig-tree of the West Indies ; of these the mulberry only requires to be cultivated.

In preparing the cloth they display a very considerable degree of ingenuity. Red and yellow are the two colours most in use for dyeing their cloth ; the red is stated to be exceedingly brilliant and beautiful, approaching nearest to our full scarlet ; it is produced by the mixture of the juices of two vegetables, neither of which separately has the least tendency to that hue : one is the *Cordia Sebestina,* the other a species of *Ficus;* of the former the leaves, of the latter the fruits yield the juices. The yellow dye is extracted from the bark of the root of the *Morinda citrifolia,* by scraping and infusing it in water.

Their matting is exceedingly beautiful, particularly that which is made from the bark of the *Hibiscus tiliaceus,* and of a species of *Pandanus.* Others are made of rushes and grass with amazing facility and dispatch. . In the same manner their basket and wicker work are most ingeniously

D 2

made; the former in patterns of a thousand different kinds. Their nets and fishing-lines are strong and neatly made, so are their fish-hooks of pearl-shell; and their clubs are admirable specimens of wood-carving.

A people so lively, sprightly, and good-humoured as the Otaheitans are, must necessarily have their amusements. They are fond of music, such as is derived from a rude flute and a drum; of dancing, wrestling, shooting with the bow, and throwing the lance. They exhibit frequent trials of skill and strength in wrestling; and Cook says it is scarcely possible for those who are acquainted with the athletic sports of very remote antiquity, not to remark a rude resemblance of them in a wrestling-match (which he describes) among the natives of a little island in the midst of the Pacific Ocean.

But these simple-minded people have their vices, and great ones too. Chastity is almost unknown among a certain description of women: there is a detestable society called *Arreoy*, composed, it would seem, of a particular class, who are supposed to be the chief warriors of the island. In this society the men and women live in common; and on the birth of a child it is immediately smothered, that its bringing up may not interfere with the brutal pleasures of either father or mother. Another savage practice, is that of immolating human beings at the *Morais*, which serve as temples as well as sepulchres, and yet, by the report of the missionaries, they entertain a due sense and reverential awe of the Deity. 'With regard to their worship,' Captain Cook does the Otaheitans but justice in saying, 'they reproach many who bear the name of Christians. You see no instances of an Otaheitan drawing near the Eatooa with carelessness and inattention; he is all devotion; he approaches the place of worship with reverential awe; uncovers when he treads on sacred ground; and prays with a fervour that would do honour to a better profession. He firmly credits the traditions of his ancestors. None dares dispute the existence of the Deity.' Thieving may also be reckoned as one of their vices; this, however, is common to all uncivilized nations, and, it may be added, civilized too. But to judge them fairly in this respect, we should compare their situation with that of a more civilized people. A native of Otaheite goes on board a ship and finds himself in the midst of iron bolts, nails, knives, scattered about, and is tempted to carry off a few of them. If we could suppose a ship from El Dorado to arrive in the Thames, and that the custom-house officers, on boarding her, found themselves in the midst of bolts, hatchets, chissels, all of solid gold, scattered about the deck, one need scarcely say what would be likely to happen. If the former found the temptation irresistible to supply himself with what was essentially useful—the latter would be as little able to resist that which would contribute to the indulgence of his avarice or the gratification of his pleasures, or of both.

Such was the state of this beautiful island and its interesting and fascinating natives at the time when Captain Wallis first discovered and Lieutenant Cook shortly afterwards visited it. What they now are, as described by Captain Beechey, it is lamentable to reflect. All their usual and innocent amusements have been denounced by the missionaries, and, in lieu of them, these poor people have been driven to seek for resources in habits of indolence and apathy : that simplicity of character, which atoned for many of their faults, has been converted into cunning and hypocrisy ; and drunkenness, poverty, and disease have thinned the island of its former population to a frightful degree. By a survey of the first missionaries, and a census of the inhabitants, taken in 1797, the population was estimated at 16,050 souls ; Captain Waldegrave, in 1830, states it, on the authority of a census also taken by the missionaries, to amount only to 5000—and there is but too much reason to ascribe this diminution to praying, psalm-singing, and dram-drinking*.

The island of Otaheite is in shape two circles united by a low and narrow isthmus. The larger circle is named Otaheite Mooé, and is about thirty miles in diameter; the lesser, named Tiaraboo, about ten miles in diameter. A belt of low land, terminating in numerous valleys, ascending by gentle slopes to the central mountain, which is about seven thousand feet high, surrounds the

* Cook appears not to have exercised his usual judgment in estimating the population of this island. After stating the number of war-canoes at seventeen hundred and twenty, and able men to man them, at sixty-eight thousand eight hundred, he comes to the conclusion that the population must consist of two hundred and four thousand souls; and reflecting on the vast swarms which everywhere appeared, 'I was convinced,' he says, ' that this estimate was not much, if at all, too great.'

Drawn & Etched by Lieut.Col.Batty.

Creek in Matavai Bay, Otaheite.

From an Original Drawing by Webber.

Published by John Murray, Albemarle Street 1831

larger circle, and the same is the case with the smaller circle on a proportionate scale. Down these valleys flow streams and rivulets of clear water, and the most luxuriant and verdant foliage fills their sides and the hilly ridges that separate them, among which were once scattered the smiling cottages and little plantations of the natives. All these are now destroyed, and the remnant of the population has crept down to the flats and swampy ground on the sea shore, completely subservient to the seven establishments of missionaries, who have taken from them what little trade they used to carry on, to possess themselves of it ; who have their warehouses, act as agents, and monopolize all the cattle on the island—but, in return, they have given them a new religion and a *parliament* (*risum teneatis?*) and reduced them to a state of complete pauperism—and all, as they say, and probably have so persuaded themselves, for the honour of God, and the salvation of their souls! How much is such a change brought about by such conduct to be deprecated ! how lamentable is it to reflect, that an island on which Nature has lavished so many of her bounteous gifts, with which neither Cyprus nor Cythera, nor the fanciful island of Calypso, can compete in splendid and luxuriant beauties, should be doomed to such a fate,—in an enlightened age, and by a people that call themselves civilized !

CHAPTER II.

THE BREAD-FRUIT.

—— ' The happy shores without a law.
.   .   .   .   .   .
Where all partake the earth without dispute,
And bread itself is gather'd as a fruit;
Where none contest the fields, the woods, the streams.
The goldless age, where gold disturbs no dreams,
Inhabits or inhabited the shore,
Till Europe taught them better than before,
Bestow'd her customs, and amended theirs,
But left her vices also to their heirs.'   BYRON.

In the year 1787, being seventeen years after
Cook's return from his first voyage, the merchants
and planters resident in London, and interested in
the West India possessions, having represented to
his Majesty, that the introduction of the bread-
fruit tree into the islands of those seas, to consti-
tute an article of food, would be of very essential
benefit to the inhabitants, the king was graciously
pleased to comply with their request ; and a vessel
was accordingly purchased, and fitted at Deptford
with the necessary fixtures and preparations, for
carrying into effect the benevolent object of the
voyage.   The arrangements for disposing the
plants were undertaken, and completed in a most
ingenious and effective manner, by Sir Joseph
Banks, who superintended the whole equipment
of the ship with the greatest attention and assi-

duity till she was in all respects ready for sea.
He named the ship the Bounty, and recommended
Lieutenant Bligh, who had been with Captain
Cook, to command her. Her burden was about
two hundred and fifteen tons; and her establishment consisted of one lieutenant, who was commanding officer, one master, three warrant officers, one surgeon, two master's mates, two midshipmen, and thirty-four petty officers and seamen,
making in all forty-four; to which were added
two skilful and careful men, recommended by
Sir Joseph Banks, to have the management of
the plants intended to be carried to the West Indies,
and others to be brought home for his Majesty's
garden at Kew : one was David Nelson, who had
served in a similar situation in Captain Cook's
last voyage; the other William Brown, as an
assistant to him.

The object of all the former voyages to the
South Seas, undertaken by command of his Majesty George III., was the increase of knowledge
by new discoveries, and the advancement of
science, more particularly of natural history and
geography : the intention of the present voyage
was to derive some practical benefit from the distant discoveries that had already been made; and
no object was deemed more likely to realise the
expectation of benefit than the bread-fruit, which
afforded to the natives of Otaheite so very considerable a portion of their food, and which it was
hoped it might also do for the black population of
the West India Islands. The bread-fruit plant
was no new discovery of either Wallis or Cook.
So early as the year 1688, that excellent old navi-

gator, Dampier, thus describes it:—' The bread-fruit, as we call it, grows on a large tree, as big and high as our largest apple-trees; it hath a spreading head, full of branches and dark leaves. The fruit grows on the boughs like apples; it is as big as a penny-loaf, when wheat is at five shillings the bushel; it is of a round shape, and hath a thick tough rind; when the fruit is ripe it is yellow and soft, and the taste is sweet and pleasant. The natives of Guam use it for bread. They gather it, when full grown, while it is green and hard; then they bake it in an oven, which scorcheth the rind and makes it black, but they scrape off the outside black crust, and there remains a tender thin crust; and the inside is soft, tender, and white, like the crumb of a penny-loaf. There is neither seed nor stone in the inside, but all is of a pure substance like bread. It must be eaten new; for if it is kept above twenty-four hours, it grows harsh and choaky; but it is very pleasant before it is too stale. This fruit lasts in season eight months in the year, during which the natives eat no other sort of food of bread kind. I did never see of this fruit anywhere but here. The natives told us that there is plenty of this fruit growing on the rest of the Ladrone Islands; and I did never hear of it anywhere else.'

Lord Anson corroborates this account of the bread-fruit, and says that, while at Tinian, it was constantly eaten by his officers and ship's company during their two months' stay, instead of bread; and so universally preferred, that no ship's bread was expended in that whole interval. The only essential difference between Dampier's and Cook's description is, where the latter says, which is true, that this fruit has a *core*, and that the eatable part lies between the skin and the core. Cook says also that its taste is insipid, with a slight sweetness, somewhat resembling that of the crumb of wheaten bread mixed with a Jerusalem artichoke. From such a description, it is not surprising that the West India planters should have felt desirous of introducing it into those islands; and accordingly the introduction of it was subsequently accomplished, notwithstanding the failure of the present voyage; it has not, however, been found to answer the expectation that had reasonably been entertained. The climate, as to latitude, ought to be the same, or nearly so, as that of Otaheite, but there would appear to be some difference in the situation or nature of the soil, that prevents it from thriving in the West India Islands. At Otaheite and on several of the Pacific Islands,

'The bread-tree, which, without the ploughshare, yields
The unreap'd harvest of unfurrow'd fields,
And bakes its unadulterated loaves
Without a furnace in unpurchased groves,
And flings off famine from its fertile breast,
A priceless market for the gathering guest—'

is to the natives of those islands a most invaluable gift, but it has not been found to yield similar benefits to the West India Islands.

On the 23rd December, 1787, the Bounty sailed from Spithead, and on the 26th it blew a severe storm of wind from the eastward, which continued to the 29th, in the course of which the ship suf-

fered greatly. One sea broke away the spare-
yards and spars out of the starboard main-chains.
Another heavy sea broke into the ship and stove
all the boats. Several casks of beer that had been
lashed upon deck, were broke loose and washed
overboard ; and it was not without great difficulty
and risk that they were able to secure the boats
from being washed away entirely. Besides other
mischief done to them in this storm, a large quantity of bread was damaged and rendered useless,
for the sea had stove in the stern and filled the
cabin with water.

This made it desirable to touch at Teneriffe to
put the ship to rights, where they arrived on the
5th January, 1788, and having refitted and refreshed, they sailed again on the 10th.

' I now,' says Bligh, ' divided the people into
three watches, and gave the charge of the third
watch to Mr. Fletcher Christian, one of the mates.
I have always considered this a desirable regula-
tion when circumstances will admit of it, and I am
persuaded that unbroken rest not only contributes
much towards the health of the ship's company,
but enables them more readily to exert themselves
in cases of sudden emergency.'

Wishing to proceed to Otaheite without stopping, and the late storm having diminished their
supply of provisions, it was deemed expedient to
put all hands on an allowance of two-thirds of
bread. It was also decided that water for drinking should be passed through filtering stones that
had been procured at Teneriffe. ' I now,' says
Bligh, ' made the ship's company acquainted with
the object of the voyage, and gave assurances of

the certainty of promotion to every one whose
endeavours should merit it.' Nothing, indeed,
seemed to be neglected on the part of the commander to make his officers and men comfortable
and happy. He was himself a thorough-bred
sailor, and availed himself of every possible means
of preserving the health of his crew. Continued
rain and a close atmosphere had covered everything in the ship with mildew. She was therefore
aired below with fires, and frequently sprinkled
with vinegar, and every interval of dry weather
was taken advantage of to open all the hatchways,
and clean the ship, and to have all the people's
wet things washed and dried. With these pre-
cautions to secure health, they passed the hazy
and sultry atmosphere of the low latitudes without
a single complaint.

On Sunday, the 2d of March, Lieutenant Bligh
observes, ' after seeing that every person was
clean, Divine service was performed, according to
my usual custom. On this day I gave to Mr.
Fletcher Christian, whom I had before desired to
take charge of the third watch, a written order to
act as lieutenant.'

Having reached as far as the latitude of 36°
south, on the 9th March, ' the change of temperature,' he observes, ' began now to be sensibly felt,
there being a variation in the thermometer,
since yesterday, of eight degrees. That the people might not suffer by their own negligence, I
gave orders for their light tropical clothing to be
put by, and made them dress in a manner more
suited to a cold climate. I had provided for this
before I left England, by giving directions for such

clothes to be purchased as would be found necessary.   On this day, on a complaint of the master,
I found it necessary to punish Matthew Quintal,
one of the seamen, with two dozen lashes, for
insolence and mutinous behaviour.   Before this I
had not had occasion to punish any person on
board.'

The sight of New Year's Harbour, in Staaten
Land, almost tempted him, he says, to put in ; but
the lateness of the season, and the people being
in good health, determined him to lay aside all
thoughts of refreshment until they should reach
Otaheite.   Indeed the extraordinary care he had
taken to preserve the health of the ship's company
rendered any delay in this cold and inhospitable
region unnecessary.

They soon after this had to encounter tremendous weather off Cape Horn, storms of wind, with
hail and sleet, which made it necessary to keep a
constant fire night and day ; and one of the watch
always attended to dry the people's wet clothes.
This stormy weather continued for nine days ; the
ship began to complain, and required pumping
every hour ; the decks became so leaky that the
commander was obliged to allot the great cabin
to those who had wet berths, to hang their hammocks in.   Finding they were losing ground
every day, and that it was hopeless to persist in
attempting a passage by this route, at this season
of the year, to the Society Islands, and after
struggling for thirty days in this tempestuous
ocean, it was determined to bear away for the
Cape of Good Hope.   The helm was accordingly
put a-weather, to the great joy of every person on
board.

They arrived at the Cape on the 23rd of May, and having remained there thirty-eight days to refit the ship, replenish provisions, and refresh the crew, they sailed again on the 1st July, and anchored in Adventure Bay, in Van Dieman's Land, on the 20th August. Here they remained taking in wood and water till the 4th September, and on the evening of the 25th October they saw Otaheite; and the next day came to anchor in Matavai Bay, after a distance which the ship had run over, by the log, since leaving England, of twenty-seven thousand and eighty-six miles, being on an average one hundred and eight miles each twenty-four hours. Of their proceedings in Otaheite a short abstract from Bligh's Journal will suffice.

Many inquiries were made by the natives after Captain Cook, Sir Joseph Banks, and others of their former friends. 'One of my first questions,' says Bligh, 'was after our friend Omai; and it was a sensible mortification and disappointment to me to hear, that not only Omai, but both the New Zealand boys who had been left with him, were dead. There appeared among the natives in general great good-will towards us, and they seemed to be much rejoiced at our arrival. The whole day we experienced no instance of dishonesty; and we were so much crowded, that I could not undertake to remove to a more proper station, without danger of disobliging our visiters, by desiring them to leave the ship.'

Otoo, the chief of the district, on hearing of the arrival of the Bounty, sent a small pig and a young plantain tree, as a token of friendship.

The ship was now plentifully supplied with provisions; every man on board having as much as he could consume.

As soon as the ship was secured, Lieutenant Bligh went on shore with the chief, Poeeno, passing through a walk delightfully shaded with breadfruit trees, to his own house, where his wife and her sister were busily employed staining a piece of cloth red. They desired him to sit down on a mat, and with great kindness offered him refreshments. Several strangers were now introduced, who came to offer their congratulations, and behaved with great decorum and attention. On taking leave, he says, ' the ladies, for they deserve to be called such from their natural and unaffected manners, and elegance of deportment, got up, and taking some of their finest cloth and a mat, clothed me in the Otaheitan fashion, and then said, " We will go with you to your boat;" and each taking me by the hand, amidst a great crowd, led me to the water side, and then took their leave.' In this day's walk, Bligh had the satisfaction to see that the island had received some benefit from the former visits of Captain Cook. Two shaddocks were brought to him, a fruit which they had not till Cook introduced it; and among the articles which they brought off to the ship, and offered for sale, were capsicums, pumkins, and two young goats. ' In the course of two or three days,' says he, ' an intimacy between the natives and the ship's company was become so general, that there was scarcely a man in the ship who had not already his *tayo* or friend.'

Nelson, the gardener, and his assistant, being

sent out to look for young plants, it was no small
degree of pleasure to find them report on their
return, that, according to appearances, the object
of the voyage would probably be accomplished
with ease; the plants were plentiful, and no apparent objection on the part of the natives to collect
as many as might be wanted. Nelson had the
gratification to meet with two fine shaddock trees
which he had planted in 1777, and which were
now full of fruit, but not ripe.

Presents were now given to Otoo, the Chief of
Matavai, who had changed his name to Tinah.
He was told that, on acccount of the kindness of
his people to Captain Cook, and from a desire to
serve him and his country, King George had sent
out those valuable presents to him ; and 'will you
not, Tinah,' said Bligh, ' send something to King
George in return?' 'Yes,' he said, ' I will send
him anything I have ; ' and then began to enu-
merate the different articles in his power, among
which he mentioned the bread-fruit. This was the
exact point to which Bligh was endeavouring to
lead him, and he was immediately told that the
bread-fruit trees were what King George would
like very much, on which he promised that a great
many should be put on board.

Hitherto no thefts had been committed, and
Bligh was congratulating himself on the improvement of the Otaheitans in this respect, as the same
facilities and the same temptations were open to
them as before. The ship, as on former occasions,
was constantly crowded with visiters. One day,
however, the gudgeon of the rudder belonging to
the large cutter was drawn out and stolen, without

E

being perceived by the man who was stationed to take care of her; and as this and some other petty thefts, mostly owing to the negligence of the men, were commencing, and would have a tendency to interrupt the good terms on which they were with the chiefs, ' I thought,' says Bligh, ' it would have a good effect to punish the boat-keeper in their presence, and accordingly I ordered him a dozen lashes. All who attended the punishment interceded very earnestly to get it mitigated : the women shewed great sympathy, and that degree of feeling which characterizes the amiable part of their sex.'

The longer they remained on the island, the more they had occasion to be pleased with the conduct of the islanders, and the less incommoded either on board or when on shore, by the natives following them as at first. Into every house they wished to enter, they always experienced a kind reception. The Otaheitans, we are told, have the most perfect easiness of manner, equally free from forwardness and formality ; and that ' there is a candour and sincerity about them that is quite delightful.' When they offer refreshments, for instance, if they are not accepted, they do not think of offering them a second time ; for they have not the least idea of that ceremonious kind of refusal which expects a second invitation. ' Having one day,' says Bligh, ' exposed myself too much in the sun, I was taken ill, on which all the powerful people, both men and women, collected round me, offering their assistance. For this short illness I was made ample amends by the pleasure I received from the attention and appearance of affection in these kind people.'

On one occasion the Bounty had nearly gone ashore in a tremendous gale of wind, and on another did actually get aground; on both which accidents, these kind-hearted people came in crowds to congratulate the captain on her escape; and many of them are stated to have been affected in the most lively manner, shedding tears while the danger in which the ship was placed continued.

On the 9th December, the surgeon of the Bounty died from the effects of intemperance and indolence. This unfortunate man is represented to have been in a constant state of intoxication, and was so averse from any kind of exercise, that he never could be prevailed on to take half a dozen hours upon deck at a time in the whole course of the voyage. Lieutenant Bligh had obtained permission to bury him on shore; and on going with the chief Tinah to the spot intended for his burial place, ' I found,' says he, ' the natives had already begun to dig his grave.' Tinah asked if they were doing it right? ' There,' says he, ' the sun rises, and there it sets.' Whether the idea of making the grave east and west is their own, or whether they learnt it from the Spaniards, who buried the captain of their ship on the island in 1774, there were no means of ascertaining; but it was certain they had no intimation of that kind from any body belonging to the Bounty. When the funeral took place, the chiefs and many of the natives attended the ceremony, and shewed great attention during the service. Many of the principal natives attended divine service on Sundays, and behaved with great decency. Some of the women at one time betrayed an inclination to laugh at the general responses ; but, the captain says, on looking at them they appeared much ashamed.

The border of low land, which is of the breadth of about three miles, between the sea-coast and the foot of the hills, consists of a very delightful country, well covered with bread-fruit and cocoa-trees, and strewed with houses in which are swarms of children playing about. ' It is delightful,' Bligh observes, ' to see the swarms of little children that are every where to be seen employed at their several amusements ; some flying kites, some swinging in ropes suspended from the boughs of trees, others walking on stilts, some wrestling, and others playing all manner of antic tricks such as are common to boys in England. The little girls have also their amusements, consisting generally of heivahs or dances. On an evening, just before sunset, the whole beach abreast the ship is described as being like a parade, crowded with men, women, and children, who go on with their sports and amusements till nearly dark, when every one peaceably returns to his home. At such times, we are told, from three to four hundred people are assembled together, and all happily diverted, good humoured, and affectionate to one another, without a single quarrel having ever happened to disturb the harmony that existed among these amiable people. Both boys and girls are said to be handsome and very sprightly.

It did not appear that much pains were taken in their plantations, except those of the ava and the cloth-plant; many of the latter are fenced with stone, and surrounded with a ditch. In fact, Nature has done so much for them, that they have

no great occasion to use exertion in obtaining a
sufficient supply of either food or raiment. Yet
when Bligh commenced taking up the bread-fruit
plants, he derived much assistance from the natives in collecting and pruning them, which they
understood perfectly well.

The behaviour of these people on all occasions
was highly deserving of praise. One morning, at
the relief of the watch, the small cutter was missing. The ship's company were immediately mus-
tered, when it appeared that three men were absent.
They had taken with them eight stand of arms
and ammunition; but what their plan was, or
which way they had gone, no one on board
seemed to have the least knowledge. Information
being given of the route they had taken, the
master was despatched to search for the cutter,
and one of the chiefs went with him; but before
they had got half way, they met the boat with five
of the natives, who were bringing her back to the
ship. For this service they were handsomely rewarded. The chiefs promised to use every possible
means to detect and bring back the deserters,
which, in a few days, some of the islanders had
so far accomplished as to seize and bind them,
but let them loose again on a promise that they
would return to their ship, which they did not exactly fulfil, but gave themselves up soon after on
a search being made for them.

A few days after this, a much more serious
occurrence happened, that was calculated to give
to the commander great concern. The wind had
blown fresh in the night, and at day-light it was

discovered that the cable, by which the ship rode,
had been cut near the water's edge, in such a
manner, that only one strand remained whole.
While they were securing the ship, Tinah came on
board ; and though there was no reason whatever
to suppose otherwise than that he was perfectly
innocent of the transaction, nevertheless, says the
commander, ' I spoke to him in a very peremptory
manner, and insisted upon his discovering and
bringing to me the offender. He promised to use
his utmost endeavours to discover the guilty person.
The next morning he and his wife came to me,
and assured me that they had made the strictest
inquiries without success. This was not at all satisfactory, and I behaved towards them with great
coolness, at which they were much distressed ;
and the lady at length gave vent to her sorrow by
tears. I could no longer keep up the appearance
of mistrusting them, but I earnestly recommended
to them, as they valued the King of England's
friendship, that they would exert their utmost endeavours to find out the offenders, which they faithfully promised to do.'

Here Bligh observes, it had since occurred to
him, that this attempt to cut the ship adrift was
most probably the act of some of his own people ;
whose purpose of remaining at Otaheite might
have been effectually answered without danger,
if the ship had been driven on shore. At the
time it occurred, he says, he entertained not the
least thought of this kind, nor did the possibility
of it enter into his ideas, having no suspicion
that so general an indication, or so strong an

attachment to these islands, could prevail among
his people, as to induce them to abandon every
prospect of returning to their native country.

This after-thought of Bligh will appear in the
sequel to be wholly gratuitous, and yet he might
naturally enough have concluded that so long and
unrestrained an intercourse with a people among
whom every man had his *tayo* or friend; among
whom every man was free to indulge every wish of
his heart; where, from the moment he set his foot
on shore, he found himself surrounded by female
allurements in the midst of ease and indolence,
and living in a state of luxury without submitting
to any kind of labour—such enticements to a common sailor might naturally enough be supposed
to create a desire for a longer residence in such a
country ; but this supposition is not borne out by
subsequent events.   The damage done to the
cable was, in all probability, owing to its chafing
over the rocky bottom.

The Bounty arrived on the 26th October, 1788,
and remained till the 4th April, 1789.   On the
31st March, the Commander says, ' To-day, all
the plants were on board, being in seven hundred
and seventy-four ` pots, thirty-nine tubs, and
twenty-four boxes.   The number of bread-fruit
plants were one thousand and fifteen ;   besides
which, we had collected a number of other plants :
the *avee*, which is one of the finest flavoured
fruits in the world ; the *ayyah*, which is a fruit
not so rich, but of a fine flavour and very refreshing ; the *rattah*, not much unlike a chestnut,
which grows on a large tree in great quantities;
they are singly in large pods, from one to two

inches broad, and may be eaten raw, or boiled
in the same manner as Windsor beans, and so
dressed are equally good; the *orai-ab*, which is
a very superior kind of plantain. All these I
was particularly recommended to collect, by my
worthy friend Sir Joseph Banks.'

While these active preparations for departure
were going on, the good chief Tinah, on bringing
a present for King George, could not refrain
from shedding tears. During the remainder of
their stay, there appeared among the natives an
evident degree of sorrow that they were so soon
to leave them, which they showed by a more than
usual degree of kindness and attention. The
above-mentioned excellent chief, with his wife,
brothers, and sister, requested permission to remain on board for the night previous to the
sailing of the Bounty. The ship was crowded
the whole day with the natives, and she was
loaded with presents of cocoa-nuts, plantains,
bread-fruits, hogs, and goats. Contrary to what
had been the usual practice, there was this
evening no dancing or mirth on the beach, such
as they had long been accustomed to, but all was
silent.

At sunset, the boat returned from landing
Tinah and his wife, and the ship made sail, bid-
ding farewell to Otaheite, where, Bligh observes,
' for twenty-three weeks we had been treated with
the utmost affection and regard, and which seemed
to increase in proportion to our stay. That we
were not insensible to their kindness, the events
which followed more than sufficiently prove ; for
to the friendly and endearing behaviour of these

people, may be ascribed the motives for that event which effected the ruin of an expedition, that there was every reason to hope would have been completed in the most fortunate manner.'

The morning after their departure, they got sight of Huaheine; and a double canoe soon coming alongside, containing ten natives, among them was a young man who recollected Captain Bligh, and called him by name; having known him when here in the year 1780, with Captain Cook in the Resolution. Several other canoes arrived with hogs, yams, and other provisions, which they purchased. This person confirmed the account that had already been received of Omai, and said that, of all the animals which had been left with Omai, the mare only remained alive; that the seeds and plants had been all destroyed, except one tree : but of what kind that was, he could not satisfactorily explain. A few days after sailing from this island, the weather became squally, and a thick body of black clouds collected in the east. A water-spout was in a short time seen at no great distance from the ship, which appeared to great advantage from the darkness of the clouds behind it. The upper part is described as being about two feet in diameter; and the lower about eight inches. It advanced rapidly towards the ship, when it was deemed expedient to alter the course, and to take in all the sails, except the foresail; soon after which it passed within ten yards of the stern, making a rustling noise, but without their feeling the least effect from its being so near. The rate at which it travelled was judged to be about ten miles per hour, going towards the west, in the direction of the wind ; and in a quarter of an hour after passing the ship, it dispersed. As they passed several low islands, the natives of one of them came out in their canoes, and it was observed that they all spoke the language of Otaheite. Presents of iron, beads, and a looking-glass were given to them ; but it was observed that the chief, on leaving the ship, took possession of everything that had been distributed. One of them showed some signs of dissatisfaction ; but after a little altercation, they joined noses and were reconciled.

The Bounty anchored at Anamooka on the 23rd April ; and an old lame man, named Tepa, whom Bligh had known here in 1777, and immediately recollected, came on board along with others from different islands in the vicinity. This man having formerly been accustomed to the English manner of speaking their language, the Commander found he could converse with him tolerably well. He told him that the cattle which had been left at Tongataboo had all bred, and that the old ones were yet living. Being desirous of seeing the ship, he and his companions were taken below, and the bread-fruit and other plants were shown to them, on seeing which they were greatly surprised.

' I landed,' says Bligh, ' in order to procure some bread-fruit plants to supply the place of one that was dead, and two or three others that were a little sickly. I walked to the west part of the bay, where some plants and seeds had been sown by Captain Cook ; and had the satisfaction to see, in a plantation close by, about twenty fine pine-

apple plants, but no fruit, this not being the proper
season. They told me that they had eaten many
of them, that they were very fine and large, and
that at Tongataboo there were great numbers.'

Numerous were the marks of mourning with
which these people disfigure themselves, such as
bloody temples, their heads deprived of most of
the hair, and, which was worse, almost all of them
with the loss of some of their fingers. Several
fine boys, not above six years of age, had lost
both their little fingers ; and some of the men
had parted with the middle finger of the right hand.

A brisk trade soon began to be carried on for
yams ; some plantains and bread-fruit were likewise brought on board, but no hogs. Some of
the sailing canoes, which arrived in the course of
the day, were large enough to contain not less
than ninety passengers. From these the officers
and crew purchased hogs, dogs, fowls, and shaddocks ; yams, very fine and large; one of them
actually weighed above forty-five pounds. The
crowd of natives had become so great the next day,
Sunday 26th, that it became impossible to do anything. The watering party were therefore ordered
to go on board, and it was determined to sail ; the
ship was accordingly unmoored and got under
weigh. A grapnel, however, had been stolen, and
Bligh informed the chiefs that were still on board,
that unless it was returned, they must remain in
the ship, at which they were surprised and not a
little alarmed. ' I detained them,' he says, ' till
sunset, when their uneasiness and impatience increased to such a degree, that they began to beat
themselves about the face and eyes, and some of
them cried bitterly. As this distress was more

than the grapnel was worth, I could not think of detaining them longer, and called their canoes alongside. I told them they were at liberty to go, and made each of them a present of a hatchet, a saw, with some knives, gimblets and nails. This unexpected present, and the sudden change in their situation, affected them not less with joy than they had before been with apprehension. They were unbounded in their acknowledgments; and I have little doubt but that we parted better friends than if the affair had never happened.'

From this island the ship stood to the northward all night, with light winds; and on the next day, the 27th, at noon, they were between the islands Tofoa and Kotoo.

' Thus far,' says Bligh, ' the voyage had advanced in a course of uninterrupted prosperity, and had been attended with many circumstances equally pleasing and satisfactory. A very different scene was now to be experienced. A conspiracy had been formed, which was to render all our past labour productive only of extreme misery and distress. The means had been concerted and prepared with so much secrecy and circumspection, that no one circumstance appeared to occasion the smallest suspicion of the impending calamity, the result of an act of piracy the most consummate and atrocious that was probably ever committed.'

How far Bligh was justified in ascribing the calamity to a conspiracy will be seen hereafter. The following chapter will detail the facts of the mutinous proceedings as stated by the Lieutenant, in his own words.

CHAPTER III.

THE MUTINY.

'That, Captain Bligh; that is the thing; I am in hell !—I am in hell !'—FLETCHER CHRISTIAN.

————' Horror and doubt distract
His troubled thoughts, and from the bottom stir
The hell within him ; for within him hell
He brings, and round about him, nor from hell
One step no more than from himself can fly
By change of place ; now conscience wakes despair
That slumber'd, wakes the bitter memory
Of what he was, what is, and what must be
Worse ; of worse deeds worse sufferings must ensue.'

' In the morning of the 28th April, the north-westernmost of the Friendly Islands, called Tofoa, bearing north-east, I was steering to the westward with a ship in most perfect order, all my plants in a most flourishing condition, all my men and officers in good health, and in short, everything to flatter and insure my most sanguine expectations. On leaving the deck I gave directions for the course to be steered during the night. The master had the first watch ; the gunner, the middle watch ; and Mr. Christian the morning watch. This was the turn of duty for the night.

' Just before sun-rising on Tuesday the 28th, while I was yet asleep, Mr. Christian, officer of the watch, Charles Churchill, ship's corporal, John Mills, gunner's mate, and Thomas Burkitt, seaman,

came into my cabin, and seizing me, tied my hands
with a cord behind my back, threatening me with
instant death if I spoke or made the least noise.
I called, however, as loud as I could in hopes of
assistance; but they had already secured the
officers who were not of their party, by placing
sentinels at their doors. There were three men at
my cabin door, besides the four within ; Christian
had only a cutlass in his hand, the others had muskets and bayonets. I was hauled out of bed, and
forced on deck in my shirt, suffering great pain
from the tightness with which they had tied my
hands* [behind my back, held by Fletcher Christian, and Charles Churchill, with a bayonet at my
breast, and two men, Alexander Smith and Thomas
Burkitt behind me, with loaded muskets cocked and
bayonets fixed]. I demanded the reason of such
violence, but received no other answer than abuse,
for not holding my tongue. The master, the gunner, Mr. Elphinstone, the master's mate, and Nelson, were kept confined below; and the fore-
hatchway was guarded by sentinels. The boatswain and carpenter, and also Mr. Samuel the
clerk, were allowed to come upon deck, where they
saw me standing abaft the mizen-mast, with my
hands tied behind my back, under a guard, with
Christian at their head. The boatswain was ordered to hoist the launch out, with a threat, if he
did not do it instantly, to take care of himself.

'When the boat was out, Mr. Hayward and Mr.
Hallet, two of the midshipmen, and Mr. Samuel,
were ordered into it. I demanded what their intention was in giving this order, and endeavoured

* The words within brackets are in the original despatch.

to persuade the people near me not to persist in such acts of violence; but it was to no effect— " Hold your tongue, Sir, or you are dead this instant," was constantly repeated to me.

The master by this time had sent to request that he might come on deck, which was permitted; but he was soon ordered back again to his cabin.

' [When I exerted myself in speaking loud, to try if I could rally any with a sense of duty in them, I was saluted with—" d—n his eyes, the ——, blow his brains out;" while Christian was threatening me with instant death, if I did not hold my tongue.]

' I continued my endeavours to turn the tide of affairs, when Christian changed the cutlass which he had in his hand, for a bayonet that was brought to him, and holding me with a strong gripe by the cord that tied my hands, he threatened, with many oaths, to kill me immediately, if I would not be quiet; the villains round me had their pieces cocked and bayonets fixed. Particular persons were called on to go into the boat and were hurried over the side; whence I concluded that with these people I was to be set adrift. I therefore made another effort to bring about a change, but with no other effect than to be threatened with having my brains blown out.

' The boatswain and seamen who were to go in the boat, were allowed to collect twine, canvas, lines, sails, cordage, an eight-and-twenty gallon cask of water; and Mr. Samuel got one hundred and fifty pounds of bread, with a small quantity of rum and wine, also a quadrant and compass; but he was forbidden, on pain of death, to touch

either map, ephemeris, book of astronomical observations, sextant, time-keeper, or any of my
surveys or drawings.

'The mutineers having forced those of the seamen whom they meant to get rid of into the boat,
Christian directed a dram to be served to each of
his own crew. I then unhappily saw that nothing
could be done to effect the recovery of the ship:
there was no one to assist me, and every endeavour on my part was answered with threats of
death.

'The officers were next called upon deck, and
forced over the side into the boat, while I was
kept apart from every one, abaft the mizen-mast;
Christian, armed with a bayonet, holding me by
the bandage that secured my hands. The guard
round me had their pieces cocked, but on my daring
the ungrateful wretches to fire, they uncocked
them.

'Isaac Martin, one of the guard over me, I saw
had an inclination to assist me, and as he fed me
with shaddock (my lips being quite parched) we
explained our wishes to each other by our looks;
but this being observed, Martin was removed from
me. He then attempted to leave the ship, for
which purpose he got into the boat; but with
many threats they obliged him to return.

'The armourer, Joseph Coleman, and two of the
carpenters, M'Intosh and Norman, were also kept
contrary to their inclination; and they begged of
me, after I was astern in the boat, to remember
that they declared they had no hand in the transaction. Michael Byrne, I am told, likewise
wanted to leave the ship.

' It is of no moment for me to recount my endeavours to bring back the offenders to a sense of their duty; all I could do was by speaking to them in general; but it was to no purpose, for I was kept securely bound, and no one except the guard suffered to come near me.

' To Mr. Samuel (clerk) I am indebted for securing my journals and commission, with some material ship papers. Without these I had nothing to certify what I had done, and my honour and character might have been suspected, without my possessing a proper document to have defended them. All this he did with great resolution, though guarded and strictly watched. He attempted to save the timekeeper, and a box with my surveys, drawings, and remarks, for fifteen years past, which were numerous; when he was hurried away with " D—n your eyes, you are well off to get what you have."

' It appeared to me that Christian was some time in doubt whether he should keep the carpenter, or his mates; at length he determined on the latter, and the carpenter was ordered into the boat. He was permitted, but not without some opposition, to take his tool-chest.

' Much altercation took place among the mutinous crew during the whole business: some swore " I'll be d—d if he does not find his way home, if he gets anything with him;" and when the carpenter's chest was carrying away, " D—n my eyes, he will have a vessel built in a month;" while others laughed at the helpless situation of the boat, being very deep, and so little room for those who were in her. As for Christian, he

F

seemed as if meditating destruction on himself and every one else.

'I asked for arms, but they laughed at me, and said I was well acquainted with the people among whom I was going, and therefore did not want them; four cutlasses, however, were thrown into the boat, after we were veered astern.

'The officers and men being in the boat, they only waited for me, of which the master-at-arms informed Christian; who then said—"Come, Captain Bligh, your officers and men are now in the boat, and you must go with them; if you attempt to make the least resistance, you will instantly be put to death;" and without further ceremony, with a tribe of armed ruffians about me, I was forced over the side, when they untied my hands. Being in the boat, we were veered astern by a rope. A few pieces of pork were thrown to us, and some clothes, also the cutlasses I have already mentioned; and it was then that the armourer and carpenters called out to me to remember that they had no hand in the transaction. After having undergone a great deal of ridicule, and been kept for some time to make sport for these unfeeling wretches, we were at length cast adrift in the open ocean.

'I had with me in the boat the following persons :

Names.	*Stations.*
JOHN FRYER	Master.
THOMAS LEDWARD . . .	Acting Surgeon.
DAVID NELSON	Botanist.
WILLIAM PECKOVER . . .	Gunner.
WILLIAM COLE	Boatswain.
WILLIAM PURCELL . . .	Carpenter,

Names.	Stations.
WILLIAM ELPHINSTONE . .	Master's Mate.
THOMAS HAYWARD } JOHN HALLET	. . . Midshipmen.
JOHN NORTON } PETER LENKLETTER	. . Quarter-Masters.
LAWRENCE LEBOGUE . . .	Sailmaker.
JOHN SMITH } THOMAS HALL	. . . . Cooks.
GEORGE SIMPSON	Quarter-Master's Mate.
ROBERT TINKLER . . .	A boy.
ROBERT LAMB	Butcher.
MR. SAMUEL	Clerk.

In all eighteen.

' There remained in the Bounty:

Names.	Stations.
FLETCHER CHRISTIAN . . .	Master's Mate.
PETER HEYWOOD } EDWARD YOUNG } GEORGE STEWART	. . . Midshipmen.
CHARLES CHURCHILL . . .	Master-at-Arms.
JOHN MILLS	Gunner's Mate.
JAMES MORRISON	Boatswain's Mate.
THOMAS BURKITT MATTHEW QUINTAL JOHN SUMNER JOHN MILLWARD WILLIAM M'KOY HENRY HILLBRANT MICHAEL BYRNE WILLIAM MUSPRAT ALEXANDER SMITH JOHN WILLIAMS THOMAS ELLISON ISAAC MARTIN RICHARD SKINNER MATTHEW THOMPSON	. Able Seamen.
WILLIAM BROWN	Gardener.
JOSEPH COLEMAN	Armourer.
CHARLES NORMAN . . .	Carpenter's Mate.
THOMAS M'INTOSH . . .	Carpenter's Crew.

In all twenty-five—and the most able of the ship's company.

'Christian, the chief of the mutineers, is of a respectable family in the North of England. This was the third voyage he had made with me; and as I found it necessary to keep my ship's company at three watches, I 'had given him an order to take charge of the third, his abilities being thoroughly equal to the task; and by this means the master and gunner were not at watch and watch.

'Heywood is also of a respectable family in the North of England *, and a young man of abilities as well as Christian. These two had been objects of my particular regard and attention, and I had taken great pains to instruct them, having entertained hopes that, as professional men, they would have become a credit to their country.

'Young was well recommended, and had the look of an able, stout seaman ; he, however, fell short of what his appearance promised. [In the account sent home he is thus described: Edward Young, midshipman, aged twenty-two years. Dark complexion and rather a bad look—strong made—has lost several of his fore teeth, and those that remain are all rotten.]

'Stewart was a young man of creditable parents in the Orkneys; at which place, on the return of the Resolution from the South Seas, in 1780, we received so many civilities that, on that account only, I should gladly have taken him with me: but, independent of this recommendation, he was a seaman, and had always borne a good character.

'Notwithstanding the roughness with which I was treated, the remembrance of past kindnesses

* He was born in the Isle of Man, his father being Deemster of Man, and Seneschal to the Duke of Athol.

produced some signs of remorse in Christian.
When they were forcing me out of the ship, I
asked him if this treatment was a proper return
for the many instances he had received of my
friendship? he appeared disturbed at my question,
and answered with much emotion, "That,—Captain Bligh,—that is the thing;—I am in hell—I
am in hell!"

'As soon as I had time to reflect, I felt an
inward satisfaction, which prevented any depres-
sion of my spirits: conscious of my integrity, and
anxious solicitude for the good of the service in
which I had been engaged, I found my mind
wonderfully supported, and I began to conceive
hopes, notwithstanding so heavy a calamity, that
I should one day be able to account to my king
and country for the misfortune. A few hours
before my situation had been peculiarly flattering.
I had a ship in the most perfect order, and well
stored with every necessary both for service and
health; by early attention to those particulars I
had, as much as lay in my power, provided against
any accident in case I could not get through
Endeavour Straits, as well as against what might
befall me in them; add to this, the plants had
been successfully preserved in the most flourishing
state: so that, upon the whole, the voyage was
two-thirds completed, and the remaining part, to
all appearance, in a very promising way; every
person on board being in perfect health, to establish which was ever amongst the principal objects
of my attention.

'It will very naturally be asked, what could be
the reason for such a revolt? In answer to which

I can only conjecture, that the mutineers had flattered themselves with the hopes of a more happy life among the Otaheitans than they could possibly enjoy in England ; and this, joined to some female connections, most probably occasioned the whole transaction. The ship, indeed, while within our sight, steered to the W.N.W., but I considered this only as a feint; for when we were sent away,—" Huzza for Otaheite !"—was frequently heard among the mutineers.

'The women of Otaheite are handsome, mild and cheerful in their manners and conversation, possessed of great sensibility, and have sufficient delicacy to make them admired and beloved. The chiefs were so much attached to our people, that they rather encouraged their stay among them than otherwise, and even made them promises of large possessions. Under these and many other attendant circumstances, equally desirable, it is now perhaps not so much to be wondered at, though scarcely possible to have been foreseen, that a set of sailors, most of them void of connections, should be led away; especially when, in addition to such powerful inducements, they imagined it in their power to fix themselves in the midst of plenty, on one of the finest islands in the world, where they need not labour, and where the allurements of dissipation are beyond anything that can be conceived. The utmost, however, that any commander could have supposed to have happened is, that some of the people would have been tempted to desert. But if it should be asserted that a commander is to guard against an act of mutiny and piracy in his

own ship, more than by the common rules of service, it is as much as to say that he must sleep
locked up, and when awake, be girded with
pistols.

' Desertions have happened, more or less, from
most of the ships that have been at the Society
Islands ; but it has always been in the commander's power to make the chiefs return their
people ; the knowledge, therefore, that it was unsafe to desert, perhaps first led mine to consider
with what ease so small a ship might be surprized,
and that so favourable an opportunity would
never offer to them again.

' The secrecy of this mutiny is beyond all conception. Thirteen of the party, who were with
me, had always lived forward among the seamen ;
yet neither they, nor the messmates of Christian,
Stewart, Heywood and Young, had ever observed
any circumstance that made them in the least
suspect what was going on. To such a close-
planned act of villainy, my mind being entirely free
from any suspicion, it is not wonderful that I fell
a sacrifice. Perhaps, if there had been marines
on board, a sentinel at my cabin-door might have
prevented it ; for I slept with the door always
open, that the officer of the watch might have
access to me on all occasions, the possibility of
such a conspiracy being ever the farthest from
my thoughts. Had their mutiny been occasioned
by any grievances, either real or imaginary, I
must have discovered symptoms of their discontent, which would have put me on my guard :
but the case was far otherwise. Christian, in particular, I was on the most friendly terms with :

that very day he was engaged to have dined with
me ; and the preceding night he excused himself
from supping with me, on pretence of being unwell ; for which I felt concerned, having no suspicions of his integrity and honour.'

Such is the story published by Lieutenant
Bligh immediately on his return to England,
after one of the most distressing and perilous
passages over nearly four thousand miles of the
wide ocean, with eighteen persons, in an open
boat. The story obtained implicit credit; and
though Lieutenant Bligh's character never stood
high in the navy for suavity of manners or mild-
ness of temper, he was always considered as an
excellent seamen, and his veracity stood unim-
peached. But in this age of refined liberality,
when the most atrocious criminals find their
apologists, it is not surprising it should now be
discovered, when all are dead that could either
prove or disprove it, that it was the tyranny of
the commander alone, and not the wickedness of
the ringleader of the mutineers of the Bounty,
that caused that event. ' We all know,' it is
said, ' that mutiny can arise but from one of these
two sources, excessive folly or excessive tyranny ;
therefore'—the logic is admirable—' as it is
admitted that Bligh was no idiot, the inference is
obvious *.' If this be so, it may be asked to which
of the two causes must be ascribed the mutiny
at the Nore, &c. ? The true answer will be, to
neither. ' Not only,' continues the writer, ' was
the *narrative* which he published proved to be
false in many material bearings, by evidence

* United Service Journal for April, 1831.

before a court martial, but every act of his public
life after this event, from his successive command
of the Director, the Glatton, and the Warrior, to
his disgraceful expulsion from New South Wales,—
was stamped with an insolence, an inhumanity,
and coarseness, which fully developed his character.'

There is no intention, in narrating this eventful
history, to accuse or defend either the character or
the conduct of the late Admiral Bligh ; it is well
known his temper was irritable in the extreme;
but the circumstance of his having been the friend
of Captain Cook, with whom he sailed as his
master,—of his ever afterwards being patronized by
Sir Joseph Banks—of the Admiralty promoting him
to the rank of commander, appointing him immediately to the Providence, to proceed on the same
expedition to Otaheite,—and of his returning in a
very short time to England with complete success,
and recommending all his officers for promotion
on account of their exemplary conduct ;—of his
holding several subsequent employments in the
service—of his having commanded ships of the
line in the battles of Copenhagen and Camperdown,
—and risen to the rank of a flag-officer,—these
may perhaps be considered to speak something in
his favour, and be allowed to stand as some proof
that, with all his failings, he had his merits.
That he was a man of coarse habits, and entertained very mistaken notions with regard to discipline, is quite true : yet he had many redeeming
qualities.   The accusation, by the writer in question, of Bligh having falsified his ' narrative,' is a
very heavy charge, and, it is to be feared, is not

wholly without foundation; though it would perhaps be more correct to say, that in the printed narrative of his voyage, and the narrative on which the mutineers were tried, there are many important omissions from his original manuscript journal, some of which it will be necessary to notice presently.

The same writer further says, ' We know that the officers fared in every way worse than the men, and that even young Heywood was kept at the mast head no less than eight hours at one spell, in the worst weather which they encountered off Cape Horn.'

Perhaps Heywood may himself be brought forward as authority, if not to disprove, at least to render highly improbable, his experiencing any such treatment on the part of his captain. This young officer, in his defence, says, ' Captain Bligh, in his narrative, acknowledges that he had left some friends on board the Bounty, and no part of my conduct could have induced him to believe that I ought not to be reckoned of the number. Indeed, from his attention to, *and very kind treatment of me personally*, I should have been a monster of depravity to have betrayed him. The idea alone is sufficient to disturb a mind, where humanity and gratitude have, I hope, ever been noticed as its characteristic features.' Bligh, too, has declared in a letter to Heywood's uncle, Holwell, after accusing him of ingratitude, that ' he never once had an angry word from me during the whole course of the voyage, as his conduct always gave me much pleasure and satisfaction.'

In looking over a manuscript journal, kept by

Morrison, the boatswain's mate, who was tried and convicted as one of the mutineers, but received the king's pardon, the conduct of Bligh appears in a very unfavourable point of view. This Morrison was a person, from talent and education, far above the situation he held in the Bounty; he had previously served in the navy as midshipman, and, after his pardon, was appointed gunner of the Blenheim, in which he perished with Sir Thomas Troubridge. In comparing this journal with other documents, the dates and transactions appear to be correctly stated, though the latter may occasionally be somewhat too highly coloured. How he contrived to preserve this journal, in the wreck of the Pandora, does not appear; but there can be no doubt of its authenticity, having been kept among the late Captain Heywood's papers; various passages in it have been corrected either by this officer or some other person, but without altering their sense.

It would appear from this important document that the seeds of discord, in the unfortunate ship Bounty, were sown at a very early period of the voyage. It happened, as was the case in all small vessels, that the duties of commander and purser were united in the person of Lieutenant Bligh; and it would seem that this proved the cause of very serious discontent among the officers and crew; of the mischief arising out of this union, the following statement of Mr. Morrison may serve as a specimen. At Teneriffe, Lieutenant Bligh ordered the cheese to be hoisted up and exposed to the air; which was no sooner done, than he pretended to miss a certain quantity, and declared that it had been stolen. The cooper, Henry Hillbrant, informed him that the cask in question had been opened by the orders of Mr. Samuel, his clerk, who acted also as steward, and the cheese sent on shore to his own house, previous to the Bounty leaving the river on her way to Portsmouth. Lieutenant Bligh, without making any further inquiry, immediately ordered the allowance of that article to be stopped, both from *officers* and *men*, until the deficiency should be made good, and told the cooper he would give him a d——d good flogging, if he said another word on the subject. It can hardly be supposed that a man of Bligh's shrewdness, if disposed to play the rogue, would have placed himself so completely in the hands of the cooper, in a transaction which, if revealed, must have cost him his commission.

Again, on approaching the equator, some decayed pumpkins, purchased at Teneriffe, were ordered to be issued to the crew, at the rate of *one* pound of pumpkin for *two* pounds of biscuit. The reluctance of the men to accept this proposed substitute, *on such terms*, being reported to Lieutenant Bligh, he flew upon deck in a violent rage, turned the hands up, and ordered the first man on the list of each mess to be called by name ; at the same time saying, ' I'll see who will dare to refuse the pumpkin, or any thing else I may order to be served out ;' to which he added, ' You d——d infernal scoundrels, I'll make you eat grass, or any thing you can catch, before I have done with you.' This speech had the desired effect, every one receiving the pumpkins, even the *officers*.

Next comes a complaint respecting the mode of issuing beef and pork; but when a representation was made to Lieutenant Bligh in the quiet and orderly manner prescribed by the twenty-first article of war, he called the crew aft, told them that every thing relative to the provisions was transacted by his orders; that it was therefore needless for them to complain, as they would get no redress, he being the fittest judge of what was right or wrong, and that he would flog the first man who should dare attempt to make any complaint in future. To this imperious menace they bowed in silence, and not another murmur was heard from them during the remainder of the voyage to Otaheite, it being their determination to seek legal redress on the Bounty's return to England. Happy would it have been had they kept their resolution. By so doing, if the story be true, they would amply have been avenged, a vast number of human lives spared, and a world of misery avoided.

According to this Journalist, ' the seeds of eternal discord were sown between Lieutenant Bligh and some of his officers,' while in Adventure Bay, Van Dieman's Land; and on arriving at Matavai Bay, in Otaheite, he is accused of taking the officers' hogs and bread-fruit, and serving them to the ship's company; and when the master remonstrated with him on the subject, he replied that ' he would convince him that every thing became *his* as soon as it was brought on board; that he would take nine-tenths of every man's property, and let him see who dared to say any thing to the contrary.' The sailors' pigs were

seized without ceremony, and it became a favour
for a man to obtain an extra pound of his own meat.

The writer then says, ' the object of our visit to
the Society Islands being at length accomplished,
we weighed on the 4th April, 1789. Every one
seemed in high spirits, and began to talk of home,
as though they had just left Jamaica instead of
Otaheite, so far onward did their flattering fancies
waft them. On the 23rd, we anchored off Anna-
mooka, the inhabitants of which island were very
rude, and attempted to take the casks and axes from
the parties sent to fill water and cut wood. A
musket pointed at them produced no other effect
than a return of the compliment, by poising their
clubs or spears with menacing looks ; and, as it
was Lieutenant's Bligh's orders, that no person
should affront them on any occasion, they were
emboldened by meeting with no check to their insolence. They at length became so troublesome,
that Mr. Christian, who commanded the watering
party, found it difficult to carry on his duty ; but
on acquainting Lieutenant Bligh with their behaviour, he received a volley of abuse, was d—d
as a cowardly rascal, and asked if he were afraid
of naked savages whilst he had weapons in his
hand? To this he replied in a respectful manner,
' The arms are of no effect, Sir, while your orders
prohibit their use.'

This happened but three days before the mutiny, and the same circumstance is noticed, but
somewhat differently, in Bligh's MS. Journal,
where he says, ' the men cleared themselves, and
they therefore merit no punishment. As to
the officers I have no resource, nor do I ever

feel myself safe in the few instances I trust to them.' A perusal of all the documents certainly leads to the conclusion that all his officers were of a very inferior description ; they had no proper feeling of their own situation ; and this, together with the contempt in which they were held by Bligh, and which he could not disguise, may account for that perfect indifference, with regard both to the captain and the ship, which was manifested on the day of the mutiny.

That sad catastrophe, if the writer of the Journal be correct, was hastened, if not brought about by, the following circumstance, of which Bligh takes no notice. ' In the afternoon of the 27th, Lieutenant Bligh came upon deck, and missing some of the cocoa-nuts, which had been piled up between the guns, said they had been stolen, and could not have been taken away without the knowledge of the officers, all of whom were sent for and questioned on the subject. On their declaring that they had not seen any of the people touch them, he exclaimed, "Then you must have taken them yourselves ;" and proceeded to inquire of them separately, how many they had purchased. On coming to Mr. Christian, that gentleman answered, " I do not know, Sir, but I hope you do not think me so mean as to be guilty of stealing yours.". Mr. Bligh replied, " Yes, you d—d hound, I do—you must have stolen them from me, or you would be able to give a better account of them ;" then turning to the other officers, he said, " God d—n you, you scoundrels, you are all thieves alike, and combine with the men to rob me : I suppose you will steal my yams next; but I'll sweat you for it, you rascals—I'll make half of you jump overboard, before you get through Endeavour Straits." This threat was followed by an order to the clerk " to stop the villains' grog, and give them but half a pound of yams to-morrow; if they steal them, I'll reduce them to a quarter." '

It is difficult to believe that an officer in his majesty's service could condescend to make use of such language to the meanest of the crew, much less to gentlemen; it is to be feared, however, that there is sufficient ground for the truth of these statements: with regard to the last, it is borne out by the evidence of Mr. Fryer, the master, on the court-martial. This officer, being asked, ' what did you suppose to be Mr. Christian's meaning, when he said he had been in hell for a fortnight?' answered, ' From the frequent quarrels they had had, and the abuse which he had received from Mr. Bligh.'—' Had there been any very recent quarrel?'—' The day before Mr. Bligh challenged all the young gentlemen and people with stealing his cocoa-nuts.' It was on the evening of this day that Lieutenant Bligh, according to his printed narrative, says Christian was to have supped with him; but excused himself on account of being unwell; and that he was invited to dine with him on the day of the mutiny.

Every one of these circumstances, and many others, which might be stated from Mr. Morrison's Journal, are omitted in Bligh's published narrative; but many of them are alluded to in his original Journal, and others that prove distinctly the constant reproofs to which his officers were

subject, and the bad terms on which they stood
with their commander.   A few extracts from this
Journal will sufficiently establish this point.

In so early a part of the voyage as their arrival
in Adventure Bay, he found fault with his officers,
and put the carpenter into confinement.   Again,
at Matavai Bay, on the 5th December, Bligh
says, ' I ordered the carpenter to cut a large stone
that was brought off by one of the natives, re-
questing me to get it made fit for them to grind
their hatchets on, but to my astonishment he refused, in direct terms, to comply, saying, " I will
not cut the stone, for it will spoil my chisel; and
though there may be law to take away my clothes,
there is none to take away my tools."   This man
having before shewn his mutinous and insolent
behaviour, I was under the necessity of confining
him to his cabin.'

On the 5th January three men deserted in the
cutter, on which occasion Bligh says, ' Had the
mate of the watch been awake, no trouble of this
kind would have happened.   I have therefore dis-
rated and turned him before the mast : such neglectful and worthless petty officers, I believe, never
were in a ship as are in this.   No orders for a few
hours together are obeyed by them, and their conduct in general is so bad, that no confidence or
trust can be reposed in them ; in short, they have
driven me to every thing but corporal punishment, and that must follow if they do not improve.'

By Morrison's journal it would appear that
' corporal punishment' was not long delayed ; for,
on the very day, he says, the midshipman was put

G

in irons, and confined from the 5th January to the
23rd March—eleven weeks!

On the 17th January, orders being given to
clear out the sail-room and to air the sails, many
of them were found very much mildewed and rotten
in many places, on which he observes, ' If I had
any officers to supersede the master and boatswain, or was capable of doing without them, considering them as common seamen, they should no
longer occupy their respective stations; scarcely
any neglect of duty can equal the criminality of
this.'

On the 24th January, the three deserters were
brought back and flogged, then put in irons for
further punishment. ' As this affair,' he says,
' was solely caused by the neglect of the officers
who had the watch, I was induced to give them
all a lecture on this occasion, and endeavour to
shew them that, however exempt they were at
present from the like punishment, yet they were
equally subject, by the articles of war, to a condign one.' He then tells them, that it is only
necessity that makes him have recourse to repri-
mand, because there are no means of trying them
by court-martial; and adds a remark, not very
intelligible, but what he calls an unpleasant one,
about *such* offenders having no feelings of honour
or sense of shame.

On the 7th March, a native Otaheitan, whom
Bligh had confined in irons, contrived to break the
lock of the bilboa-bolt and make his escape. ' I
had given,' says Bligh, ' a written order that the
mate of the watch was to be answerable for the
prisoners, and to visit and see that they were safe

in his watch, but I have such a neglectful set
about me, that I believe nothing but condign punishment can alter their conduct. Verbal orders,
in the course of a month, were so forgotten, that
they would impudently assert, no such thing or
directions were given, and I have been at last
under the necessity to trouble myself with writing,
what, by decent young officers, would be complied
with as the common rules of the service. Mr.
Stewart was the mate of the watch.'

These extracts shew the terms on which Bligh
was with his officers ; and these few instances,
with others from Morrison's Journal, make it
pretty clear, that though Christian, as fiery and
passionate a youth as his commander could well
be, and with feelings too acute to bear the foul
and opprobrious language constantly addressed to
him, was the sole instigator of the mutiny;—
and that the captain had no support to expect,
and certainly received none, from the rest of his
officers. That Christian was the sole author
appears still more strongly from the following
passage in Morrison's Journal. ' When Mr.
Bligh found he must go into the boat, he
begged of Mr. Christian to desist, saying " I'll
pawn my honour, I'll give my bond, Mr. Christian, never to think of this, if you'll desist," and
urged his wife and family ; to which Mr. Christian
replied, " No, Captain Bligh, if you had any
honour, things had not come to this; and if you
had any regard for your wife and family, you
should have thought on them before, and not behaved so much like a villain." Lieutenant Bligh
again attempted to speak, but was ordered to be

G 2

silent. The boatswain also tried to pacify Mr.
Christian, to whom he replied, " It is too late, I
have been in hell for this fortnight past, and am
determined to bear it no longer ; and you know,
Mr. Cole, that I have been used like a dog all the
voyage."'

It is pretty evident, therefore, that the mutiny
was not, as Bligh in his narrative states it to
have been, the result of a conspiracy. It will be
seen by the minutes of the court-martial, that the
whole affair was planned and executed between the
hours of four and eight o'clock, on the morning
of the 28th April, when Christian had the watch
upon deck ; that Christian, unable longer to bear
the abusive and insulting language, had medi-
tated his own escape from the ship the day before,
choosing to trust himself to fate, rather than sub-
mit to the constant upbraiding to which he had
been subject; but the unfortunate business of the
cocoa-nuts drove him to the commission of the
rash and felonious act, which ended, as such criminal acts usually do, in his own destruction, and
that of a great number of others, many of whom
were wholly innocent.

Lieutenant Bligh, like most passionate men,
whose unruly tempers get the better of their reason, having vented his rage about the cocoa-nuts,
became immediately calm, and by inviting Christian
to sup with him the same evening, evidently wished
to renew their friendly intercourse; and happy
would it have been for all parties had he accepted the invitation. On the same night, towards ten o'clock, when the master had the
watch, Bligh came on deck, as was his cus-

tom, before retiring to sleep. It was one of
those calm and beautiful nights, so frequent in
tropical regions, whose soothing influence can be
appreciated only by those who have felt it, when,
after a scorching day, the air breathes a most refreshing coolness,—it was an evening of this sort,
when Bligh for the last time came upon deck, in
the capacity of commander; a gentle breeze
scarcely rippled the water, and the moon, then in
its first quarter, shed its soft light along the surface
of the sea. The short and quiet conversation that
took place between Bligh and the master on this
evening, after the irritation of the morning had subsided, only to burst forth again in all the horrors
of mutiny and piracy, recalls to one's recollection
that beautiful passage of Shakspeare, where, on
the evening of the murder, Duncan, on approaching the castle of Macbeth, observes to Banquo—

————' The air
Nimbly and sweetly recommends itself
Unto our gentle senses, &c.'—

a passage which Sir Joshua Reynolds considers as
a striking instance of what in painting is termed
repose. ' The subject,' he says, ' of this quiet and
easy conversation, gives that repose so necessary
to the mind, after the tumultuous bustle of the
preceding scenes, and beautifully contrasts the
scene of terror that immediately succeeds.' While,
on this lovely night, Bligh and his master were
congratulating themselves on the pleasing prospect of fine weather and a full moon, to light
them through Endeavour's dangerous straits, the
unhappy and deluded Christian was, in all probability, brooding over his wrongs, and meditating

on the criminal act he was to perpetrate the following morning; for he has himself stated, that he had just fallen asleep about half after three in the morning, and was much out of order.

The evidence on the court-martial is sufficiently explicit as to the mode in which this act of piracy was committed. By the journal of James Morrison, the following is the account of the transaction, as given by Christian himself to the two midshipmen, Heywood and Stewart, (both of whom had been kept below,) the moment they were allowed to come upon deck, after the boat, in which were Bligh and his companions, had been turned adrift.

He said, that, ' finding himself much hurt by the treatment he had received from Lieutenant Bligh, he had determined to quit the ship the preceding evening, and had informed the boatswain, carpenter, and two midshipmen (Stewart and *Hayward*), of his intention to do so ; that by them he was supplied with part of a roasted pig, some nails, beads, and other articles of trade, which he put into a bag that was given him by the last-named gentleman; that he put this bag into the clue of Robert Tinkler's hammock, where it was discovered by that young gentleman when going to bed at night, but the business was smothered, and passed off without any further notice. He said he had fastened some staves to a stout plank, with which he intended to make his escape; but finding he could not effect it during the first and middle watches, as the ship had no way through the water, and the people were all moving about, he laid down to rest about half-past three in the morning ; that when Mr. Stewart called him to

relieve the deck at four o'clock, he had but just
fallen asleep, and was much out of order; upon
observing which, Mr. Stewart strenuously advised
him to abandon his intention; that as soon as he
had taken charge of the deck, he saw Mr. Hayward, the mate of his watch, lie down on the arm-
chest to take a nap; and finding that Mr. Hallet,
the other midshipman, did not make his appearance, he suddenly formed the resolution of seizing
the ship. Disclosing his intention to Matthew
Quintal, and Isaac Martin, both of whom had been
flogged by Lieutenant Bligh, they called up
Charles Churchill, who had also tasted the cat,
and Matthew Thompson, both of whom readily
joined in the plot. That Alexander Smith (*alias*
John Adams), John Williams, and William
M'Koy, evinced equal willingness, and went with
Churchill to the armourer, of whom they obtained
the keys of the arm-chest, under pretence of wanting a musket to fire at a shark, then alongside; that
finding Mr. Hallet asleep on an arm-chest in the
main-hatchway, they roused and sent him on deck.
Charles Norman, unconscious of their proceedings, had in the mean time awaked Mr. *Hayward*,
and directed his attention to the shark, whose
movements he was watching at the moment that
Mr. Christian and his confederates came up the
fore-hatchway, after having placed arms in the
hands of several men who were not aware of their
design. One man, Matthew Thompson, was left
in charge of the chest, and he served out arms to
Thomas Burkitt and Robert Lamb. Mr. Christian said he then proceeded to secure Lieutenant
Bligh, the master, gunner, and botanist.'

' When Mr. Christian,' observes Morrison in
his journal, ' related the above circumstances, I
recollected having seen him fasten some staves to
a plank lying on the larboard gangway, as also
having heard the boatswain say to the carpenter,
" it will not do to-night." I likewise remembered
that Mr. Christian had visited the fore-cockpit
several times that evening, although he had very
seldom, if ever, frequented the warrant-officers'
cabins before.'

If this be a correct statement, and the greater
part of it is borne out by evidence on the court-
martial, it removes every doubt of Christian being
the sole instigator of the mutiny, and that no conspiracy nor preconcerted measures had any existence, but that it was suddenly conceived by a hot-
headed young man, in a state of great excitement
of mind, amounting to a temporary aberration of
intellect, caused by the frequent abusive and insulting language of his commanding officer.
Waking out of a short half hour's disturbed sleep,
to take the command of the deck—finding the two
mates of the watch, Hayward and Hallet asleep,
(for which they ought to have been dismissed the
service instead of being, as they were, promoted)
—the opportunity tempting, and the ship completely in his power, with a momentary impulse
he darted down the fore-hatchway, got possession
of the keys of the arm-chest, and made the hazardous experiment of arming such of the men as
he thought he could trust, and effected his purpose.

There is a passage in Captain Beechey's account of Pitcairn Island, which, if correct, would
cast a stain on the memory of the unfortunate

Stewart—he who, if there was one innocent man in the ship, was that man. Captain Beechey says (speaking of Christian), ' His plan, strange as it must appear for a young officer to adopt, who was fairly advanced in an honourable profession, was to set himself adrift upon a raft, and make his way to the island (Tofoa) then in sight. As quick in the execution as in the design, the raft was soon constructed, various useful articles were got together, and he was on the point of launching it, when a young officer, *who afterwards perished in the Pandora*, to whom Christian communicated his intention, recommended him, rather than risk his life on so hazardous an expedition, *to endeavour to take possession of the ship*, which he thought would not be very difficult, as many of the ship's company were not well disposed towards the commander, and would all be very glad to return to Otaheite, and reside among their friends in that island. This daring proposition is even more extraordinary than the premeditated scheme of his companion, and, if true, certainly relieves Christian from part of the odium which has hitherto attached to him as the sole instigator of the mutiny.' Relieve him?—not a jot—but on the best authority it may boldly be stated, that it is *not* true —the authority of Stewart's friend and messmate, the late Captain Heywood.

Captain Beechey, desirous of being correct in his statement, very properly sent his chapter on Pitcairn's Island for any observations Captain Heywood might have to make on what was said therein regarding the mutiny; observing in his note which accompanied it, that this account, re-

ceived from Adams, differed materially from a foot-
note in ' Marshall's Naval Biography ;' to which
Captain Heywood returned the following reply.

' 5th April, 1830.

' Dear Sir,—I have perused the account you received from Adams of the mutiny in the Bounty,
which does indeed differ very materially from a
foot-note in Marshall's Naval Biography, by the
editor, to whom I verbally detailed the facts, which
are strictly true.

' That Christian informed the boatswain and the
carpenter, Messrs. Hayward and Stewart, of his
determination to leave the ship upon a raft, on
the night preceding the mutiny, is certain ; but
that any one of them (Stewart in particular) should
have " recommended, rather than risk his life on
so hazardous an expedition, that he should try the
expedient of taking the ship from the captain, &c.,"
is entirely at variance with the whole character
and conduct of the latter, both before and after the
mutiny ; as well as with the assurance of Christian
himself, the very night he quitted Taheité, that the
idea of attempting to take the ship had never entered his distracted mind, until the moment he relieved the deck, and found his mate and midshipman asleep *.

' At that last interview with Christian he also
communicated to me, for the satisfaction of his
relations, other circumstances connected with that
unfortunate disaster, which, after their deaths,
may or may not be laid before the public. And
although they can implicate none but himself,

* Hayward and Hallet, who may thus be considered as
the *passive* cause of the mutiny.

either living or dead, they may extenuate but will
contain not a word of his in defence of the crime
he committed against the laws of his country.

'I am, &c.—P. HEYWOOD.'

Captain Beechey stated only what he had heard
from old Adams, who was not always correct in
the information he gave to the visiters of his
island; but this part of his statement gave great
pain to Heywood, who adverted to it on his
death-bed, wishing, out of regard for Stewart's
memory and his surviving friends, that it should
be publicly contradicted; and with this view the
above reply of Captain Heywood is here inserted.

The temptations, therefore, which it was supposed Otaheite held out to the deluded men of
the Bounty, had no more share in the transaction
than the supposed conspiracy; it does not appear,
indeed, that the cry of 'Huzza for Otaheite!' was
ever uttered; if this island had been the object of
either Christian or the crew, they would not have
left it three hundred miles behind them, before
they perpetrated the act of piracy; but after the
deed had been committed, it would be natural
enough that they should turn their minds to the
lovely island and its fascinating inhabitants, which
they had but just quitted, and that in the moment
of excitement some of them should have so called
out; but Bligh is the only person who has said
they did so.

If, however, the recollection of the 'sunny isle'
and its 'smiling women' had really tempted the
men to mutiny, Bligh would himself not be free
from blame, for having allowed them to indulge
for six whole months among this voluptuous

and fascinating people ; for though he was one of
the most active and anxious commanders of his
time, ' the service,' as is observed by a naval
officer, ' was carried on in those days in a very
different spirit from that which regulates its movements now, otherwise the Bounty would never
have passed six whole months at one island
" stowing away the fruit," during which time the
officers and seamen had free access to the shore.
Under similar circumstances nowadays, if the
fruit happened not to be ready, the ship would
have been off, after ten days' relaxation, to survey
other islands, or speculate on coral reefs, or make
astronomical observations ; in short, to do something or other to keep the devil out of the heads
of the crew *.'   Bligh would appear to have been
sensible of this on his next expedition in the
Providence, for on that occasion he collected more
bread-fruit plants than on the former, and spent
only half the time in doing so.

Be that as it may, Bligh might naturally
enough conclude that the seamen were casting ' a
lingering look behind' towards Otaheite. ' If,'
says Forster (who accompanied Cook), ' we fairly
consider the different situations of a common
sailor on board the Resolution, and of a Taheitan
on his island, we cannot blame the former if he
attempt to rid himself of the numberless discom-
forts of a voyage round the world, and prefer an
easy life, free from cares, in the happiest climate
of the world, to the frequent vicissitudes which are
entailed upon the mariner. The most favourable
prospects of future success in England, which he

* Quarterly Review, No. 89.

might form in idea, could never be so flattering
to his senses as the lowly hope of living like the
meanest Taheitan.   And supposing him to escape
the misfortunes incident to seamen, still he must
earn his subsistence in England at the expense of
labour, and " in the sweat of his brow," when this
oldest curse on mankind is scarcely felt at Taheité.
Two or three bread-fruit trees, which grow almost
without any culture, and which flourish as long as
he himself can expect to live, supply him with
abundant food during three-fourths of the year.
The cloth-trees and eddo-roots are cultivated
with much less trouble than our cabbages and
kitchen-herbs.   The banana, the royal palm, the
golden apple, all thrive with such luxuriance, and
require so little trouble, that I may venture to call
them spontaneous.   Most of their days are therefore spent in a round of various enjoyments, where
Nature has lavished many a pleasing landscape ;
where the temperature of the air is warm, but
continually refreshed by a wholesome breeze from
the sea ; and where the sky is almost constantly
serene.   A kind of happy uniformity runs through
the whole life of the Taheitans. They rise with the
sun, and hasten to rivers and fountains to perform an ablution equally reviving and cleanly.
They pass the morning at work, or walk about
till the heat of the day increases, when they retreat to their dwellings, or repose under some
tufted tree.   There they amuse themselves with
smoothing their hair, and anoint it with fragrant
oils ; or they blow the flute, and sing to it, or
listen to the songs of the birds.   At the hour of
noon, or a little later, they go to dinner.   After
their meals they resume their domestic amuse-

ments, during which the flame of mutual affection spreads in every heart, and unites the rising generation with new and tender ties. The lively jest, without any ill-nature, the artless tale, the jocund dance and frugal supper, bring on the evening; and another visit to the river concludes the actions of the day. Thus contented with their simple way of life, and placed in a delightful country, they are free from cares, and happy in their ignorance.'

Such is the picture drawn of the happy people of Otaheite by a cold, philosophical, German doctor, and such, with very little change, Bligh found them. As far, however, as the mutiny of his people was concerned, we must wholly discard the idea thrown out by him, that the seductions of Otaheite had any share in producing it. It could not have escaped a person of Christian's sagacity, that certain interrogatories would unquestionably be put by the natives of Otaheite, on finding the ship return so soon without her commander, without the bread-fruit plants, and with only about half her crew; questions he knew to which no satisfactory answer could be made; and though, at subsequent periods, he twice visited that island, it was some time afterwards, and not from choice but necessity; his object was to find a place of concealment, where he might pass the remainder of his days, unheard of and unknown, and where it is to be hoped he had time for sincere repentance, the only atonement he could make for the commission of a crime, which involved so many human beings in misery, and brought others to an untimely end—but of this hereafter.

CHAPTER IV.

THE OPEN-BOAT NAVIGATION.

' The boat is lower'd with all the haste of hate,
With its slight plank between thee and thy fate;
Her only cargo such a scant supply
As promises the death their hands deny;
And just enough of water and of bread
To keep, some days, the dying from the dead:
Some cordage, canvas, sails and lines and twine,
But treasures all to hermits of the brine,
Were added after, to the earnest prayer
Of those who saw no hope save sea and air;
And last, that trembling vassal of the Pole,
The feeling compass, Navigation's soul.

　　.　　　.　　　.　　　.　　　.

The launch is crowded with the faithful few
That wait their Chief—a melancholy crew :
But some remain'd reluctant on the deck
Of that proud vessel, now a moral wreck—
And view'd their Captain's fate with piteous eyes ;
While others scoff'd his augur'd miseries,
Sneer'd at the prospect of his pigmy sail,
And the slight bark, so laden and so frail.'

CHRISTIAN had intended to send away his captain and associates in the cutter, and ordered that it should be hoisted out for that purpose, which was done—a small wretched boat, that could hold but eight or ten men at the most, with a very small additional weight ; and, what was still worse, she was so worm-eaten and decayed, especially in the bottom planks, that the probability was, she would have gone down before she had proceeded a mile from the ship. In this ' rotten carcass of a boat,'

not unlike that into which Prospero and his lovely
daughter were ' hoist,'

> ' not rigg'd,
> Nor tackle, sail, nor mast; the very rats
> Instinctively had quit it,'

did Christian intend to cast adrift his late commander and his eighteen innocent companions,
or as many of them as she would stow, to find, as
they inevitably must have found, a watery grave.
But the remonstrances of the master, boatswain
and carpenter, prevailed on him to let those unfortunate men have the launch, into which nineteen
persons were thrust, whose weight, together with
that of the few articles they were permitted to
take, brought down the boat so near to the water,
as to endanger her sinking with but a moderate
swell of the sea—and to all human appearance, in
no state to survive the length of voyage they were
destined to perform over the wide ocean, but
which they did most miraculously survive.

The first consideration of Lieutenant Bligh and
his eighteen unfortunate companions, on being
cast adrift in their open boat, was to examine the
state of their resources. The quantity of provisions
which they found to have been thrown into the
boat, by some few kind-hearted messmates,
amounted to one hundred and fifty pounds of
bread, sixteen pieces of pork, each weighing two
pounds, six quarts of rum, six bottles of wine,
with twenty-eight gallons of water, and four
empty barricoes. Being so near to the island of
Tofoa, it was resolved to seek there a supply of
bread-fruit and water, to preserve if possible the
above-mentioned stock entire; but after rowing

along the coast, they discovered only some cocoa-nut trees on the top of high precipices, from which, with much danger owing to the surf, and great difficulty in climbing the cliffs, they succeeded in obtaining about twenty nuts. The second day they made excursions into the island, but without success. They met however with a few natives, who came down with them to the cove where the boat was lying; and others presently followed. They made inquiries after the ship, and Bligh unfortunately advised they should say that the ship had overset and sunk, and that they only were saved. The story might be innocent, but it was certainly indiscreet to put the people in possession of their defenceless situation; however, they brought in small quantities of bread-fruit, plantains and cocoa-nuts, but little or no water could be procured. These supplies, scanty as they were, served to keep up the spirits of the men: ' They no longer,' says Bligh, ' regarded me with those anxious looks, which had constantly been directed towards me, since we lost sight of the ship : every countenance appeared to have a degree of cheerfulness, and they all seemed determined to do their best.'

The numbers of the natives having so much increased as to line the whole beach, they began knocking stones together, which was known to be the preparatory signal for an attack. With some difficulty on account of the surf, our seamen succeeded in getting the things that were on shore into the boat, together with all the men, except John Norton, quarter-master, who was casting off the stern-fast. The natives immediately rushed

H

upon this poor man, and actually stoned him to death. A volley of stones was also discharged at the boat, and every one in it was more or less hurt. This induced the people to push out to sea with all the speed they were able to give to the launch, but to their surprize and alarm, several canoes, filled with stones, followed close after them and renewed the attack ; against which, the only return the unfortunate men in the boat could make, was with the stones of the assailants that lodged in her, a species of warfare in which they were very inferior to the Indians. The only expedient left was to tempt the enemy to desist from the pursuit, by throwing overboard some clothes, which fortunately induced the canoes to stop and pick them up; and night coming on, they returned to the shore, leaving the party in the boat to reflect on their unhappy situation.

The men now intreated their commander to take them towards home ; and on being told that no hope of relief could be entertained till they reached Timor, a distance of full twelve hundred leagues, they all readily agreed to be content with an allowance, which, on calculation of their resources, the commander informed them would not exceed one ounce of bread, and a quarter of a pint of water, per day. Recommending them, therefore, in the most solemn manner, not to depart from their promise in this respect, ' we bore away,' says Bligh, ' across a sea where the navigation is but little known, in a small boat twenty-three feet long from stem to stern, deeply laden with eighteen men. I was happy, however, to see that every one seemed better satisfied with our

Drawn & Etched by

Isaac G.tt Batt.

The open Boat with Bligh and his Companions.

Published by John Murray, Albemarle St. 1831.

situation than myself. It was about eight o'clock at night on the 2nd May, when we bore away under a reefed lug-foresail; and having divided the people into watches, and got the boat into a little order, we returned thanks to God for our miraculous preservation, and, in full confidence of his gracious support, I found my mind more at ease than it had been for some time past.'

At day-break on the 3rd, the forlorn and almost hopeless navigators saw with alarm the sun to rise fiery and red,—a sure indication of a severe gale of wind; and accordingly, at eight o'clock it blew a violent storm, and the sea ran so very high, that the sail was becalmed when between the seas, and too much to have set when on the top of the sea; yet it is stated that they could not venture to take it in, as they were in very imminent danger and distress, the sea curling over the stern of the boat, and obliging them to bale with all their might. ' A situation,' observes the commander, ' more distressing has, perhaps, seldom been experienced.'

The bread, being in bags, was in the greatest danger of being spoiled by the wet, the consequence of which, if not prevented, must have been fatal, as the whole party would inevitably be starved to death, if they should fortunately escape the fury of the waves. It was determined, therefore, that all superfluous clothes, with some rope and spare sails, should be thrown overboard, by which the boat was considerably lightened. The carpenter's tool-chest was cleared, and the tools stowed in the bottom of the boat, and the bread secured in the chest. All the people being thoroughly wet and cold, a tea-spoonful of rum was served out to each person, with a quarter of a bread-fruit, which is stated to have been scarcely eatable, for dinner ; Bligh having determined to preserve sacredly, and at the peril of his life, the engagement they entered into, and to make their small stock of provisions last eight weeks, let the daily proportion be ever so small.

The sea continuing to run even higher than in the morning, the fatigue of baling became very great ; the boat was necessarily kept before the sea. The men were constantly wet, the night very cold, and at daylight their limbs were so benumbed, that they could scarcely find the use of them. At this time a tea-spoonful of rum served out to each person was found of great benefit to all. Five small cocoa-nuts were distributed for dinner, and every one was satisfied ; and in the evening, a few broken pieces of bread-fruit were served for supper, after which prayers were performed.

On the night of the 4th and morning of the 5th, the gale had abated ; the first step to be taken was to examine the state of the bread, a great part of which was found to be damaged and rotten—but even this was carefully preserved for use. The boat was now running among some islands, but after their reception at Tofoa, they did not venture to land. On the 6th, they still continued to see islands at a distance ; and this day, for the first time, they hooked a fish, to their great joy; ' but,' says the commander, ' we were miserably disappointed by its being lost in trying to get it into the boat.' In the evening, each person had an

ounce of the damaged bread, and a quarter of a
pint of water for supper.

Lieutenant Bligh observes, ' it will readily be
supposed our lodgings were very miserable, and
confined for want of room ;' but he endeavoured
to remedy the latter defect, by putting themselves at watch and watch ; so that one half
always sat up, while the other lay down on the
boat's bottom, or upon a chest, but with nothing
to cover them except the heavens.   Their limbs,
he says, were dreadfully cramped, for they could
not stretch them. out ; and the nights were so
cold, and they were so constantly wet, that, after
a few hours sleep, they were scarcely able to
move.   At dawn of day on the 7th, being very
wet and cold, he says, ' I served a spoonful of
rum and a morsel of bread for breakfast.'

In the course of this day they passed close to
some rocky isles, from which two large sailing-
canoes came swiftly after them, but in the afternoon gave over the chase.   They were of the same
construction as those of the Friendly Islands, and
the land seen for the last two days was supposed
to be the Fejee Islands.   But being constantly wet,
Bligh says, ' it is with the utmost difficulty I can
open a book to write, and I feel truly sensible I can
do no more than point out where these lands are to
be found, and give some idea of their extent.' Heavy
rain came on in the afternoon, when every person in
the boat did his utmost to catch some water, and
thus succeeded in increasing their stock to thirty-
four gallons, besides quenching their thirst for the
first time they had been able to do so since they
had been at sea : but it seems an attendant con-

sequence of the heavy rain caused them to pass the night very miserably; for being extremely wet, and having no dry things to shift or cover them-selves, they experienced cold and shiverings scarcely to be conceived.

On the 8th, the allowance issued was an ounce and a half of pork, a tea spoonful of rum, half a pint of cocoa-nut milk, and an ounce of bread. The rum, though so small in quantity, is stated to have been of the greatest service. In the after-noon they were employed in cleaning out the boat, which occupied them until sunset before they got every thing dry and in order. ' Hitherto,' Bligh says, ' I had issued the allowance by guess, but I now made a pair of scales with two cocoa-nut shells; and having accidentally some pistol-balls in the boat, twenty-five of which weighed one pound or sixteen ounces, I adopted one of these balls as the proportion of weight that each person should receive of bread at the times I served it. I also amused all hands with describing the situa-tions of New Guinea and New Holland, and gave them every information in my power, that in case any accident should happen to me, those who sur-vived might have some idea of what they were about, and be able to find their way to Timor, which at present they knew nothing of more than the name, and some not even that. At night I served a quarter of a pint of water and half an ounce of bread for supper.

On the morning of the 9th, a quarter of a pint of cocoa-nut milk and some of the decayed bread were served for breakfast; and for dinner, the kernels of four cocoa-nuts, with the remainder of the rotten bread, which, he says, was eatable only by such distressed people as themselves. A storm of thunder and lightning gave them about twenty gallons of water. ' Being miserably wet and cold, I served to the people a tea-spoonful of rum each, to enable them to bear with their distressing situation. The weather continued extremely bad, and the wind increased; we spent a very miserable night, without sleep, except such as could be got in the midst of rain.'

The following day, the 10th, brought no relief, except that of its light. The sea broke over the boat so much, that two men were kept constantly baling; and it was necessary to keep the boat before the waves for fear of its filling. The allowance now served regularly to each person was one twenty-fifth part of a pound of bread and a quarter of a pint of water, at eight in the morning, at noon, and at sunset. To-day was added about half an ounce of pork for dinner, which, though any moderate person would have considered only as a mouthful, was divided into three or four.

The morning of the 11th did not improve. ' At day-break I served to every person a tea-spoonful of rum, our limbs being so much cramped that we could scarcely move them. Our situation was now extremely dangerous, the sea frequently running over our stern, which kept us baling with all our strength. At noon the sun appeared, which gave us as much pleasure as is felt when it shows itself on a winter's day in England.

' In the evening of the 12th it still rained hard, and we again experienced a dreadful night. At length the day came, and showed a miserable set of beings, full of wants, without any thing to relieve them. Some complained of great pain in their bowels, and every one of having almost lost the use of his limbs. The little sleep we got was in no way refreshing, as we were constantly covered with the sea and rain. The weather continuing, and no sun affording the least prospect of getting our clothes dried, I recommended to every one to strip and wring them through the sea-water, by which means they received a warmth that, while wet with rain-water, they could not have.' The shipping of seas and constant baling continued; and though the men were shivering with wet and cold, the commander was under the necessity of informing them, that he could no longer afford them the comfort they had derived from the tea-spoonful of rum.

On the 13th and 14th the stormy weather and heavy sea continued unabated, and on these days they saw distant land, and passed several islands. The sight of these islands, it may well be supposed, served only to increase the misery of their situation. They were as men very little better than starving with plenty in their view; yet, to attempt procuring any relief was considered to be attended with so much danger, that the prolongation of life, even in the midst of misery, was thought preferable, while there remained hopes of being able to surmount their hardships.

The whole day and night of the 15th were still rainy; the latter was dark, not a star to be seen by which the steerage could be directed, and the sea was continually breaking over the boat. On the next day, the 16th, was issued for dinner an

ounce of salt pork, in addition to their miserable
allowance of one twenty-fifth part of a pound of
bread. The night was again truly horrible, with
storms of thunder, lightning, and rain ; not a star
visible, so that the steerage was quite uncertain.

On the morning of the 17th, at dawn of day,
' I found,' says the commander, ' every person
complaining, and some of them solicited extra
allowance, which I positively refused. Our situation was miserable ; always wet, and suffering
extreme cold in the night, without the least shelter
from the weather. The little rum we had was of
the greatest service : when our nights were particularly distressing, I generally served a tea-spoonful or two to each person, and it was always joyful
tidings when they heard of my intentions. The
night was again a dark and dismal one, the sea
constantly breaking over us, and nothing but the
wind and waves to direct our steerage. It was
my intention, if possible, to make the coast of
New Holland to the southward of Endeavour
Straits, being sensible that it was necessary to preserve such a situation as would make a southerly
wind a fair one ; that we might range along the
reefs till an opening should be found into smooth
water, and we the sooner be able to pick up some
refreshments.'

On the 18th the rain abated, when, at their
commander's recommendation, they all stripped
and wrung their clothes through the sea-water,
from which, as usual, they derived much warmth
and refreshment ; but every one complained of
violent pains in their bones. At night the heavy
rain recommenced, with severe lightning, which

obliged them to keep baling without intermission. The same weather continued through the 19th and 20th; the rain constant—at times a deluge—the men always baling; the commander, too, found it necessary to issue for dinner only half an ounce of pork.

At dawn of day, Lieutenant Bligh states, that some of his people seemed half dead; that their appearances were horrible; ' and I could look,' says he, ' no way, but I caught the eye of some one in distress. Extreme hunger was now too evident, but no one suffered from thirst, nor had we much inclination to drink, that desire perhaps being satisfied through the skin. The little sleep we got was in the midst of water, and we constantly awoke with severe cramps and pains in our bones. At noon the sun broke out and revived every one.'

' During the whole of the afternoon of the 21st we were so covered with rain and salt water, that we could scarcely see. We suffered extreme cold, and every one dreaded the approach of night. Sleep, though we longed for it, afforded no comfort ; for my own part, I almost lived without it. On the 22nd, our situation was extremely calamitous. We were obliged to take the course of the sea, running right before it, and watching with the utmost care, as the least error in the helm would in a moment have been our destruction. It continued through the day to blow hard, and the foam of the sea kept running over our stern and quarters.

'The misery we suffered this night exceeded the preceding. The sea flew over us with great force,

and kept us baling with horror and anxiety. At
dawn of day I found every one in a most distressed
condition, and I began to fear that another such
night would put an end to the lives of several, who
seemed no longer able to support their sufferings.
I served an allowance of *two* tea-spoonsful of rum ;
after drinking which, and having wrung our
clothes and taken our breakfast of bread and water,
we became a little refreshed.

'On the evening of the 24th, the wind mode-
rated and the weather looked much better, which
rejoiced all hands, so that they ate their scanty
allowance with more satisfaction than for some
time past. The night also was fair ; but being
always wet with the sea, we suffered much from
the cold. I had the pleasure to see a fine morning
produce some cheerful countenances ; and for the
first time, during the last fifteen days, we experienced comfort from the warmth of the sun. We
stripped and hung up our clothes to dry, which
were by this time become so threadbare, that they
could not keep out either wet or cold. In the
afternoon we had many birds about us, which are
never seen far from land, such as boobies and
noddies.'

As the sea now began to run fair, and the boat
shipped but little water, Lieutenant Bligh took
the opportunity to examine into the state of their
bread ; and it was found that, according to the
present mode of living, there was a sufficient quantity remaining for twenty-nine days allowance, by
which time there was every reason to expect they
would be able to reach Timor. But as this was
still uncertain, and it was possible that, after all,

they might be obliged to go to Java, it was determined to proportion the allowance, so as to
make the stock hold out six weeks. ' I was apprehensive,' he says, ' that this would be ill received, and that it would require my utmost resolution to enforce it ; for, small as the quantity was
which I intended to take away for our future good,
yet it might appear to my people like robbing
them of life ; and some who were less patient than
their companions, I expected would very ill brook
it. However, on my representing the necessity of
guarding against delays that might be occasioned
by contrary winds, or other causes, and promising
to enlarge upon the allowance as we got on, they
cheerfully agreed to my proposal.' It was accordingly settled that every person should receive one
twenty-fifth part of a pound of bread for breakfast,
and the same quantity for dinner as usual, but that
the proportion for supper should be discontinued;
this arrangement left them forty-three days consumption.

On the 25th about noon, some noddies came so
near to the boat, that one of them was caught by
hand. This bird was about the size of a small
pigeon. ' I divided it,' says Bligh, ' with its entrails, into eighteen portions, and by a well-known
method at sea, of " *Who shall have this?*"* it was

* One person turns his back on the object that is to be
divided ; another then points separately to the portions, at
each of them asking aloud, ' Who shall have this?' to
which the first answers by naming somebody. This impartial method of distribution gives every man an equal
chance of the best share. Bligh used to speak of the great
amusement the poor people had at the beak and claws fall-
ing to his share.

distributed, with the allowance of bread and water for dinner, and eaten up, bones and all, with salt water for sauce. In the evening, several boobies flying very near to us, we had the good fortune to catch one of them. This bird is as large as a duck. They are the most presumptive proof of being near land, of any sea-fowl we are acquainted with. I directed the bird to be killed for supper, and the blood to be given to three of the people who were the most distressed for want of food. The body, with the entrails, beak, and feet, I divided into eighteen shares, and with the allowance of bread, which I made a merit of granting, we made a good supper compared with our usual fare.

' On the next day, the 26th, we caught another booby, so that Providence appeared to be relieving our wants in an extraordinary manner. The people were overjoyed at this addition to their dinner, which was distributed in the same manner as on the preceding evening ; giving the blood to those who were the most in want of food. To make the bread a little savoury, most of the men frequently dipped it in salt water, but I generally broke mine into small pieces, and ate it in my allowance of water, out of a cocoa-nut shell, with a spoon ; economically avoiding to take too large a piece at a time, so that I was as long at dinner as if it had been a much more plentiful meal.'

The weather was now serene, which, nevertheless, was not without its inconveniences, for, it appears, they began to feel distress of a different kind from that which they had hitherto been accustomed to suffer. The heat of the sun was now

so powerful, that several of the people were seized
with a languor and faintness, which made life indifferent.   But the little circumstance of catching
two boobies in the evening, trifling as it may
appear, had the effect of raising their spirits.
The stomachs of these birds contained several
flying-fish, and small cuttle-fish, all of which were
carefully saved to be divided for dinner the next
day; which were accordingly divided with their
entrails, and the contents of their maws, into
eighteen portions, and, as the prize was a very
valuable one, it was distributed as before, by calling out, ' *Who shall have this?*'—' so that to-day,'
says the Lieutenant, ' with the usual allowance
of bread at breakfast and at dinner, I was happy
to see that every person thought he had feasted.'
From the appearance of the clouds in the evening,
Mr. Bligh had no doubt they were then near the
land, and the people amused themselves with conversing on the probability of what they would meet
with on it.

Accordingly, at one in the morning of the 28th,
the person at the helm heard the sound of breakers.
It was the ' barrier reef' which runs along the
eastern coast of New Holland, through which it
now became the anxious object to discover a passage; Mr. Bligh says this was now become absolutely necessary, without a moment's loss of time.
The idea of getting into smooth water and finding
refreshments kept up the people's spirits.   The
sea broke furiously over the reef in every part;
within, the water was so smooth and calm, that every
man already anticipated the heartfelt satisfaction
he was about to receive, as soon as he should have

passed the barrier.   At length a break in the reef
was discovered, a quarter of a mile in width, and
through this the boat rapidly passed with a strong
stream running to the westward, and came immediately into smooth water, and all the past hardships seemed at once to be forgotten.

They now returned thanks to God for his generous protection, and with much content took their
miserable allowance of the twenty-fifth part of a
pound of bread, and a quarter of a pint of water,
for dinner.

The coast now began to shew itself very distinctly, and in the evening they landed on the
sandy point of an island, when it was soon discovered there were oysters on the rocks, it being
low water.   The party sent out to reconnoitre
returned highly rejoiced at having found plenty of
oysters and fresh water.   By help of a small
magnifying glass a fire was made, and among
the things that had been thrown into the boat was
a tinder-box and a piece of brimstone, so that in
future they had the ready means of making a fire.
One of the men too had been so provident as to
bring away with him from the ship a copper pot;
and thus with a mixture of oysters, bread, and
pork, a stew was made, of which each person received a full pint.   It is remarked that the oysters
grew so fast to the rocks, that it was with great
difficulty they could be broken off; but they at
length discovered it to be the most expeditious
way to open them where they were fixed.

The general complaints among the people
were a dizziness in the head, great weakness
in the joints, and violent tenesmus, but none

of them are stated to have been alarming; and notwithstanding their sufferings from cold and hunger, all of them retained marks of strength. Mr. Bligh had cautioned them not to touch any kind of berry or fruit that they might find; yet it appears they were no sooner out of sight, than they began to make free with three different kinds that grew all over the island, eating without any reserve. The symptoms of having eaten too much began at last to frighten some of them; they fancied they were all poisoned, and regarded each other with the strongest marks of apprehension, uncertain what might be the issue of their imprudence: fortunately the fruit proved to be wholesome and good.

'This day (29th May) being,' says Lieutenant Bligh, 'the anniversary of the restoration of King Charles II., and the name not being inapplicable to our present situation, (for we were *restored* to fresh life and strength,) I named this "Restoration Island;" for I thought it probable that Captain Cook might not have taken notice of it.'

With oysters and palm-tops stewed together the people now made excellent meals, without consuming any of their bread. In the morning of the 30th, Mr. Bligh saw with great delight a visible alteration in the men for the better, and he sent them away to gather oysters, in order to carry a stock of them to sea, for he determined to put off again that evening. They also procured fresh water, and filled all their vessels to the amount of nearly sixty gallons. On examining the bread, it was found there still remained about thirty-eight days' allowance.

Being now ready for sea, every person was ordered to attend prayers; but just as they were embarking, about twenty naked savages made their appearance, running and hallooing, and beckoning the strangers to come to them ; but, as each was armed with a spear or lance, it was thought prudent to hold no communication with them. They now proceeded to the northward, having the continent on their left, and several islands and reefs on their right.

On the 31st they landed on one of these islands, to which was given the name of ' Sunday.' ' I sent out two parties (says Bligh), one to the northward and the other to the southward, to seek for supplies, and others I ordered to stay by the boat. On this occasion fatigue and weakness so far got the better of their sense of duty, that some of the people expressed their discontent at having worked harder than their companions, and declared that they would rather be without their dinner than go in search of it. One person, in particular, went so far as to tell me, with a mutinous look, that he was as good a man as myself. It was not possible for one to judge where this might have an end, if not stopped in time; to prevent therefore such disputes in future, I determined either to preserve my command or die in the attempt ; and seizing a cutlass, I ordered him to lay hold of another and defend himself; on which he called out that I was going to kill him, and immediately made concessions. I did not allow this to interfere further with the harmony of the boat's crew, and every thing soon became quiet.'

*

On this island they obtained oysters, and clams, and dog-fish; also a small bean, which Nelson, the botanist, pronounced to be a species of dolichos. On the 1st of June, they stopped in the midst of some sandy islands, such as are known by the name of *keys*, where they procured a few clams and beans. Here Nelson was taken very ill with a violent heat in his bowels, a loss of sight, great thirst, and an inability to walk. A little wine, which had carefully been saved, with some pieces of bread soaked in it, was given to him in small quantities, and he soon began to recover. The boatswain and carpenter were also ill, and complained of head-ache and sickness of the stomach. Others became shockingly distressed with tenesmus; in fact, there were few without complaints.

A party was sent out by night to catch birds; they returned with only twelve noddies, but it is stated, that, had it not been for the folly and obstinacy of one of the party, who separated from the others and disturbed the birds, a great many more might have been taken. The offender was Robert Lamb, who acknowledged, when he got to Java, that he had that night eaten *nine* raw birds, after he separated from his two companions. The birds, with a few clams, were the whole of the supplies afforded at these small islands.

On the 3d of June, after passing several keys and islands, and doubling Cape York, the north-easternmost point of New Holland, at eight in the evening the little boat and her brave crew once more launched into the open ocean.

' Miserable,' says Lieutenant Bligh, ' as our situation was in every respect, I was secretly surprised to see that it did not appear to affect any one so strongly as myself; on the contrary, it seemed as if they had embarked on a voyage to Timor in a vessel sufficiently calculated for safety and convenience. So much confidence gave me great pleasure, and I may venture to assert that to this cause our preservation is chiefly to be attributed. I encouraged every one with hopes that eight or ten days would bring us to a land of safety ; and, after praying to God for a continuance of his most gracious protection, I served out an allowance of water for supper, and directed our course to the west south-west.

' We had been just six days on the coast of New Holland, in the course of which we found oysters, a few clams, some birds and water. But a benefit, probably not less than this, was that of being relieved from the fatigue of sitting constantly in the boat, and enjoying good rest at night. These advantages certainly preserved our lives; and small as the supply was, I am very sensible how much it alleviated our distresses. Before this time nature must have sunk under the extremes of hunger and fatigue. Even in our present situation, we were most deplorable objects, but the hopes of a speedy relief kept up our spirits. For my own part, incredible as it may appear, I felt neither extreme hunger nor thirst. My allowance contented me, knowing that I could have no more.' In his manuscript journal, he adds, ' This, perhaps, does not permit me to be a proper judge on a story of miserable people like

us being at last driven to the necessity of destroying one another for food—but, if I may be allowed, I deny the fact in its greatest extent. I
say, I do not believe that, among us, such a
thing could happen, but death through famine
would be received in the same way as any mortal
disease *.'

On the 5th a booby was caught by the hand,
the blood of which was divided among three of the
men who were weakest, and the bird kept for next
day's dinner ; and on the evening of the 6th the
allowance for supper was recommenced, according
to a promise made when it had been discontinued.
On the 7th, after a miserably wet and cold night,
nothing more could be afforded than the usual
allowance for breakfast; but at dinner each person
had the luxury of an ounce of dried clams, which
consumed all that remained. The sea was running high and breaking over the boat the whole of
this day. Mr. Ledward, the surgeon, and Law-
rence Lebogue, an old hardy seaman, appeared to
be giving way very fast. No other assistance
could be given to them than a tea-spoonful or two
of wine, that had been carefully saved for such

* If Bligh here meant to deny the fact of men, in
extreme cases, destroying each other for the sake of ap-
peasing hunger, he is greatly mistaken. The fact was but
too well established, and to a great extent, on the raft of
the French frigate *Meduse*, when wrecked on the coast of
Africa, and also on the rock in the Mediterranean, when
the Nautilus frigate was lost. There may be a difference
between men, in danger of perishing by famine, when in
robust health, and men like those of the Bounty, worn by
degrees to skeletons, by protracted famine, who may thus
have become equally indifferent to life or death.

a melancholy occasion, which was not at all unexpected.

; On the 8th the weather was more moderate,
and a small dolphin was caught, which gave about
two ounces to each man : in the night it again
blew strong, the boat shipped much water, and
they all suffered greatly from wet and cold. The
surgeon and Lebogue still continued very ill, and
the only relief that could be afforded them was a
small quantity of wine, and encouraging them
with the hope that a very few days more, at the
rate they were then sailing, would bring them to
Timor.

'In the morning of the 10th, after a very com-
fortless night, there was a visible alteration for the
worse,' says Mr. Bligh, ' in many of the people,
which gave me great apprehensions.   An extreme
weakness, swelled legs, hollow and ghastly countenances, a more than common inclination to
sleep, with an apparent debility of understanding,
seemed to me the melancholy presages of an
approaching dissolution.   The surgeon and Lebogue, in particular, were most miserable objects.
I occasionally gave them a few tea-spoonfuls of
wine, out of the little that remained, which greatly
assisted them.   The hopes of being able to accomplish the voyage was our principal support.   The
boatswain very innocently told me that he really
thought I looked worse than any in the boat.
The simplicity with which he uttered such an opinion amused me, and I returned him a better
compliment.'

On the 11th Lieutenant Bligh announced to
his wretched companions that he had no doubt

they had now passed the meridian of the eastern part of Timor, a piece of intelligence that diffused universal joy and satisfaction. Accordingly at three in the morning of the following day Timor was discovered at the distance only of two leagues from the shore.

' It is not possible for me,' says this experienced navigator, ' to describe the pleasure which the blessing of the sight of this land diffused among us. It appeared scarcely credible to ourselves that, in an open boat, and so poorly provided, we should have been able to reach the coast of Timor in forty-one days after leaving Tofoa, having in that time run, by our log, a distance of three thousand six hundred and eighteen nautical miles; and that, notwithstanding our extreme distress, no one should have perished in the voyage.'

On Sunday the 14th they came safely to anchor in Coupang Bay, where they were received with every mark of kindness, hospitality, and humanity. The houses of the principal people were thrown open for their reception. The poor sufferers when landed were scarcely able to walk; their condition is described as most deplorable. ' The abilities of a painter could rarely, perhaps, have been displayed to more advantage than in the delineation of the two groupes of figures which at this time presented themselves to each other. An indifferent spectator (if such could be found) would have been at a loss which most to admire, the eyes of famine sparkling at immediate relief, or the horror of their preservers at the sight of so many spectres, whose ghastly countenances, if the cause had been unknown, would rather have excited terror than pity. Our bodies were nothing but skin and bones, our limbs were full of sores, and we were clothed in rags ; in this condition, with the tears of joy and gratitude flowing down our cheeks, the people of Timor beheld us with a mixture of horror, surprise, and pity.

' When,' continues the commander, ' I reflect how providentially our lives were saved at Tofoa, by the Indians delaying their attack ; and that, with scarcely anything to support life, we crossed a sea of more than twelve hundred leagues, without shelter from the inclemency of the weather ; when I reflect that in an open boat, with so much stormy weather, we escaped foundering, that not any of us were taken off by disease, that we had the great good fortune to pass the unfriendly natives of other countries without accident, and at last to meet with the most friendly and best of people to relieve our distresses—I say, when I reflect on all these wonderful escapes, the remembrance of such great mercies enables me to bear with resignation and cheerfulness the failure of an expedition, the success of which I had so much at heart, and which was frustrated at a time when I was congratulating myself on the fairest prospect of being able to complete it in a manner that would fully have answered the intention of his Majesty, and the humane promoters of so benevolent a plan.'

Having recruited their strength by a residence of two months among the friendly inhabitants of Coupang, they proceeded to the westward on the 20th August in a small schooner, which was purchased and armed for the purpose, and arrived on

the 1st October in Batavia Road, where Mr.
Bligh embarked in a Dutch packet, and was
landed on the Isle of Wight on the 14th March,
1790. The rest of the people had passages provided for them in ships of the Dutch East India
Company, then about to sail for Europe. All of
them, however, did not survive to reach England.
Nelson, the botanist, died at Coupang; Mr.
Elphinstone, master's-mate, Peter Linkletter and
Thomas Hall, seamen, died at Batavia; Robert
Lamb, seaman (the booby-eater), died on the
passage; and Mr. Ledward, the surgeon, was left
behind, and not afterwards heard of. These six,
with John Norton, who was stoned to death,
left twelve of the nineteen, forced by the mutineers
into the launch, to survive the difficulties and
dangers of this unparalleled voyage, and to revisit
their native country. With great truth might
Bligh exclaim with the poet,

> ————— ' 'Tis mine to tell their tale of grief,
> Their constant peril and their scant relief;
> Their days of danger, and their nights of pain;
> Their manly courage, even when deem'd in vain;
> The sapping famine, rendering scarce a son
> Known to his mother in the skeleton;
> The ills that lessen'd still their little store,
> And starved even Hunger till he wrung no more;
> The varying frowns and favours of the deep,
> That now almost engulphs, then leaves to creep
> With crazy oar and shatter'd strength along
> The tide, that yields reluctant to the strong
> Th' incessant fever of that arid thirst
> Which welcomes, as a well, the clouds that burst
> Above their naked bones, and feels delight
> In the cold drenching of the stormy night,
> And from the outspread canvas gladly wrings
> A drop to moisten Life's all-gasping springs;

The savage foe escaped, to seek again
More hospitable shelter from the main ;
The ghastly spectres which were doom'd at last
To tell us true a tale of dangers past,
As ever the dark annals of the deep
Disclosed for man to dread or woman weep.'

It is impossible not fully to accord with Bligh when he says, ' Thus happily ended, through the assistance of Divine Providence, without accident, a voyage of the most extraordinary nature that ever happened in the world *, let it be taken either

---

* The escape of the Centaur's boat, perhaps, comes nearest to it.   When the Centaur was sinking, Captain Inglefield and eleven others, in a small leaky boat, five feet broad, with one of the gunwales stove, nearly in the middle of the Western Ocean, without compass, without quadrant, without sail, without great-coat or cloak, all very thinly clothed, in a gale of wind, with a great sea running, and the winter fast approaching,—the sun and stars, by which alone they could shape their course, sometimes hidden for twenty-four hours ;—these unhappy men, in this destitute and hopeless condition, had to brave the billows of the stormy Atlantic, for nearly a thousand miles.   A blanket, which was by accident in the boat, served as a sail, and with this they scudded before the wind, in expectation of being swallowed up by every wave ; with great difficulty the boat was cleared of water before the return of the next great sea ; all of the people were half drowned, and sitting, except the balers, at the bottom of the boat.   On quitting the ship the distance of Fayal was two hundred and sixty leagues, or about nine hundred English miles.

Their provisions were a bag of bread, a small ham, a single piece of pork, two quart bottles of water, and a few of French cordials.   One biscuit, divided into twelve morsels, was served for breakfast, and the same for dinner ; the neck of a bottle broken off, with the cork in, supplied the place of a glass ; and this filled with water was the allowance for twenty-four hours for each man.

On the fifteenth day, they had only one day's bread, and

in its extent, duration, or the want of every necessary of life.' We may go further and say, it is

one bottle of water remaining of a second supply of rain;
on this day Matthews, a quarter-master, the stoutest man in
the boat, perished of hunger and cold. This poor man, on the
day before, had complained of want of strength in his throat,
as he expressed it, to swallow his morsel; and, in the night,
drank salt-water, grew delirious, and died without a groan.
Hitherto despair and gloom had been successfully prevented,
the men, when the evenings closed in, having been encouraged by turns to sing a song, or relate a story, instead of a
supper : 'but,' says the Captain, 'this evening I found it
impossible to raise either.' The Captain had directed the
clothes to be taken from the corpse of Matthews and given
to some of the men, who were perishing with cold; but the
shocking skeleton-like appearance of his remains made such
an impression on the people, that all efforts to raise their
spirits were ineffectual. On the following day, the six-
teenth, their last breakfast was served with the bread and
water remaining, when John Gregory, the quarter-master,
declared with much confidence that he saw land in the
south-east, which turned out to be Fayal.

But the most extraordinary *feat of navigation* is that
which is related (on good authority) in a note of the *Quarterly Review*, vol. xviii., pp. 337—339 :—

Of all the feats of navigation on record, however, that of
Diogo Botelho Perreira, in the early period of 1536-7,
stands pre-eminent; it is extracted from the voluminous
Decades of Diogo de Couto, whose work, though abounding
with much curious matter, like those of most of the old Portugueze writers, has not been fortunate enough to obtain an
English translation. We are indebted to a friend for pointing it out to us, and we conceive it will be read with interest.

'In the time of the vice-royalty of Don Francisco de
Almeyda there was a young gentleman in India of the
name of Diogo Botelho Perreira, son of the commander of
Cochin, who educated him with great care, so that he
soon became skilled in the art of navigation, and an
adept in the construction of marine charts. As he grew
up, he felt anxious to visit Portugal, where, on his arrival,

impossible to read this extraordinary and unparalleled voyage, without bestowing the meed of

he was well received at court, and the king took pleasure in conversing with him on those subjects which had been the particular objects of his studies. Confident of his own talents, and presuming on the favour with which the king always treated him, he ventured one day to request his majesty to appoint him commander of the fortress of Chaul. The king smiled at his request, and replied, that "*the command of the fortress was not for pilots.*" Botelho was piqued at this answer, and, on returning into the ante-chamber, was met by Don Antonio Noronha, second son of the Marquis of Villa Real, who asked him if his suit had been granted : he answered, " Sir, I will apply where my suit will not be neglected." When this answer came to the ears of the king, he immediately ordered Botelho to be confined in the castle of Lisbon, lest he should follow the example of Megalhaens, and go over to Spain. There he remained a prisoner until the admiral viceroy, Don Vasco da Gama, solicited his release, and was permitted to take him to India ; but on the express condition that he should not return to Portugal, except by special permission. Under these unpleasant circumstances this gentleman proceeded to India, anxious for an opportunity of distinguishing himself, that he might be permitted again to visit Portugal.

' It happened about this time that the Sultan Badur, sovereign of Cambaya, gave the governor, Nuno da Cunha, permission to erect a fortress on the island of Diu, an object long and anxiously wished for, as being of the greatest importance to the security of the Portugueze possessions in India. Botelho was aware how acceptable this information would be to the king, and therefore deemed this a favourable opportunity of regaining his favour, by conveying such important intelligence ; and he resolved to perform the voyage in a vessel so small, and so unlike what had ever appeared in Portugal, that it should not fail to excite astonishment, how any man could undertake so long and perilous a navigation, in such a frail and diminutive bottom.

unqualified praise on the able and judicious conduct of its commander, who is in every respect, as

' Without communicating his scheme to any person, he
procured a *fusta*, put a deck on it from head to stern, furnished it with spare sails and spars, and every other necessary, and constructed two small tanks for water.

' As soon as the monsoon served, he embarked with some
men in his service, giving out that he was going to Melinde;
and, to give colour to this story, he proceeded to Baticala,
where he purchased some cloths and beads for that market,
and laid in provisions; some native merchants also
embarked with a few articles on board for the Melinde
market, to which he did not choose to object, lest it should
alarm his sailors.

' He set sail with the eastern monsoon, in the beginning
of October, and arrived safely at Melinde, where he landed
the native merchants, took in wood, water, and refreshments, and again put to sea, informing his crew that he
was going to Quiloa. When he had got to a distance from
the land, it would appear that some of his crew had mutinied; but this he had foreseen and provided for; putting
some of them in irons, and promising at the same time
amply to reward the services of the rest, and giving them to
understand that he was going to Sofala on account of the
trade in gold. Thus he proceeded, touching at various
places for refreshments, which he met with in great plenty
and very cheap.

' From Sofala he proceeded along the coast till he had
passed the Cabo dos Correntes, and from thence along the
shore, without ever venturing to a distance from the land,
and touching at the different rivers, until he passed the
Cape of Good Hope, which he did in January 1537.

' From thence he stretched into the ocean with gentle
breezes, steering for St. Helena; where, on arriving, he
drew his little vessel ashore, to clean her bottom and repair
her, and also to give a few days' rest to his crew, of whom
some had perished of cold, notwithstanding his having provided warm clothing for them.

' Departing from St. Helena, he boldly steered his little
bark across the wide ocean, directing his career to St.

far as this extraordinary enterprize is concerned,
fully entitled to rank with Parry, Franklin, and

Thomè, where he took in provisions, wood, and water; and
from thence he proceeded to the bar of Lisbon, where he
arrived in May, when the king was at Almeyrin.—He
entered the river with his oars, his little vessel being dressed
with flags and pendants, and anchored at Point Leira opposite to Salvaterra, not being able to get farther up the river.
This novelty produced such a sensation in Lisbon that the
Tagus was covered with boats to see the *fusta*. Diogo
Bótelho Perreira landed in a boat, and proceeded to Almeyrin, to give the king an account of his voyage, and solicit a
gratification for the good news which he brought, of his
majesty now being possessed of a fortress on the island of
Diu.

' The king was highly pleased with this intelligence, but,
as Botelho brought no letters from the governor, he did not
give him the kind of reception which he had expected.—On
the contrary, the king treated him with coldness and distance; his majesty, however, embarked to see the *fusta*, on
board of which he examined every thing with much attention, and was gratified in viewing a vessel of such a peculiar
form, and ordered money and clothes to be given to the sailors—nor could he help considering Diogo Botelho as a
man of extraordinary enterprise and courage, on whose firmness implicit reliance might be placed.

' The little vessel was ordered to be drawn ashore at
Sacabem, where it remained many years, (until it fell to
pieces,) and was visited by people from all parts of Europe,
who beheld it with astonishment. The king subsequently
received letters from the governor of Nuno da Cunha, con-
firming the news brought by Botelho; the bearer of these
letters, a Jew, was immediately rewarded with a pension of a
hundred and forty milreas; but Botelho was neglected for
many years, and at last appointed commander of St. Thomè,
and finally made captain of Cananor in India, that he
might be at a distance from Portugal.'

The vessel named *fusta* is a long, shallow, Indian-built
row-boat, which uses latine sails in fine weather. These
boats are usually open, but Botelho covered his with a
deck : its dimensions, according to Lavanha, in his edition

Richardson. Few men, indeed, were ever placed for so long a period in a more trying, distressing, and perilous situation than he was; and it may safely be pronounced, that, to his discreet management of the men and their scanty resources, and to his ability as a thorough seaman, eighteen souls were saved from imminent and otherwise inevitable destruction. It was not alone the dangers of the sea, in an open boat, crowded with people, that he had to combat, though they required the most consummate nautical skill, to be enabled to contend successfully against them; but the unfortunate situation, to which the party were exposed, rendered him subject to the almost daily murmuring and caprice of people less conscious than himself of their real danger. From the experience they had acquired at Tofoa of the savage disposition of the people against the defenceless boat's crew, a lesson was learned how little was to be trusted, even to the mildest of uncivilized people, when a conscious superiority was in their hands. A striking proof of this was experienced in the unprovoked attack made by those amiable people, the Otaheitans, on Captain Wallis's ship, of whose power they had formed no just conception; but having once experienced

of De Barros' unfinished Decade, are as follows:—length, twenty-two palmos, or sixteen feet six inches. Breadth, twelve palmos, or nine feet. Depth, six palmos, or four feet six inches. Bligh's boat was twenty-three feet long—six feet nine inches broad, and two feet nine inches deep. From the circumstance mentioned of some of his crew having perished with cold, it is probable that they were natives of India, whom the Portugueze were in the habit of bringing home as part of their crew.

the full force of it, on no future occasion was any
attempt made to repeat the attack. Lieutenant
Bligh, fully aware of his own weakness, deemed
it expedient, therefore, to resist all desires and
temptations to land at any of those islands,
among which they passed in the course of the
voyage, well knowing how little could be trusted
to the forbearance of savages, unarmed and wholly
defenceless as his party were.

But the circumstance of being tantalized with
the appearance of land, clothed with perennial ver-
dure, whose approach was forbidden to men chilled
with wet and cold, and nearly perishing with hunger, was by no means the most difficult against
which the commander had to struggle. ' It was
not the least of my distresses,' he observes,
' to be constantly assailed with the melancholy
demands of my people for an increase of allowance, which it grieved me to refuse.' He well
knew that to reason with men reduced to the last
stage of famine, yet denied the use of provisions
within their reach, and with the power to seize
upon them in their own hands, would be to no
purpose. Something more must be done to ensure
even the possibility of saving them from the effect
of their own imprudence. The first thing he set
about, therefore, was to ascertain the exact state
of their provisions, which were found to amount
to the ordinary consumption of five days, but
which were to be spun out so as to last fifty days.
This was at once distinctly stated to the men, and
an agreement entered into, and a solemn promise
made by all, that the settled allowance should
never be deviated from, as they were made clearly

to understand that on the strict observance of this
agreement rested the only hope of their safety;
and this was explained and made so evident to
every man, at the time it was concluded, that they
unanimously agreed to it; and by reminding
them of this compact, whenever they became cla-
morous for more, and shewing a firm determination not to swerve from it, Lieutenant Bligh succeeded in resisting all their solicitations.

This rigid adherence to the compact, in doling
out their miserable pittance,—the constant exposure to wet,—the imminent peril of being swallowed up by the ocean,—their cramped and confined position,—and the unceasing reflection on
their miserable and melancholy situation;—all
these difficulties and sufferings make it not less
than miraculous, that this voyage, itself a miracle,
should have been completed, not only without the
loss of a man from sickness, but with so little
loss of health. ' With respect to the preservation
of our health,' says the commander, ' during the
course of sixteen days of heavy and almost continual rain, I would recommend to every one in
a similar situation, the method we practised of
dipping their clothes in salt-water, and to wring
them out, as often as they become soaked with
rain ; it was the only resource we had, and I believe was of the greatest service to us, for it felt
more like a change of dry clothes than could well
be imagined. We had occasion to do this so
often, that at length all our clothes were wrung to
pieces.'

But the great art of all was to divert their attention from the almost hopeless situation in which

they were placed, and to prevent despondency
from taking possession of their minds; and in
order to assist in effecting this, some employment
was devised for them; among other things, a log-
line, an object of interest to all, was measured and
marked; and the men were practised in counting
seconds correctly, that the distance run on each
day might be ascertained with a nearer approach
to accuracy than by mere guessing. These little
operations afforded them a temporary amusement;
and the log being daily and hourly hove gave
them also some employment, and diverted their
thoughts for the moment from their melancholy
situation.   Then, every noon, when the sun was
out, or at other times before and after noon,
and also at night when the stars appeared, Lieutenant Bligh never neglected to take observations for the latitude, and to work the day's work
for ascertaining the ship's place. The anxiety of
the people to hear how they had proceeded, what
progress had been made, and whereabouts they
were on the wide ocean, also contributed for the
time to drive away gloomy thoughts that but too
frequently would intrude themselves. These observations were rigidly attended to, and sometimes
made under the most difficult circumstances, the
sea breaking over the observer, and the boat
pitching and rolling so much, that he was obliged
to be ' propped up,' while taking them. In this
way, with now and then a little interrupted sleep,
about a thousand long and anxious hours were
consumed in pain and peril, and a space of sea
passed over equal to four thousand five hundred

K

miles, being at the rate of four and one-fifth miles an hour, or one hundred miles a-day.

Lieutenant Bligh has expressed his conviction, that the six days spent among the coral islands, off the coast of New Holland, were the salvation of the whole party, by the refreshing sleep they here procured, by the exercise of walking about, and, above all, by the nutriment derived from the oysters and clams, the beans and berries, they procured while there ; for that such, he says, was the exhausted condition of all on their arrival at the ' barrier reef,' that a few days more at sea must have terminated the existence of many of them. This stoppage, however, had likewise been nearly productive of fatal consequences to the whole party. In fact, another mutiny was within an ace of breaking out, which, if not checked at the moment, could only, in their desperate situation, have ended in irretrievable and total destruction. Bligh mentions, in his printed narrative, the mutinous conduct of a person to whom he gave a cutlass to defend himself. This affair, as stated in his original manuscript journal, wears a far more serious aspect.

' The carpenter (Purcell) began to be insolent to a high degree, and at last told me, with a mutinous aspect, he was as good a man as I was. I did not just now see where this was to end; I therefore determined to strike a final blow at it, and either to preserve my command or die in the attempt ; and taking hold of a cutlass, I ordered the rascal to take hold of another and defend himself, when he called out that I was going to

kill him, and began to make concessions. I was
now only assisted by Mr. Nelson ; and the master
(Fryer) very deliberately called out to the boatswain, to put me under an arrest, and was stirring
up a greater disturbance, when I declared, if he
interfered, when I was in the execution of my duty
to preserve order and regularity, and that in consequence any tumult arose, I would certainly put
him to death the first person. This had a proper
effect on this man, and he now assured me that,
on the contrary, I might rely on him to support
my orders and directions for the future. This is
the outline of a tumult that lasted about a quarter
of hour ;' and he adds, ' I was told that the master and carpenter, at the last place, were endeavouring to produce altercations, and were the principal cause of their murmuring there.' This carpenter he brought to a court-martial on their arrival in England, on various charges, of which he
was found guilty in part, and reprimanded. Purcell is said to be at this time in a madhouse.

On another occasion, when a stew of oysters
was distributed among the people, Lieutenant
Bligh observes (in the MS. Journal), ' In the distribution of it, the voraciousness of some and the
moderation of others were very discernible. The
master began to be dissatisfied the first, because
it was not made into a larger quantity by the addition of water, and shewed a turbulent disposition, until I laid my commands on him to be
silent.' Again, on his refusing bread to the men,
because they were collecting oysters, he says, ' this
occasioned some murmuring with the master and
carpenter, the former of whom endeavoured to

prove the propriety of such an expenditure, and was troublesomely ignorant, tending to create disorder among those, if any were weak enough to listen to him.'

If what Bligh states with regard to the conduct of the master and the carpenter be true, it was such, on several occasions, as to provoke a man much less irritable than himself. He thus speaks of the latter, when in the ship and in the midst of the mutiny. ' The boatswain and carpenter were fully at liberty ; the former was employed, on pain of death, to hoist the boats out, but the latter I saw acting the part of an idler, with an impudent and ill-looking countenance, which led me to believe he was one of the mutineers, until he was among the rest ordered to leave the ship, for it appeared to me to be a doubt with Christian, at first, whether he should keep the carpenter or his mate (Norman), but knowing the former to be a troublesome fellow, he determined on the latter.'

The following paragraph also appears in his original journal, on the day of the mutiny, but is not alluded to in his printed narrative. ' The master's cabin was opposite to mine ; he saw them (the mutineers) in my cabin, for our eyes met each other through his door-window. He had a pair of ship's pistols loaded, and ammunition in his cabin—a firm resolution might have made a good use of them. After he had sent twice or thrice to Christian to be allowed to come on deck, he was at last permitted, and his question then was, " Will you let me remain in the ship ?"—" No." " Have *you* any objection, Captain Bligh ?" I whispered to him to knock him down—Martin is good (this is the man who gave the shaddock), for this was just before Martin was removed from me. Christian, however, pulled me back, and sent away the master, with orders to go again to his cabin, and I saw no more of him, until he was put into the boat. He afterwards told me that he could find nobody to act with him; that by staying in the ship he hoped to have retaken her, and that, as to the pistols, he was so flurried and surprised, that he did not recollect he had them.' This master tells a very different story respecting the pistols, in his evidence before the court-martial.

Whatever, therefore, on the whole, may have been the conduct of Bligh towards his officers, that of some of the latter appears to have been on several occasions provoking enough, and well calculated to stir up the irascible temper of a man, active and zealous in the extreme, as Bligh always was, in the execution of his duty. Some excuse may be found for hasty expressions uttered in a moment of irritation, when passion gets the better of reason; but no excuse can be found for one, who deeply and unfeelingly, without provocation, and in cold blood, inflicts a wound on the heart of a widowed mother, already torn with anguish and tortured with suspense for a beloved son, whose life was in imminent jeopardy : such a man was William Bligh. This charge is not loosely asserted; it is founded on documentary evidence under his own hand. Since the death of the late Captain Heywood, some papers have been brought to light, that throw a still more unfavourable stigma on the character of the two commanders, Bligh and Edwards, than any censure that has hitherto appeared in print, though the conduct of neither of them has been spared, whenever an occasion has presented itself for bringing their names before the public.

Bligh, it may be recollected, mentions young Heywood only as one of those left in the ship; he does not charge him with taking any active part in the mutiny; there is every reason, indeed, to believe that Bligh did not, and indeed could not, see him on the deck on that occasion: in point of fact, he never was within thirty feet of Captain Bligh, and the booms were between them. About the end of March, 1790, two months subsequent to the death of a most beloved and lamented husband, Mrs. Heywood received the afflicting information, but by report only, of a mutiny having taken place on board the Bounty. In that ship Mrs. Heywood's son had been serving as midshipman, who, when he left his home, in August, 1787, was under fifteen years of age, a boy deservedly admired and beloved by all who knew him, and, to his own family, almost an object of adoration, for his superior understanding and the amiable qualities of his disposition. In a state of mind little short of distraction, on hearing this fatal intelligence, which was at the same time aggravated by every circumstance of guilt that calumny or malice could invent with respect to this unfortunate youth, who was said to be one of the ringleaders, and to have gone armed into the captain's cabin, his mother addressed a letter to Captain Bligh, dictated by a mother's tenderness,

and strongly expressive of the misery she must
necessarily feel on such an occasion. The following is Bligh's reply :—

' MADAM,   ' *London, April 2nd*, 1790.
' I received your letter this day, and feel for
you very much, being perfectly sensible of the
extreme distress you must suffer from the conduct
of your son Peter. *His baseness is beyond all
description*, but I hope you will endeavour to
prevent the loss of him, heavy as the misfortune
is, from afflicting you too severely. I imagine
he is, with the rest of the mutineers, returned to
Otaheite.   ' I am, Madam,
                 (Signed)   ' Wm. Bligh.'

Colonel Holwell, the uncle of young Heywood,
had previously addressed Bligh on the same
melancholy subject, to whom he returned the
following answer :—

' Sir,   ' *26th March*, 1790.
    I have just this instant received your letter.
With much concern I inform you that your
nephew, Peter Heywood, is among the mutineers.
His ingratitude to me is of the blackest dye, for
I was a father to him in every respect, and he
never once had an angry word from me through
the whole course of the voyage, as his conduct
always gave me much pleasure and satisfaction.
I very much regret *that so much baseness formed
the character of a young man* I had a real regard
for, and it will give me much pleasure to hear

that his friends *can bear the loss of him without much concern.*   ' I am, Sir, &c.

(Signed)   ' Wm. Bligh.'

The only way of accounting for this ferocity of sentiment towards a youth, who had in point of fact no concern in the mutiny, is by a reference to certain points of evidence given by Hayward, Hallet, and Purcell on the court-martial, each point wholly unsupported. Those in the boat would no doubt, during their long passage, often discuss the conduct of their messmates left in the Bounty, and the unsupported evidence given by these three was well calculated to create in Bligh's mind a prejudice against young Heywood; yet, if so, it affords but a poor excuse for harrowing up the feelings of near and dear relatives.

As a contrast to these ungracious letters, it is a great relief to peruse the correspondence that took place, on this melancholy occasion, between this unfortunate young officer and his amiable but dreadfully afflicted family. The letters of his sister Nessy Heywood (of which a few will be inserted in the course of this narrative) exhibit so lively and ardent an affection for her beloved brother, are couched in so high a tone of feeling for his honour, and confidence in his innocence, and are so nobly answered by the suffering youth, that no apology seems to be required for their introduction, more especially as their contents are strictly connected with the story of the ill-fated crew of the Bounty. After a state of long suspense, this amiable and accomplished young lady thus addresses her brother:—

' *Isle of Man*, 2nd *June*, 1792.

' In a situation of mind only rendered supportable by the long and painful state of misery and suspense we have suffered on his account, how shall I address my dear, my fondly beloved brother!—how describe the anguish we have felt at the idea of this long and painful separation, rendered still more distressing by the terrible circumstances attending it! Oh! my ever dearest boy, when I look back to that dreadful moment which brought us the fatal intelligence that you had remained in the Bounty after Mr. Bligh had quitted her, and were looked upon by him as a *mutineer!*—when I contrast that day of horror with my present hopes of again beholding you, such as my most sanguine wishes could expect, I know not which is the most predominant sensation,—pity, compassion, and terror for your sufferings, or joy and satisfaction at the prospect of their being near a termination, and of once more embracing the dearest object of our affections.

' I will not ask you, my beloved brother, whether you are innocent of the dreadful crime of mutiny; if the transactions of that day were, as Mr. Bligh has represented them, such is my conviction of your worth and honour, that I will, without hesitation, stake my life on your innocence. If, on the contrary, you were concerned in such a conspiracy against your commander, I shall be as firmly persuaded *his* conduct was the occasion of it; but, alas! could any occasion justify so atrocious an attempt to destroy a number of our fellow-creatures? No, my ever dearest brother, nothing

but conviction from your own mouth can possibly
persuade me, that you would commit an action in
the smallest degree inconsistent with honour and
duty; and the circumstance of your having swam
off to the Pandora on her arrival at Otaheite
(which filled us with joy to which no words can
do justice), is sufficient to convince all who know
you, that you certainly staid behind either by force
or from views of preservation.

'How strange does it seem to me that I am
now engaged in the delightful task of writing to
you. Alas! my beloved brother, two years ago
I never expected again to enjoy such a felicity,
and even yet I am in the most painful uncertainty
whether you are alive. Gracious God, grant
that we may be at length blessed by your return!
but, alas! the Pandora's people have been long
expected, and are not even yet arrived. Should
any accident have happened, after all the miseries
you have already suffered, the poor gleam of hope
with which we have been lately indulged, will
render our situation ten thousand times more insupportable than if time had inured us to your
loss. I send this to the care of Mr. Hayward, of
Hackney, father to the young gentleman you so
often mention in your letters while you were on
board the Bounty, and who went out as third lieutenant of the Pandora—a circumstance which gave
us infinite satisfaction, as you would, on entering
the Pandora, meet your old friend. On discovering old Mr. Hayward's residence, I wrote to him,
as I hoped he could give me some information
respecting the time of your arrival, and in return
he sent me a most friendly letter, and has promised

this shall be given to you when you reach England, as I well know how great must be your anxiety to hear of us, and how much satisfaction it will give you to have a letter immediately on your return. Let me conjure you, my dearest Peter, to write to us the very first moment—do not lose a post—'tis of no consequence how short your letter may be, if it only informs us you are well. I need not tell you that you are the first and dearest object of our affections. Think, then, my adored boy, of the anxiety we must feel on your account; for my own part, I can know no real joy or happiness independent of you, and if any misfortune should now deprive us of you, my hopes of felicity are fled for ever.

' We are at present making all possible interest with every friend and connexion we have, to insure you a sufficient support and protection at your approaching trial; for a trial you must unavoidably undergo, in order to convince the world of that innocence, which those who know you will not for a moment doubt; but, alas! while circumstances are against you, the generality of mankind will judge severely. Bligh's representations to the Admiralty are, I am told, very unfavourable, and hitherto the tide of public opinion has been greatly in his favour. My mamma is at present well, considering the distress she has suffered since you left us; for, my dearest brother, we have experienced a complicated scene of misery from a variety of causes, which, however, when compared with the sorrow we felt on your account, was trifling and insignificant; *that* misfortune made all others light, and to see you once more returned, and safely restored to us, will be the summit of all earthly happiness.

'Farewell, my most beloved brother! God grant this may soon be put into your hands! Perhaps at this moment you are arrived in England, and I may soon have the dear delight of again beholding you. My mama, brothers, and sisters, join with me in every sentiment of love and tenderness. Write to us immediately, my ever-loved Peter, and may the Almighty preserve you until you bless with your presence your fondly affectionate family, and particularly your unalterably faithful friend and sister,

(Signed)   'Nessy Heywood*.'

* Previous to the writing of this letter, the following copy of verses shows how anxiously this young lady's mind was engaged on the unhappy circumstances under which her brother was placed.

'On the tedious and mournful Absence of a most beloved Brother, who was in the Bounty with Captain Bligh at the Time of the Fatal Mutiny, which happened April 28th, 1789, in the South Seas, and who, instead of returning with the Boat when she left the Ship, stayed behind.

'Tell me, thou busy flatt'ring Telltale, why—
Why flow these tears—why heaves this deep-felt sigh,—
Why is all joy from my sad bosom flown,
Why lost that cheerfulness I thought my own;
Why seek I now in solitude for ease,
Which once was centred in a wish to please,
When ev'ry hour in joy and gladness past,
And each new day shone brighter than the last;
When in society I loved to join;
When to enjoy, and give delight, was mine?—
Now—sad reverse! in sorrow wakes each day,
And grief's sad tones inspire each plaintive lay:

The gleam of joy which this unhappy family
derived from the circumstance, which had been

Alas! too plain these mournful tears can tell
The pangs of woe my lab'ring bosom swell!
Thou best of brothers—friend, companion, guide,
Joy of my youth, my honour, and my pride!
Lost is all peace—all happiness to me,
And fled all comfort, since deprived of thee.
In vain, my Lycidas, thy loss I mourn,
In vain indulge a hope of thy return;
Still years roll on and still I vainly sigh,
Still tears of anguish drown each gushing eye.
Ah! cruel Time! how slow thy ling'ring pace,
Which keeps me from his tender, loved embrace.
At home to see him, or to know him near,
How much I wish—and yet how much I fear!
Oh! fatal voyage! which robb'd my soul of peace
And wreck'd my happiness in stormy seas!
Why, my loved Lycidas, why did'st thou stay,
Why waste thy life from friendship far away?
Though guiltless thou of mutiny or blame,
And free from aught which could disgrace thy name;
Though thy pure soul, in honour's footsteps train'd,
Was never yet by disobedience stain'd;
Yet is thy fame exposed to slander's wound,
And fell suspicion whispering around.
In vain—to those who knew thy worth and truth,
Who watch'd each op'ning virtue of thy youth;
When noblest principles inform'd thy mind,
Where sense and sensibility were join'd;
Love to inspire, to charm, to win each heart,
And ev'ry tender sentiment impart;
Thy outward form adorn'd with ev'ry grace;
With beauty's softest charms thy heav'nly face,
Where sweet expression beaming ever proved
The index of that soul, by all beloved;
Thy wit so keen, thy genius form'd to soar,
By fancy wing'd, new science to explore;
Thy temper, ever gentle, good, and kind,
Where all but guilt an advocate could find:

related to them, of young Heywood's swimming
off to the Pandora, was dissipated by a letter
from himself to his mother, soon after his arrival
in England, in which he says:—' The question,
my dear mother, in one of your letters, concerning
my swimming off to the Pandora, is one falsity
among the too many, in which I have often
thought of undeceiving you, and as frequently
forgot. The story was this:—On the morning

To those who know this character was thine,
(And in this truth assenting numbers join)
How vain th' attempt to fix a crime on thee,
Which thou disdain'st—from which each thought is free!
No, my loved brother, ne'er will I believe
Thy seeming worth was meant but to deceive;
Still will I think (each circumstance though strange)
That thy firm principles could never change;
That hopes of preservation urged thy stay,
Or force, which those resistless must obey.
If this is error, let me still remain
In error wrapp'd—nor wake to truth again!
Come then, sweet Hope, with all thy train of joy
Nor let Despair each rapt'rous thought destroy;
Indulgent Heav'n, in pity to our tears,
At length will bless a parent's sinking years;
Again shall I behold thy lovely face,
By manhood form'd, and ripen'd ev'ry grace,
Again I'll press thee to my anxious breast,
And ev'ry sorrow shall be hush'd to rest.
Thy presence only can each comfort give.
Come then, my Lycidas, and let me live ;
Life without thee is but a wretched load,
Thy love alone can smooth its thorny road ;
But blest with thee, how light were every woe;
How would my soul with joy and rapture glow !
Kind Heav'n ! thou hast my happiness in store,
Restore him *innocent*—I ask no more !

'NESSY HEYWOOD.'

Isle of Man, Feb. 25th, 1792.'

she arrived, accompanied by two of my friends
(natives), I was going up the mountains, and
having got about a hundred yards from my own
house, another of my friends (for I was an universal favourite among those Indians, and perfectly
conversant in their language) came running after
me, and informed me there was a ship coming. I
immediately ascended a rising ground, and saw,
with indescribable joy, a ship laying-to off Ha-
piano; it was just after daylight, and thinking
Coleman might not be awake, and therefore ignorant of this pleasing news, I sent one of my
servants to inform him of it, upon which he immediately went off in a single canoe. There was a
fresh breeze, and the ship working into the bay;
he no sooner got alongside than the rippling
capsized the canoe, and he being obliged to let go
the tow-rope to get her righted, went astern, and
was picked up the next tack and taken on board
the Pandora, he being the first person. I, along
with my messmate Stewart, was then standing
upon the beach with a double canoe, manned with
twelve paddles ready for launching; and just as
she made her last tack into her berth (for we did
not think it requisite to go off sooner), we put off
and got alongside just as they streamed the buoy;
and being dressed in the country manner, tanned
as brown as themselves, and I *tattooed* like them
in the most curious manner, I do not in the least
wonder at their taking us for natives. I was tattooed, not to gratify my own desire, but theirs;
for it was my constant endeavour to acquiesce in
any little custom which I thought would be agree-
able to them, though painful in the process, provided

I gained by it their friendship and esteem, which you may suppose is no inconsiderable object in an island where the natives are so numerous. The more a man or woman there is tattooed, the more they are respected ; and a person having none of these marks is looked upon as bearing an unworthy badge of disgrace, and considered as a mere outcast of society.'

Among the many anxious friends and family connexions of the Heywoods, was Commodore Pasley, to whom this affectionate young lady addressed herself on the melancholy occasion; and the following is the reply she received from this officer.

' *Sheerness, June 8th,* 1792.

' Would to God, my dearest Nessy, that I could rejoice with you on the early prospect of your brother's arrival in England. One division of the Pandora's people has arrived, and now on board the Vengeance (my ship). Captain Edwards with the remainder, and all the prisoners late of the Bounty, in number ten, (four having been drowned on the loss of that ship), are daily expected. They have been most rigorously and closely confined since taken, and will continue so, no doubt, till Bligh's arrival. You have no chance of seeing him, for no bail can be offered. Your intelligence of his swimming off on the Pandora's arrival is not founded ; a man of the name of Coleman swam off ere she anchored—your brother and Mr. Stewart the next day; this last youth, when the Pandora was lost, refused to allow his irons to be taken off to save his life.

' I cannot conceal it from you, my dearest

Nessy, neither is it proper I should—your brother appears, by all accounts, to be the greatest culprit of all, Christian alone excepted. Every exertion, you may rest assured, I shall use to save his life, but on trial I have no hope of his not being condemned. Three of the ten who are expected are mentioned, in Bligh's narrative, as men detained against their inclination. Would to God your brother had been one of that number! I will not distress you more by enlarging on this subject; as intelligence arises on their arrival, you shall be made acquainted. Adieu! my dearest Nessy— present my affectionate remembrances to your mother and sisters, and believe me always, with the warmest affection,

' Your uncle,
' Thos. Pasley.'

How unlike is this from the letter of Bligh! while it frankly apprises this amiable lady of the real truth of the case, without disguise, as it was then understood to be from Mr. Bligh's representations, it assures her of his best exertions to save her brother's life. Every reader of sensibility will sympathise in the feeling displayed in her reply.

' Isle of Man, 22d June, 1792.

' Harassed by the most torturing suspense, and miserably wretched as I have been, my dearest uncle, since the receipt of your last, conceive, if it is possible, the heartfelt joy and satisfaction we experienced yesterday morning, when, on the arrival of the packet, the dear delightful letter from our beloved Peter (a copy of which I send you

L

enclosed) was brought to us. Surely, my excellent friend, you will agree with me in thinking there could not be a stronger proof of his innocence and worth, and that it must prejudice every person who reads it most powerfully in his favour. Such a letter in less distressful circumstances than those in which he writes, would, I am persuaded, reflect honour on the pen of a person much older than my poor brother. But when we consider his extreme youth, (only sixteen at the time of the mutiny, and now but nineteen,) his fortitude, patience and manly resignation under the pressure of sufferings and misfortunes almost unheard of, and scarcely to be supported at any age, without the assistance of that which seems to be my dear brother's greatest comfort—a quiet conscience, and a thorough conviction of his own innocence— when I add, at the same time, with real pleasure and satisfaction, that his relation corresponds in many particulars with the accounts we have hitherto heard of the fatal mutiny, and when I also add, with inconceivable pride and delight, that my beloved Peter never was known to breathe a syllable inconsistent with truth and honour ;—when these circumstances, my dear uncle, are all united, what man on earth can doubt of the innocence which could dictate such a letter? In short, let it speak for him : the perusal of his artless and pathetic story will, I am persuaded, be a stronger recommendation in his favour than any thing I can urge.*

I need not tire your patience, my ever loved

* This interesting letter is given in the following Chap-
, to which it appropriately belongs.

uncle, by dwelling longer on this subject, (the dearest and most interesting on earth to my heart;) let me conjure you only, my kind friend, to read it, and consider the innocence and defenceless situation of its unfortunate author, which calls for, and I am sure deserves, all the pity and assistance his friends can afford him, and which, I am sure also, the goodness and benevolence of your heart will prompt you to exert in his behalf. It is perfectly unnecessary for me to add, after the anxiety I feel, and cannot but express, that no benefit conferred upon myself will be acknowledged with half the gratitude I must ever feel for the smallest instance of kindness shewn to my beloved Peter. Farewell, my dearest uncle. With the firmest reliance on your kind and generous promises, I am, ever with the truest gratitude and sincerity,

'Your most affectionate niece,

' NESSY HEYWOOD.'

CHAPTER V

THE PANDORA.

——————— 'O ! I have suffer'd
With those that I saw suffer ! a brave vessel,
Who had, no doubt, some noble creature in her,
Dash'd all to pieces. O, the cry did knock
Against my very heart ! Poor souls ! they perish'd.
Had I been any god of power, I would
Have sunk the sea within the earth, or ere
It should the good ship so have swallow'd, and
The freighting souls within her.'

THE tide of public applause set as strongly in favour of Bligh, on account of his sufferings and the successful issue of his daring enterprise, as its indignation was launched against Christian and his associates, for the audacious and criminal deed they had committed. Bligh was promoted by the Admiralty to the rank of Commander, and speedily sent out a second time to transport the bread-fruit to the West Indies, which he without the least obstruction successfully accomplished; and his majesty's government were no sooner made acquainted with the atrocious act of piracy and mutiny, than it determined to adopt every possible means to apprehend and bring to condign punishment the perpetrators of so foul a deed. For this purpose, the Pandora frigate, of twenty-four guns and one hundred and sixty men, was

despatched under the command of Captain Edward
Edwards, with orders to proceed, in the first instance, to Otaheite, and not finding the mutineers
there, to visit the different groups of the Society
and Friendly Islands, and others in the neighbour-
ing parts of the Pacific, using his best endeavours
to seize and bring home in confinement the whole
or such part of the delinquents as he might be
able to discover.

This voyage was in the sequel almost as disastrous as that of the Bounty, but from a different
cause. The waste of human life was much greater,
occasioned by the wreck of the ship, and the distress experienced by the crew not much less,
owing to the famine and thirst they had to suffer
in a navigation of eleven hundred miles in open
boats; but the Captain succeeded in fulfil-
ling a part of his instructions, by taking fourteen
of the mutineers, of whom ten were brought safe
to England, the other four being drowned when
the ship was wrecked.

The only published account of this voyage is
contained in a small volume by Mr. George
Hamilton, the surgeon, who appears to have been
a coarse, vulgar, and illiterate man, more disposed
to relate licentious scenes and adventures, in which
he and his companions were engaged, than to
give any information of proceedings and occur-
rences connected with the main object of the
voyage. From this book, therefore, much information is not to be looked for. In a more modern
publication, many abusive epithets have been bestowed on Captain Edwards, and observations
made on the conduct of this officer highly inju-

rious to his reputation, in regard to his inhuman treatment of, and disgraceful acts of cruelty towards, his prisoners, which it is to be feared have but too much foundation in fact.

The account of his proceedings, rendered by himself to the Admiralty, is vague and unsatisfactory; and had it not been for the journal of Morrison, and a circumstantial letter of young Heywood to his mother, no record would have remained of the unfeeling conduct of this officer towards his unfortunate prisoners, who were treated with a rigour which could not be justified on any ground of necessity or prudence.

The Pandora anchored in Matavai Bay on the 23rd March, 1791. Captain Edwards, in his narrative, states that Joseph Coleman, the armourer of the Bounty, attempted to come on board before the Pandora had anchored; that on reaching the ship, he began to make inquiries of him after the Bounty and her people, and that he seemed to be ready to give him any information that was required; that the next who came on board, just after the ship had anchored, were Mr. Peter Heywood and Mr. Stewart, before any boat had been sent on shore; that they were brought down to his cabin, when, after some conversation, Heywood asked if Mr. Hayward (midshipman of the Bounty, but now lieutenant of the Pandora) was on board, as he had heard that he was; that Lieutenant Hayward, whom he sent for, treated Heywood with a sort of contemptuous look, and began to enter into conversation with him respecting the Bounty; but Edwards ordered him to desist, and called in the sentinel to take the

prisoners into safe custody, and to put them in
irons; that four other mutineers soon made their
appearance ; and that, from them and some of
the natives, he learned that the rest of the Bounty's
people had built a schooner, with which they had
sailed the day before from Matavai Bay to the
N.W. part of the island.

He goes on to say that, on this intelligence, he
despatched the two lieutenants, Corner and Hayward, with the pinnace and launch, to endeavour
to intercept her. They soon got sight of her and
chased her out to sea, but the schooner gained so
much upon them, and night coming on, they
were compelled to give up the pursuit and return
to the ship. It was soon made known, however,
that she had returned to Paparré, on which they
were again despatched in search of her. Lieutenant Corner had taken three of the mutineers,
and Hayward, on arriving at Paparré, found the
schooner there, but the mutineers had abandoned
her and fled to the mountains. He carried off
the schooner, and returned next day, when he
learned they were not far off; and the following
morning, on hearing they were coming down,
he drew up his party in order to receive them, and
when within hearing, called to them to lay down
their arms and to go on one side, which they did,
when they were confined and brought as prisoners
to the ship.

The following were the persons received on
board the Pandora :

PETER HEYWOOD	.	.	. Midshipman.
GEORGE STEWART	.	.	. Ditto.
JAMES MORRISON	.	.	. Boatswain's mate.

CHARLES NORMAN	. . .	Carpenter's mate.
THOMAS M'INTOSH	. . .	Carpenter's crew.
JOSEPH COLEMAN .	. . .	Armourer.
RICHARD SKINNER		
THOMAS ELLISON		
HENRY HILBRANT		
THOMAS BURKITT		
JOHN MILLWARD	} . .	Seamen.
JOHN SUMNER		
WILLIAM MUSPRATT		
RICHARD BYRN		

In all fourteen. The other two, which made up the sixteen that had been left on the island, were murdered, as will appear presently.

Captain Edwards will himself explain how he disposed of his prisoners. ' I put the pirates,' he says, ' into a round-house which I built on the after part of the quarter-deck, for their more effectual security in this airy and healthy situation, and to separate them from, and to prevent their having communication with, or to crowd and in-commode, the ship's company.' Dr. Hamilton calls it the most desirable place in the ship, and adds, that ' orders were given that the prisoners should be victualled, in every respect, the same as the ship's company, both in meat, liquor, and all the extra indulgences with which they were so liberally supplied, notwithstanding the established laws of the service, which restrict prisoners to two-thirds allowance; but Captain Edwards very humanely commiserated their unhappy and in-evitable length of confinement.' Mr. Morrison, one of the prisoners, gives a very different account of their treatment from that of Edwards or Hamilton. He says that Captain Edwards put

both legs of the two midshipmen in irons, and
that he branded them with the opprobrious
epithet of ' piratical villains :' that they, with the
rest, being strongly handcuffed, were put into a
kind of round-house only eleven feet long, built
as a prison, and aptly named ' Pandora's Box,'
which was entered by a scuttle in the roof, about
eighteen inches square. This was done in order
that they might be kept separate from the crew,
and also the more effectually to prevent them from
having any communication with the natives; that
such of those friendly creatures as ventured to
look pitifully towards them were instantly turned
out of the ship, and never again allowed to come
on board. But two sentinels were kept constantly
upon the roof of the prison, with orders to shoot
the first of its inmates who should attempt to
address another in the Otaheitan dialect.

That Captain Edwards took every precaution
to keep his prisoners in safe custody, and place
them in confinement, as by his instructions he was
directed to do, may be well imagined*, but Mr.
Morrison will probably be thought to go somewhat beyond credibility in stating that orders
were given ' to *shoot* any of the prisoners,' when
confined in irons. Captain Edwards must have
known that such an act would have cost him
his commission or something more. The fact
is, that information was given to Edwards, at

* His orders run thus : ' You are to keep the mutineers
as closely confined as may preclude all possibility of their
escaping, having, however, proper regard to the preservation
of their lives, that they may be brought home, to undergo
the punishment due to their demerits.'

least he so asserts, by the brother of the King of
Otaheite, an intelligent chief, that a conspiracy was
formed among the natives to cut the ship's cables
the first strong wind that should blow on the
shore, which was considered to be the more probable, as many of the prisoners were said to be
married to the most respectable chiefs' daughters
in the district opposite to the anchorage; that the
midshipman Stewart, in particular, had married
the daughter of a man of great landed property
near Matavai Bay. This intelligence, no doubt,
weighed with the Captain in giving his orders for
the close confinement of the prisoners; and particularly in restricting the visits of the natives;
but so far is it from being true that all communication between the mutineers and the natives was
cut off, that we are distinctly told by Mr. Hamilton,
that ' the prisoner's wives visited the ship daily,
and brought their children, who were permitted to
be carried to their unhappy fathers. To see the
poor captives in irons,' he says, ' weeping over
their tender offspring, was too moving a scene for
any feeling heart. Their wives brought them
ample supplies of every delicacy that the country
afforded, while we lay there, and behaved with the
greatest fidelity and affection to them*.'

Of the fidelity and attachment of these simple-
minded creatures an instance is afforded in the
affecting story which is told, in the first Missionary Voyage of the Duff, of the unfortunate wife
of the reputed mutineer Mr. Stewart. It would
seem also to exonerate Edwards from some part

* Voyage round the World, by Mr. George Hamilton,
p. 34.

of the charges which have been brought against him.

'The history of Peggy Stewart marks a tenderness of heart that never will be heard without emotion : she was daughter of a chief, and taken for his wife by Mr. Stewart, one of the unhappy mutineers. They had lived with the old chief in the most tender state of endearment; a beautiful little girl had been the fruit of their union, and was at the breast when the Pandora arrived, seized the criminals, and secured them in irons on board the ship. Frantic with grief, the unhappy Peggy (for so he had named her) flew with her infant in a canoe to the arms of her husband. The interview was so affecting and afflicting, that the officers on board were overwhelmed with anguish, and Stewart himself, unable to bear the heart-rending scene, begged she might not be admitted again on board. . She was separated from him by violence, and conveyed on shore in a state of despair and grief too big for utterance. Withheld from him, and forbidden to come any more on board, she sunk into the deepest dejection; it preyed on her vitals; she lost all relish for food and life, rejoiced no more, pined under a rapid decay of two months, and fell a victim to her feelings, dying literally of a broken heart. Her child is yet alive, and the tender object of our care, having been brought up by a sister, who nursed it as her own, and has discharged all the duties of an affectionate mother to the orphan infant *.'

It does not appear that young Heywood formed any matrimonial engagement during his abode in

* A Missionary Voyage to the Southern Pacific, p. 360.

Otaheite.   He was not, however, insensible to
the amiable and good qualities of these people.
In some laudatory verses which he wrote while on
the island, their numerous good qualities are
spoken of in terms of the highest commendation.

All the mutineers that were left on the island
being received on board the Pandora, that ship
proceeded in search of those who had gone away
in the Bounty.   It may be mentioned, however,
that two of the most active in the mutiny,
Churchill and Thompson, had perished on the
island before her arrival, by violent deaths. These
two men had accompanied a chief, who was the
tayo, or sworn friend, of Churchill, and having
died without children, this mutineer succeeded to
his property and dignity, according to the custom
of the country.   Thompson, for some real or
fancied insult, took an opportunity of shooting his
companion.   The natives assembled, and came to
a resolution to avenge the murder, and literally
stoned Thompson to death, and his skull was
brought on board the Pandora.   This horrible
wretch had some time before slain a man and a
child through mere wantonness, but escaped
punishment by a mistake that had nearly proved
fatal to young Heywood.   It seems that the description of a person in Otaheite is usually given
by some distinguishing figure of the *tattoo*, and
Heywood, having the same marks as Thompson,
was taken for him ; and just as the club was raised
to dash out his brains, the interposition of an old
chief, with whom he was travelling round the
island, was just in time to avert the blow.

Captain Edwards had no clue to guide him as

to the route taken by the Bounty, but he learnt
from different people and from journals kept on
board that ship, which were found in the chests of
the mutineers at Otaheite, the proceedings of
Christian and his associates after Lieutenant Bligh
and his companions had been turned adrift in the
launch, From these it appears that the pirates
proceeded in the first instance to the island of
Toobouai, in lat. 20° 13' S., long. 149° 35' W.,
where they anchored on the 25th May, 1789.
They had thrown overboard the greater part of the
bread-fruit plants, and divided among themselves
the property of the officers and men who had been
so inhumanly turned adrift. At this island they
intended to form a settlement, but the opposition
of the natives, the want of many necessary materials, and quarrels among themselves, determined
them to go to Otaheite to procure what might be
required to effect their purpose, provided they
should agree to prosecute their original intention.
They accordingly sailed from Toobouai about the
latter end of the month, and arrived at Otaheite
on the 6th June. The Otoo, or reigning sovereign,
and other principal natives, were very inquisitive
and anxious to know what had become of Lieutenant Bligh and the rest of the crew, and also
what had been done with the bread-fruit plants?
They were told they had most unexpectedly fallen
in with Captain Cook at an island he had just discovered, called Whytootakee, where he intended
to form a settlement, and where the plants had
been landed ; and that Lieutenant Bligh and the
others were stopping there to assist Captain Cook
in the business he had in hand, and that he had ap-

pointed Mr. Christian commander of the Bounty; and that he was now come by his orders for an additional supply of hogs, goats, fowls, breadfruit, and various other articles which Otaheite could supply.

This artful story was quite sufficient to impose on the credulity of these humane and simpleminded islanders; and so overcome with joy were they to hear that their old friend Captain Cook was alive, and about to settle so near them, that every possible means were forthwith made use of to procure the things that were wanted; so that in the course of a very few days the Bounty received on board three hundred and twelve hogs, thirty-eight goats, eight dozen of fowls, a bull and a cow, and a large quantity of bread-fruit, plantains, bananas, and other fruits. They also took with them eight men, nine women, and seven boys. With these supplies they left Otaheite on the 19th June, and arrived a second time at Toobouai on the 26th. They warped the ship up the harbour, landed the live stock, and set about building a fort of fifty yards square.

While this work was carrying on, quarrels and disagreements were daily happening among them, and continual disputes and skirmishes were taking place with the natives, generally brought on by the violent conduct of the invaders, and by depredations committed on their property. Retaliations were attempted by the natives without success, numbers of whom being pursued with fire-arms were put to death. Still the situation of the mutineers became so disagreeable and unsafe, the work went on so slowly and reluctantly, that the

building of the fort was agreed to be discontinued. Christian, in fact, had very soon perceived that his authority was on the wane, and
that no peaceful establishment was likely to be
accomplished at Toobouai ; he therefore held
a consultation as to what would be the most
advisable step to take. After much angry discus-
sion, it was at length determined that Toobouai
should be abandoned ; that the ship should once
more be taken to Otaheite ; and that those who
might choose to go on shore there might do so,
and those who preferred to remain in the ship
might proceed in her to whatever place they
should agree upon among themselves.

In consequence of this determination they sailed
from Toobouai on the 15th, and arrived at Matavai Bay on the 20th September, 1789. Here
sixteen of the mutineers were put on shore, at
their own request, fourteen of whom were received
on board the Pandora, and two of them, as before
mentioned, were murdered on the island. The
remaining nine agreed to continue in the Bounty.
The small arms, powder, canvass, and the small
stores belonging to the ship, were equally divided
among the whole crew. The Bounty sailed finally
from Otaheite on the night of the 21st September,
and was last seen the following morning to the
north-west of Point Venus. They took with them
seven Otaheitan men and twelve women. It was
not even conjectured whither they meant to go ; but
Christian had frequently been heard to say, that his
object was to discover some unknown or uninhabited island, in which there was no harbour for
shipping ; that he would run the Bounty on shore,

and make use of her materials to form a settlement; but this was the only account, vague as it
was, that could be procured to direct Captain
Edwards in his intended search.

It appears that when the schooner, of which we
have spoken, had been finished, six of the fourteen
mutineers that were left on Otaheite embarked in
her, with the intention of proceeding to the East
Indies, and actually put to sea; but meeting with
bad weather, and suspecting the nautical abilities of
Morrison, whom they had elected as commanding
officer, to conduct her in safety, they resolved on
returning to Otaheite.   Morrison, it seems, first
undertook the construction of this schooner, being
himself a tolerable mechanic, in which he was
assisted by the two carpenters, the cooper, and
some others.   To this little band of architects, we
are told, Morrison acted both as director and
chaplain, distinguishing the Sabbath-day by reading to them the Church Liturgy, and hoisting the
British colours on a flag-staff erected near the
scene of their operations.   Conscious of his innocence, his object is stated to have been that of
reaching Batavia in time to secure a passage
home in the next fleet bound to Holland; but that
their return was occasioned, not by any distrust of
Morrison's talents, but by a refusal, on the part of
the natives, to give them a sufficient quantity of
matting and other necessaries for so long a voyage,
being, in fact, desirous of retaining them on the
island.   Stewart and young Heywood took no part
in this transaction, having made up their minds to
remain at Otaheite, and there to await the arrival
of a king's ship, it being morally certain that ere

long one would be sent out thither to search for them, whatever might have been the fate of Bligh and his companions; and that this was really their intention is evident by the alacrity they displayed in getting on board the Pandora, the moment of her arrival.

On the 8th of May, this frigate left Otaheite, accompanied by the little schooner which the mutineers had built, and the history of which is somewhat remarkable. In point of size she was not a great deal larger than Lieutenant Bligh's launch, her dimensions being thirty feet length of keel; thirty-five feet length on deck; nine feet and a half extreme breadth; five feet depth of the hold. She parted from the Pandora near the Palmerston islands, when searching for the Bounty, and was not heard of till the arrival of the Pandora's crew at Samarang, in Java, where they found her lying at anchor, the crew having suffered so dreadfully from famine and the want of water, that one of the young gentlemen belonging to her became delirious. She was a remarkably swift sailer, and, being afterwards employed in the sea-otter trade, is stated to have made one of the quickest passages ever known from China to the Sandwich Islands. This memorable little vessel was purchased at Canton by the late Captain Broughton, to assist him in surveying the coast of Tartary, and became the means of preserving the crew of his Majesty's ship Providence, amounting to one hundred and twelve men, when wrecked to the eastward of Formosa, in the year 1797.

The Pandora called at numerous islands with-

M

out success, but on Lieutenant Corner having
landed on one of the Palmerston's group, he
found a yard and some spars with the broad
arrow upon them, and marked ' Bounty.' This
induced the captain to cause a very minute search
to be made in all these islands, in the course of
which the Pandora, being driven out to sea by
blowing weather, and very thick and hazy, lost
sight of the little tender and a jolly boat, the
latter of which was never more heard of. This
gives occasion to a little splenetic effusion from a
writer in a periodical journal*, which was hardly
called for. ' When this boat,' says the writer,
' with a midshipman and several men (four), had
been inhumanly ordered from alongside, it was
known that there was nothing in her but one piece
of salt-beef, compassionately thrown in by a seaman ; and horrid as must have been their fate,
the flippant surgeon, after detailing the disgraceful fact, adds—" that this is the way the world was
peopled"—or words to that effect, for we quote
only from memory.' The following is quoted
from the book :—

' It may be difficult to surmise,' says the surgeon, ' what has been the fate of those unfortunate
men. They had a piece of salt-beef thrown into
the boat to them on leaving the ship ; and it
rained a good deal that night and the following
day, which might satiate their thirst. It is by
these accidents the Divine Ruler of the universe
has peopled the southern hemisphere.' This is no
more than asserting an acknowledged fact that can

* United Service Journal.

hardly admit of a dispute, and there appears nothing in the paragraph which at all affects the character of Captain Edwards, against whom it is levelled.

After a fruitless search of three months, the Pandora arrived, on the 29th August, on the coast of New Holland, and close to that extraordinary reef of coral rocks called the ' Barrier Reef,' which runs along the greater part of the eastern coast, but at a considerable distance from it. The boat had been sent out to look for an opening, which was soon discovered, but in the course of the night the ship had drifted past it. ' On getting soundings,' says Captain Edwards, in his narrative laid before the court-martial, ' the topsails were filled; but before the tacks were hauled on board and other sail made and trimmed, the ship struck upon a reef; we had a quarter less two fathoms on the larboard side, and three fathoms on the starboard side; the sails were braced about different ways to endeavour to get her off, but to no purpose; they were then clewed up and afterwards furled, the top-gallant yards got down and the top-gallant masts struck. Boats were hoisted out with a view to carry out an anchor, but before that could be effected the ship struck so violently on the reef, that the carpenter reported she made eighteen inches of water in five minutes; and in five minutes after this, that there were four feet of water in the hold. Finding the leak increasing so fast, it was thought necessary to turn the hands to the pumps, and to bail at the different hatchways; but she still continued to gain upon us so fast, that in little more than an hour and half after she struck, there were eight feet and a half of water in the hold. About ten we perceived that the ship had beaten over the reef, and was in ten fathoms water; we therefore let go the small bower anchor, cleared away a cable, and let go the best bower anchor in fifteen and a half fathoms water under foot, to steady the ship. Some of her guns were thrown overboard, and the water gained upon us only in a small degree, and we flattered ourselves that by the assistance of a thrummed topsail, which we were preparing to haul under the ship's bottom, we might be able to lessen the leak, and to free her of water: but these flattering hopes did not continue long ; for, as she settled in the water, the leak increased again, and in so great a degree, that there was reason to apprehend she would sink before daylight. During the night two of the pumps were unfortunately for some time rendered useless ; one of them, however, was repaired, and we continued baling and pumping the remainder of the night; and every effort that was thought of was made to keep afloat and preserve the ship. Daylight fortunately appeared, and gave us the opportunity of seeing our situation and the surrounding danger, and it was evident the ship had been carried to the northward by a tide or current.

' The officers, whom I had consulted on the subject of our situation, gave it as their opinion that nothing more could be done for the preservation of the ship ; it then became necessary to endeavour to provide and to find means for the preservation of the people. Our four boats, which consisted of one launch, one eight-oared pinnace, and two six-oared yawls, with careful hands in them,

were kept astern of the ship; a small quantity of
bread, water, and other necessary articles, were
put into them; two canoes, which we had on
board, were lashed together and put into the water;
rafts were made, and all floating things upon
deck were unlashed.

'About half-past six in the morning of the
29th the hold was full, and the water was between
decks, and it also washed in at the upper deck
ports, and there were strong indications that the
ship was on the very point of sinking, and we
began to leap overboard and take to the boats,
and before everybody could get out of her she
actually sunk. The boats continued astern of the
ship in the direction of the drift of the tide from
her, and took up the people that had hold of rafts
and other floating things that had been cast loose,
for the purpose of supporting them on the water.
The double canoe, that was able to support a considerable number of men, broke adrift with only
one man, and was bulged upon a reef, and afforded
us no assistance when she was so much wanted
on this trying and melancholy occasion. Two of
the boats were laden with men and sent to a small
sandy island (or key) about four miles from the
wreck; and I remained near the ship for some
time with the other two boats, and picked up all
the people that could be seen, and then followed
the two first boats to the key; and having landed
the men and cleared the boats, they were immediately despatched again to look about the wreck and
the adjoining reef for any that might be missing,
but they returned without having found a single
person. On mustering the people that were saved,

it appeared that eighty-nine of the ship's company,
and ten of the mutineers that had been prisoners
on board, answered to their names; but thirty-
one of the ship's company, and four mutineers,
were lost with the ship.'

It is remarkable enough that so little notice is
taken of the mutineers in this narrative of the
captain; and as the following statement is supposed to come from the late Lieutenant Corner,
who was second lieutenant of the Pandora, it is
entitled to be considered as authentic, and if so,
Captain Edwards must have deserved the character, ascribed to him, of being altogether destitute of the common feelings of humanity.

'Three of the Bounty's people, Coleman, Norman, and M'Intosh, were now let out of irons, and
sent to work at the pumps. The others offered
their assistance, and begged to be allowed a chance
of saving their lives; instead of which, two additional sentinels were placed over them, with orders
to shoot any who should attempt to get rid of
their fetters. Seeing no prospect of escape, they
betook themselves to prayer, and prepared to meet
their fate, every one expecting that the ship
would soon go to pieces, her rudder and part of
the stern-post being already beat away.'

When the ship was actually sinking, and every
effort making for the preservation of the crew, it
is asserted that ' no notice was taken of the prisoners, as is falsely stated by the author of the
" Pandora's Voyage," although Captain Edwards
was entreated by Mr. Heywood to have mercy
upon them, when he passed over their prison, to
make his own escape, the ship then lying on her

broadside, with the larboard bow completely under water.   Fortunately the master-at-arms, either by accident or design, when slipping from the roof of " Pandora's Box " into the sea, let the keys of the irons fall through the scuttle or entrance, which he had just before opened, and thus enabled them to commence their own liberation, in which they were generously assisted, at the imminent risk of his own life, by William Moulter, a boatswain's mate, who clung to the coamings, and pulled the long bars through the shackles, saying he would set them free, or go to the bottom with them.

' Scarcely was this effected when the ship went down, leaving nothing visible but the top-mast cross-trees.   The master-at-arms and all the sentinels sunk to rise no more.   The cries of them and the other drowning men were awful in the extreme ; and more than half an hour had elapsed before the survivors could be taken up by the boats.   Among the former were Mr. Stewart, John Sumner, Richard Skinner, and Henry Hillbrant, the whole of whom perished with their hands still in manacles.

' On this melancholy occasion Mr. Heywood was the last person but three who escaped from the prison, into which the water had already found its way through the bulk-head scuttles.   Jumping overboard, he seized a plank, and was swimming towards a small sandy quay (key) about three miles distant, when a boat picked him up, and conveyed him thither in a state of nudity.   It is worthy of remark, that James Morrison endeavoured to follow his young companion's example, and, although handcuffed, managed to keep afloat until a boat came to his assistance.'

This account would appear almost incredible. It is true men are sometimes found to act the part of inhuman monsters, but then they are generally actuated by some motive or extraordinary excitement ; here, however, there was neither; but on the contrary, the condition of the poor prisoners appealed most forcibly to the mercy and humanity of their jailor. The surgeon of the ship states, in his account of her loss, that as soon as the spars, booms, hen-coops, and other buoyant articles were cut loose, ' the prisoners were ordered to be let out of irons.' One would imagine, indeed, that the officers on this dreadful emergency would not be witness to such inhumanity, without remonstrating effectually against keeping these unfortunate men confined a moment beyond the period when it became evident that the ship must sink. It will be seen, however, presently, from Mr. Heywood's own statement, that they were so kept, and that the brutal and unfeeling conduct which has been imputed to Captain Edwards is but too true.

It is an awful moment when a ship takes her last heel, just before going down. When the Pandora sunk, the surgeon says, ' the crew had just time to leap overboard, accompanying it with a most dreadful yell. The cries of the men drowning in the water was at first awful in the extreme; but as they sunk and became faint, they died away by degrees.' How accurately has Byron described the whole progress of a shipwreck to the final catastrophe ! He might have been a specta-

tor of the Pandora, at the moment of her foundering, when

> She gave a heel, and then a lurch to port,
> And, going down head foremost—sunk. . . . .
>
> Then rose from sea to sky the wild farewell!
> Then shriek'd the timid and stood still the brave;
> Then some leap'd overboard with dreadful yell,
> As eager to anticipate their grave;
> And the sea yawn'd around her like a hell,
> And down she suck'd with her the whirling wave,
> Like one who grapples with his enemy,
> And strives to strangle him before he die.
>
> And first one universal shriek there rush'd
> Louder than the loud ocean, like a crash
> Of echoing thunder; and then all was hush'd,
> Save the wild wind and the remorseless dash
> Of billows; but at intervals there gush'd,
> Accompanied with a convulsive splash,
> A solitary shriek—the bubbling cry
> Of some strong swimmer in his agony.

On the sandy key which fortunately presented
itself, the shipwrecked seamen hauled up the
boats, to repair those that were damaged, and
to stretch canvas round the gunwales, the better to
keep out the sea from breaking into them. The
heat of the sun and the reflection from the sand
are described as excruciating, and the thirst of
the men was rendered intolerable, from their
stomachs being filled with salt water in the length
of time they had to swim before being picked up.
Mr. Hamilton says they were greatly disturbed in
the night, by the irregular behaviour of one of the
seamen, named Connell, which made them suspect
he had got drunk with some wine that had been
saved; but it turned out that the excruciating
torture he suffered from thirst had induced him to

drink salt water; ' by which means he went mad,
and died in the sequel of the voyage.' It seems, a
small keg of water, and some biscuits, had been
thrown into one of the boats, which they found, by
calculation, would be sufficient to last sixteen
days, on an allowance of two wine-glasses of
water per day to each man, and a very small
quantity of bread, the weight of which was accurately ascertained by a musket-ball, and a pair of
wooden scales made for each boat.

The crew and the prisoners were now distributed
among the four boats. At Bligh's ' Mountainous
Island,' they entered a bay where swarms of natives came down and made signs for their landing;
but this they declined to do; on which an arrow
was discharged and struck one of the boats; and
as the savages were seen to be collecting their
bows and arrows, a volley of muskets, a few of
which happened to be in the boats, was discharged, which put them to flight. While sailing
among the islands and near the shore, they now
and then stopped to pick up a few oysters, and
procure a little fresh water. On the 2nd September, they passed the N.W. point of New Holland, and launched into the great Indian Ocean,
having a voyage of about a thousand miles still to
perform.

It will be recollected that Captain Bligh's people
received warmth and comfort by wringing out
their clothes in salt-water. The same practice was
adopted by the crews of the Pandora's boats; but
the doctor observes, that ' this wetting their bodies
with salt-water is not advisable, if protracted beyond three or four days, as, after that time, the

great absorption from the skin that takes place,
taints the fluids with the bitter part of salt-water,
so that the saliva becomes intolerable in the
mouth.' Their mouths, indeed, he says, became
so parched, that few attempted to eat the slender
allowance of bread. He also remarks, that as the
sufferings of the people continued, their temper
became cross and savage. In the Captain's boat,
it is stated, one of the mutineers took to praying;
but that ' the captain, suspecting the purity of
his doctrines, and unwilling that he should have
a monopoly of the business, gave prayers himself.'

On the 13th, they saw the island of Timor, and
the next morning landed and got some water, and
a few small fish from the natives; and on the
night of the 15th, anchored opposite the fort of
Coupang. Nothing could exceed the kindness
and hospitality of the governor and other Dutch
officers of this settlement, in affording every possible assistance and relief in their distressed condition. Having remained here three weeks, they
embarked, on the 6th October, on board the Rem-
bang Dutch Indiaman, and on the 30th, anchored
at Samarang, where they were agreeably surprised
to find their little Tender, which they had so long
given up for lost. On the 7th November they
arrived at Batavia, where Captain Edwards agreed
with the Dutch East India Company, to divide the
whole of the ship's company and prisoners among
four of their ships proceeding to Europe. The
latter the captain took with him in the Vreeden-
burgh ; but finding his Majesty's ship Gorgon at
the Cape, he transhipped himself and prisoners,

and proceeded in her to Spithead, where he arrived on the 19th June, 1792.

Captain Edwards, in his meagre narrative, takes no more notice of his prisoners with regard to the mode in which they were disposed of at Coupang and Batavia, than he does when the Pandora went down. In fact, he suppresses all information respecting them, from the day in which they were consigned to ' Pandora's Box.' From this total indifference towards these unfortunate men, and their almost unparalleled sufferings, Captain Edwards must be set down as a man, whose only feeling was to stick to the letter of his instructions, and rigidly to adhere to what he considered the strict line of his duty; that he was a man of a cold phlegmatic disposition, whom no distress could move, and whose feelings were not easily disturbed by the sufferings of his fellow-creatures. He appears to have been one of those mortals, who might say, with Manfred—

My spirit walk'd not with the souls of men;

. . . .

My joys, my griefs, my passions, and my powers,
Made me a stranger; though I wore the form,
I had no sympathy with breathing flesh !

There seems to have been a general feeling at and before the court-martial, that Captain Edwards had exercised a harsh, unnecessary, and undue degree of severity on his prisoners. It is the custom, sanctioned no doubt by long usage, to place in irons all such as may have been guilty of mutiny in a ship of war, and the necessity of so doing is obvious enough—to prevent, in the

most effectual manner, communication with the
rest of the ship's company, who might be contami-
nated by their intercourse with such mischievous
and designing men ; men whose crime is of that
dye, that, if found guilty, they have little hope to
escape the punishment of death, to which a mutineer must, by the naval articles of war, be sentenced ; no alternative being left to a court-martial, in such a case, but to pronounce a sentence
of acquittal or of death.

In the present case, however, most of the prisoners had surrendered themselves ; many of
them had taken no active part in the mutiny ; and
others had been forcibly compelled to remain in
the ship. It was not likely, therefore, that any
danger could arise from indulging them occasionally, and in turns, with a few hours of fresh air on
deck. As little danger was there of their escaping ;
where indeed could they escape to—especially
when the ship was going down, at a great distance from any shore, and the nearest one known
to be inhabited by savages ? All or most of them
were desirous of getting home, and throwing
themselves on God and their country. The captain, however, had no ' compunctious visitings
of nature' to shake his purpose, which seems to
have been, to keep them strictly in irons during
the whole passage, and to deliver them over in
that state on his arrival in England.

Perhaps the circumstance of the crime of piracy,
being superadded to that of mutiny, may have
operated on his stern nature, and induced him to
inflict a greater severity of punishment than he
might otherwise have done, and which he certainly

did far beyond the letter and spirit of his instructions. He might have considered that, in all ages
and among all nations, with the exception of some
of the Greek states*, piracy has been held in the
utmost abhorrence, and those guilty of it treated
with singular and barbarous severity ; and that the
most sanguinary laws were established for the protection of person and property in maritime adventure. The laws of Oleron, which were composed
under the immediate direction of our Richard I.,
and became the common usage among maritime
states, whose vessels passed through British seas,
are conceived in a spirit of the most barbarous
crueltyf. Thus, if a poor pilot, through ignorance, lost the vessel, he was either required to
make full satisfaction to the merchant for damages
sustained, or to lose his head. In the case of
wrecks, where the lord of the coast (something
like our present vice-admiral) should be found to
be in league with the pilots, and run the ships on
rocks, in order to get salvage, the said lord, the

* The Phoceans, on account of the sterility of their country, were in the habit of practising piracy, which, according
to Justin, was held to be an honourable profession.

† These laws are contained in an ancient authentic book,
called 'The Black Book of the Admiralty,' in which all things
therein comprehended are engrossed on vellum, in an ancient
character ; which hath been from time to time kept in the
registry of the High Court of Admiralty, for the use of the
Judges. When Mr. Luders made enquiry at the office in
Doctors' Commons, in 1808, he was informed by the proper
officers there, that they had never seen such book, and knew
nothing of it, nor where to find it. The fact is, the book in
question was put into Lord Thurlow's hands when Attorney-
General, and never returned. There is a copy of it in the
Admiralty.

salvers, and all concerned, are declared to be accursed and excommunicated, and punished as thieves and robbers; and the pilot condemned to be hanged upon a high gibbet, which is to abide and remain to succeeding ages, on the place where erected, as a visible caution to other ships sailing thereby. Nor was the fate of the lord of the coast less severe,—his property was to be confiscated, and himself, fastened to a post in the midst of his own mansion, which being fired at the four corners, were all to be burned together; the walls thereof demolished; and the spot on which it stood be converted into a market-place, for the sale only of hogs and swine, to all posterity.

These and many other barbarous usages were transferred into the institutions of Wisbuy, which formed the *jus mercatorum* for a long period, and in which great care was taken for the security of ships against their crews. Among other articles are the following.—Whoever draws a sword upon the master of a vessel, or wilfully falsifies the compass, shall have his right hand nailed to the mast.—Whoever behaves riotously shall be punished by being keel-hauled.—Whoever is guilty of rebellion (or mutiny) shall be thrown overboard.

For the suppression of piracy, the Portuguese, in their early intercourse with India, had a summary punishment, and accompanied it with a terrible example to deter others from the commission of the crime. Whenever they took a pirate ship, they instantly hanged every man, carried away the sails, rudder, and every thing that was valuable in the ship, and left her to be buffeted about by the winds and the waves, with the carcasses of the criminals dangling from the yards, a horrid object of terror to all who might chance to fall in with her. Even to this day, a spice of the laws of Oleron still remains in the maritime code of European nations, as far as regards mutiny and piracy; and a feeling of this kind may have operated on the mind of Captain Edwards, especially as a tendency even to mutiny, or mutinous expressions, are considered, by the usage of the service, as justifying the commander of a ship of war to put the offenders in irons. Besides, the treatment of Bligh, whose admirable conduct under the unparalleled sufferings of himself and all who accompanied him in the open boat, had roused the people of England to the highest pitch of indignation against Christian and his associates, in which Edwards no doubt participated.

The following letter of Mr. Peter Heywood to his mother removes all doubt as to the character and conduct of this officer. It is an artless and pathetic tale, and, as his amiable sister says, 'breathes not a syllable inconsistent with truth and honour.'

' *Batavia, November* 20*th*, 1791.

' My ever-honoured and dearest Mother,

' At length the time has arrived when you are once more to hear from your ill-fated son, whose conduct at the capture of that ship, in which it was my fortune to embark, has I fear, from what has since happened to me, been grossly misrepresented to you by Lieutenant Bligh, who, by not knowing the real cause of my remaining on board, natu-

rally suspected me, unhappily for me, to be a coad-
jutor in the mutiny; but I never, to my knowledge, whilst under his command, behaved myself
in a manner unbecoming the station I occupied,
nor so much as even entertained a thought deroga-
tory to his honour, so as to give him the least
grounds for entertaining an opinion of me so un-
generous and undeserved; for I flatter myself he
cannot give a character of my conduct, whilst I
was under his tuition, that could merit the slightest
scrutiny. Oh! my dearest mother, I hope you
have not so easily credited such an account of me;
do but let me vindicate my conduct, and declare
to you the true cause of my remaining in the ship,
and you will then see how little I deserve censure,
and how I have been injured by so gross an as-
persion. I shall then give you a short and cursory
account of what has happened to me since; but
I am afraid to say a hundredth part of what I have
got in store, for I am not allowed the use of
writing materials, if known, so that this is done
by stealth; but if it should ever come to your
hands, it will, I hope, have the desired effect of
removing your uneasiness on my account, when I
assure you, before the face of God, of my innocence of what is laid to my charge. How I
came to remain on board was thus :—

'The morning the ship was taken, it being my
watch below, happening to awake just after daylight, and looking out of my hammock, I saw a
man sitting upon the arm-chest in the main hatchway, with a drawn cutlass in his hand, the reason
of which I could not divine; so I got out of bed
and inquired of him what was the cause of it.

He told me that Mr. Christian, assisted by some
of the ship's company, had seized the captain and
put him in confinement; had taken the command
of the ship and meant to carry Bligh home a prisoner, in order to try him by court-martial, for his
long tyrannical and oppressive conduct to his
people. I was quite thunderstruck; and hurrying
into my berth again, told one of my messmates,
whom I awakened out of his sleep, what had happened. Then dressing myself, I went up the
fore-hatchway, and saw what he had told me was
but too true; and again, I asked some of the
people, who were under arms, what was going to
be done with the captain, who was then on the
larboard side of the quarter-deck, with his hands
tied behind his back, and Mr. Christian alongside
him with a pistol and drawn bayonet. I now
heard a very different story, and that the Captain
was to be sent ashore to Tofoa in the launch, and
that those who would not join Mr. Christian,
might either accompany the captain, or would be
taken in irons to Otaheite and left there. The
relation of two stories so different, left me unable
to judge which could be the true one; but seeing
them hoisting the boats out, it seemed to prove
the latter.

' In this trying situation, young and inexperienced
as I was, and without an adviser, (every person
being as it were infatuated, and not knowing what
to do,) I remained for awhile a silent spectator of
what was going on ; and after revolving the matter in my mind, I determined to choose what I
thought the lesser of two evils and stay by the
ship; for I had no doubt that those who went on

shore, in the launch, would be put to death by the savage natives, whereas the Otaheitans being a humane and generous race, one might have a hope of being kindly received, and remain there until the arrival of some ship, which seemed, to silly me, the most consistent with reason and rectitude.

'While this resolution possessed my mind, at the same time lending my assistance to hoist out the boats, the hurry and confusion affairs were in, and thinking my intention just, I never thought of going to Mr. Bligh for advice; besides, what confirmed me in it was, my seeing two experienced officers, when ordered into the boat by Mr. Christian, desire his permission to remain in the ship, (one of whom, my own messmate, Mr. Hayward,) and I being assisting to clear the launch of yams, he asked me what I intended to do? I told him, to remain in the ship. Now this answer, I imagine, he has told Mr. Bligh I made to him; from which, together with my not speaking to him that morning, his suspicions of me have arisen, construing my conduct into what is foreign to my nature.

'Thus, my dearest mother, it was all owing to my youth and unadvised inexperience, but has been interpreted into villany and disregard of my country's laws, the ill effects of which I at present, and still am to, labour under for some months' longer. And now, after what I have asserted, I may still once more retrieve my injured reputation, be again reinstated in the affection and favour of the most tender of mothers, and be still considered as her ever dutiful son.

' I was not undeceived in my erroneous decision till too late, which was after the captain was in the launch; for while I was talking to the master-at-arms, one of the ringleaders in the affair, my other messmate whom I had left in his hammock in the berth, (Mr. Stewart,) came up to me, and asked me, if I was not going in the launch? I replied, No—upon which he told me not to think of such a thing as remaining behind, but take his advice and go down below with him to get a few necessary things, and make haste to go with him into the launch; adding that, by remaining in the ship, I should incur an equal share of guilt with the mutineers themselves. I reluctantly followed his advice—I say *reluctantly*, because I knew no better, and was foolish; and the boat swimming very deep in the water—the land being far distant —the thoughts of being sacrificed by the natives —and the self-consciousness of my first intention being just—all these considerations almost staggered my resolution; however, I preferred my companion's judgment to my own, and we both jumped down the main-hatchway to prepare ourselves for the boat—but, no sooner were we in the berth, than the master-at-arms ordered the sentry to keep us both in the berth till he should receive orders to release us. We desired the master-at-arms to acquaint Mr. Bligh of our intention, which we had reason to think he never did, nor were we permitted to come on deck until the launch was a long way astern. I now, when too late, saw my error.

At the latter end of May, we got to an island to the southward of Taheité, called Tooboui, where they intended to make a settlement, but finding no stock there of any kind, they agreed to go to Taheité, and, after procuring hogs and fowls, to return to Tooboui and remain. So, on the 6th June, we arrived at Taheité, where I was in hopes I might find an opportunity of running away, and remaining on shore, but I could not effect it, as there was always too good a look-out kept to prevent any such steps being taken. And besides, they had all sworn that should any one make his escape, they would force the natives to restore him, and would then shoot him as an example to the rest; well knowing, that any one by remaining there might be the means (should a ship arrive) of discovering their intended place of abode. Finding it therefore impracticable, I saw no other alternative but to rest as content as possible and return to Tooboui, and there wait till the masts of the Bounty should be taken out, and then take the boat which might carry me to Taheité, and disable those remaining from pursuit [*]. But Providence so ordered it, that we had no occasion to try our fortune at such a hazard, for, upon returning there and remaining till the latter end of August, in which time a fort was almost built, but nothing could be effected; and as the natives could not be brought to friendly terms, and with whom we had many skirmishes, and narrow escapes from being cut off by them, and, what was

---

[*] Morrison mentions, in his Journal, a plan to this effect, contrived by Heywood, Stewart, and himself, but observes, 'it was a foolish attempt, as, had we met with bad weather, our crazy boat would certainly have made us a coffin.'

still worse, internal broils and discontent,—these
things determined part of the people to leave the
island and go to Taheité, which was carried by a
majority of votes.

‘ This being carried into execution on the 22d
September, and having anchored in Matavai bay,
the next morning my messmate (Mr. Stewart) and
I went on shore, to the house of an old landed
proprietor, our former friend; and being now set
free from a lawless crew, determined to remain as
much apart from them as possible, and wait patiently for the arrival of a ship. Fourteen more
of the Bounty’s people came likewise on shore,
and Mr. Christian and eight men went away with
the ship, but God knows whither. Whilst we remained here, we were treated by our kind and
friendly natives with a generosity and humanity
almost unparalleled, and such as we could hardly
have expected from the most civilized people.

‘ To be brief—having remained here till the
latter end of March, 1791, on the 26th of that
month, his Majesty’s ship Pandora arrived, and
had scarcely anchored, when my messmate and I
went on board and made ourselves known ; and
having learnt from one of the natives who had
been off in a canoe, that our former messmate
Mr. Hayward, now promoted to the rank of lieutenant, was on board, we asked for him, supposing he might prove the assertions of our innocence. But he (like all worldlings when raised a
little in life) received us very coolly, and pretended ignorance of our affairs ; yet formerly, he
and I were bound in brotherly love and friendship.
Appearances being so much against us, we were

ordered to be put in irons, and looked upon—oh, infernal words !—as *piratical villains.* A rebuff so severe as this was, to a person unused to troubles, would perhaps have been insupportable, but to me, who had now been long inured to the frowns of fortune, and feeling myself supported by an inward consciousness of not deserving it, it was received with the greatest composure, and a full determination to bear it with patience.

' My sufferings, however, I have not power to describe; but though they are great, yet I thank God for enabling me to bear them without repining. I endeavour to qualify my affliction with these three considerations, first, my innocence not deserving them; secondly, that they cannot last long; and thirdly, that the change may be for the better. The first improves my hopes; the second, my patience; and the third, my courage. I am young in years, but old in what the world calls adversity; and it has had such an effect, as to make me consider it the most beneficial incident that could have occurred at my age. It has made me acquainted with three things which are little known, and as little believed by any but those who have felt their effects : first, the villainy and censoriousness of mankind; secondly, the futility of all human hopes; and thirdly, the happiness of being content in whatever station it may please Providence to place me. In short, it has made me more of a philosopher, than many years of a life spent in ease and pleasure would have done.

' As they will no doubt proceed to the greatest lengths against me, I being the only surviving officer, and they most inclined to believe a prior story, all that can be said to confute it will probably be looked upon as mere falsity and invention. Should that be my unhappy case, and they resolved upon my destruction as an example to futurity, may God enable me to bear my fate with the fortitude of a man, conscious that misfortunc, not any misconduct, is the cause, and that the Almighty can attest my innocence. Yet why should I despond? I have, I hope, still a friend in that Providence which hath preserved me amidst many greater dangers, and upon whom alone I now depend for safety. God will always protect those who deserve it. These are the sole considerations which have enabled me to make myself easy and content under my past misfortunes.

' Twelve more of the people who were at Otaheite having delivered themselves up, there was a sort of prison built on the after-part of the quarter-deck, into which we were all put in close confinement with both legs and both hands in irons, and were treated with great rigour, not being allowed ever to get out of this den; and, being obliged to eat, drink, sleep, and obey the calls of nature here, you may form some idea of the disagreeable situation I must have been in, unable as I was to help myself, (being deprived of the use of both my legs and hands,) but by no means adequate to the reality.

' On the 9th May we left Otaheite, and proceeded to the Friendly Islands, and about the beginning of August, got in among the reefs of New Holland, to endeavour to discover a passage through them; but it was not effected, for the Pandora,

ever unlucky, and as if devoted by heaven to destruction, was driven by a current upon the patch
of a reef, and on which, there being a heavy surf,
she was soon almost bulged to pieces; but having
thrown all the guns on one side overboard, and
the tide flowing at the same time, she beat over
the reef into a basin and brought up in fourteen or
fifteen fathoms; but she was so much damaged
while on the reef, that imagining she would go to
pieces every moment, we had contrived to wrench
ourselves out of our irons, and applied to the captain to have mercy on us, and suffer us to take our
chance for the preservation of our lives; but it
was all in vain—he was even so inhuman as to order
us all to be put in irons again, though the ship
was expected to go down every moment, being
scarcely able to keep her under with all the pumps
at work.

' In this miserable situation, with an expected
death before our eyes, without the least hope of
relief, and in the most trying state of suspense,
we spent the night, the ship being by the hand of
Providence kept up till the morning. The boats
by this time had all been prepared; and as the
captain and officers were coming upon the poop or
roof of our prison, to abandon the ship, the water
being then up to the combings of the hatchways,
we again implored his mercy; upon which he sent
the corporal and an armourer down to let some of
us out of irons, but three only were suffered to go
up, and the scuttle being then clapped on, and the
master-at-arms upon it, the armourer had only
time to let two persons out of irons, the rest,
except three, letting themselves out; two of these

three went down with them on their hands, and
the third was picked up. She now began to heel
over to port so very much, that the master-at-
arms, sliding overboard, and leaving the scuttle
vacant, we all tried to get up, and I was the last
out but three. The water was then pouring in at
the bulk-head scuttles, yet I succeeded in getting
out, and was scarcely in the sea when I could see
nothing above it but the cross-trees, and nothing
around me but a scene of the greatest distress. I
took a plank (being stark-naked) and swam towards an island about three miles off, but was
picked up on my passage by one of the boats.
When we got ashore to the small sandy key, we
found there were thirty-four men drowned, four of
whom were prisoners, and among these was my
unfortunate messmate (Mr. Stewart); ten of us,
and eighty-nine of the Pandora's crew, were saved.

' When a survey was made of what provisions
had been saved, they were found to consist of
two or three bags of bread, two or three breakers of water, and a little wine; so we subsisted
three days upon two wine-glasses of water,
and two ounces of bread per day. On the 1st September we left the island, and on the 16th, arrived
at Coupang in the island of Timor, having been
on short allowance eighteen days. We were put
in confinement in the castle, where we remained
till October, and on the 5th of that month were
sent on board a Dutch ship bound for Batavia.

' Though I have been eight months in close
confinement in a hot climate, I have kept my
health in a most surprising manner, without the
least indisposition, and am still perfectly well in

Drawn & Etched by

H. M. Ship Pandora in the act of foundering.

From a sketch by the late M.r Peter Heywood.

Published by John Murray, Albemarle S.t 1831.

Etched Gec.r B day.

every respect, in mind as well as body ; but without a friend, and only a shirt and pair of trousers
to put on, and carry me home. Yet with all this
I have a contented mind, entirely resigned to the
will of Providence, which conduct alone enables
me to soar above the reach of unhappiness.'

In a subsequent letter to his sister he says,
' I send you two little sketches of the manner in
which his Majesty's ship Pandora went down on
the 29th August, and of the appearance which we
who survived made on the small sandy key within
the reef, about ninety yards long and sixty broad,
in all ninety-nine souls ; here we remained three
days, subsisting on a single wine-glass of wine or
water, and two ounces of bread a day, with no
shelter from the meridian and then vertical sun.
Captain Edwards had tents erected for himself
and his people, and we prisoners petitioned him
for an old sail which was lying useless, part of
the wreck, but he refused it ; and the only shelter
we had was to bury ourselves up to the neck in
the burning sand, which scorched the skin entirely off our bodies, for we were quite naked, and
we appeared as if dipped in large tubs of boiling
water. We were nineteen days in the same miserable situation before we landed at Coupang.
I was in the ship, in irons, hands and feet, much
longer than till the position you now see her in,
the poop alone being above water (and that knee
deep), when a kind Providence assisted me to get
out of irons and escape from her.'

The treatment of these unhappy men was almost
as bad at Batavia as in the Pandora, being closely
confined in irons in the castle, and fed on very

bad provisions ; and the hardships they endured on their passage to England, in Dutch ships, were very severe, having, as he says, slept on nothing but hard boards on wet canvas, without any bed, for seventeen months, always subsisting on short allowance of execrable provisions, and without any clothes for some time, except such as the charity of two young men in the ship supplied him with. He had during his confinement at Batavia learned to make straw hats, and finished several with both his hands in fetters, which he sold for half-a-crown a-piece ; and with the produce of these he procured a suit of coarse clothes, in which, with a cheerful and light heart, notwithstanding all his sufferings, he arrived at Portsmouth. How he preserved his health under the dreadful sufferings he endured, and in eight months' close confinement in a hot climate, is quite wonderful.

On the second day after the arrival of the Gorgon at Spithead the prisoners were transferred to the Hector, commanded by Captain (the late Admiral Sir George) Montague, where they were treated with the greatest humanity, and every indulgence allowed that could with propriety be extended to men in their unhappy situation, until the period when they were to be arraigned before the competent authority, and put on their trials for mutiny and piracy, which did not take place until the month of September.

In this period of anxious and awful suspense, a most interesting correspondence was carried on between this unfortunate youth and his numerous friends, which exhibits the character of himself and the whole family in the most amiable and affectionate colours, and in a more particular manner, of that adorable creature, his sister Nessy, who, in one of her letters, accounts for the peculiar warmth of her attachment and expressions by their being nearly of the same age, and engaged in the same pursuits, whether of study or amusement, in their juvenile years. The poor mother, on hearing of his arrival, thus addresses her unfortunate son :—

Isle of Man, June 29th, 1792.

' Oh! my ever dearly-beloved and long-lost son, with what anxiety have I waited for this period! I have counted the days, hours, and even minutes, since I first heard of the horrid and unfortunate mutiny which has so long deprived me of my dearest boy: but now the happy time is come when, though I cannot have the unspeakable pleasure of seeing and embracing you, yet I hope we may be allowed to correspond; surely there can be nothing improper in a liberty of this sort between an affectionate mother and her dutiful and beloved son, who, I am perfectly convinced, was never guilty of the crime he has been suspected of by those who did not know his worth and truth. I have not the least doubt but that the all-gracious God, who of his good providence has protected you so long, and brought you safe through so many dangers and difficulties, will still protect you, and at your trial make your innocence appear as clear as the light. All your letters have come safe to me, and to my very dear good Nessy. Ah! Peter, with what real joy did

we all receive them, and how happy are we that
you are now safe in England! I will endeavour,
my dearest lad, to make your present situation as
comfortable as possible, for so affectionate and
good a son deserves my utmost attention. Nessy
has written to our faithful and kind friend, Mr.
Heywood, of Plymouth, for his advice, whether it
would be proper for her to come up to you; if he
consents to her so doing, not a moment shall be
lost, and how happy shall I be when she is with
you! Such a sister as she is! Oh! Peter, she is
a most valuable girl,' &c.

On the same day this 'most valuable girl' thus
writes* :—

* The following shows how much her fond mind was
fixed on her unfortunate brother:—

*On the Arrival of my dearly-beloved Brother, Peter Hey-
wood, in England, written while a Prisoner, and waiting
the Event of his Trial on board his Majesty's Ship Hector.*

COME, gentle Muse, I woo thee once again,
Nor woo thee now in melancholy strain;
Assist my verse in cheerful mood to flow,
Nor let this tender bosom Anguish know;
Fill all my soul with notes of Love and Joy,
No more let Grief each anxious thought employ:
With Rapture now alone this heart shall burn,
And Joy, my Lycidas, for thy return!
Return'd with every charm, accomplish'd youth,
Adorn'd with Virtue, Innocence, and Truth;
Wrapp'd in thy conscious merit still remain,
Till I behold thy lovely form again.
Protect him, Heav'n, from dangers and alarms,
And oh! restore him to a sister's arms;
Support his fortitude in that dread hour
When he must brave Suspicion's cruel pow'r;
Grant him to plead with Eloquence divine,
In ev'ry word let Truth and Honour shine;

' My dearest and most beloved brother—Thanks
to that Almighty Providence which has so miraculously preserved you, your fond, anxious, and,
till now, miserable Nessy, is at last permitted to
address the object of her tenderest affection in
England! Oh! my admirable, my heroic boy,
what have we felt on your account! yet how small,
how infinitely trifling was the misery of our situation when compared with the horror of yours!
Let me now, however, with confidence hope that
the God of all mercies has not so long protected
you in vain, but will at length crown your fortitude
and pious resignation to his will with that peace
and happiness you so richly merit. How blest did
your delightful and yet dreadful letter from Batavia make us all! Surely, my beloved boy, you
could not for a moment imagine we ever supposed
you guilty of the crime of mutiny. No, no;
believe me, no earthly power could have persuaded us that it was possible for you to do anything inconsistent with strict honour and duty. So
well did we know your amiable, steady principles,
that we were assured your reasons for staying
behind would turn out such as you represent them;
and I firmly trust that Providence will at length
restore you to those dear and affectionate friends,

Through each sweet accent let Persuasion flow,
With manly Firmness let his bosom glow,
Till strong Conviction, in each face exprest,
Grants a reward by Honour's self confest.
Let thy Omnipotence preserve him still,
And all his future days with Pleasure fill;
And oh! kind Heav'n, though now in chains he be,
Restore him soon to Friendship, Love, and me.
August 5th, 1792, *Isle of Man*.   NESSY HEYWOOD.

who can know no happiness until they are blest
with your loved society. Take care of your precious health, my angelic boy. I shall soon be
with you ; I have written to Mr. Heywood (your
and our excellent friend and protector) for his
permission to go to you immediately, which my
uncle Heywood, without first obtaining it, would
not allow, fearing lest any precipitate step might
injure you at present; and I only wait the arrival
of his next letter to fly into your arms. Oh ! my
best beloved Peter, how I anticipate the rapture
of that moment!—for alas ! I have no joy, no happiness, but in your beloved society, and no hopes,
no fears, no wishes, but for you.'

Mr. Heywood's sisters all address their unfortunate brother in the same affectionate, but less
impassioned strain ; and a little trait of good
feeling is mentioned, on the part of an old female
servant, that shows what a happy and attached
family the Heywoods were, previous to the melancholy affair in which their boy became entangled.
Mrs. Heywood says, 'my good honest Birket is
very well, and says your safe return has made her
more happy than she has been for these two and
forty years she has been in our family.' And
Miss Nessy tells him, ' Poor Birket, the most
faithful and worthiest of servants, desires me to
tell you that she almost dies with joy at the
thought of your safe arrival in England. What
agony, my dear boy, has she felt on your account!
her affection for you knows no bounds, and her
misery has indeed been extreme ; but she still
lives to bless your virtues.'

The poor prisoner thus replies, from his Ma-

jesty's ship Hector, to his 'beloved sisters
all:'—

'This day I had the supreme happiness of your
long expected letters, and I am not able to express the pleasure and joy they afforded me; at
the sight of them my spirits, low and dejected,
were at once exhilarated; my heart had long and
greatly suffered from my impatience to hear of
those most dear to me, and was tossed and tor-
mented by the storms of fearful conjecture—but
they are now subsided, and my bosom has at
length attained that long-lost serenity and calm-
ness it once enjoyed: for you may believe me
when I say it never yet has suffered any disquiet
from my own misfortunes, but from a truly anxious
solicitude for, and desire to hear of, your welfare.
God be thanked, you still entertain such an opinion
of me as I will flatter myself I have deserved; but
why do I say so? can I make myself too worthy
the affectionate praises of such amiable sisters?
Oh! my Nessy, it grieves me to think I must be
under the necessity, however heart-breaking to
myself, of desiring you will relinquish your most
affectionate design of coming to see me; it is too
long and tedious a journey, and even on your
arrival, you would not be allowed the wished-for
happiness, both to you and myself, of seeing,
much less conversing with, your unfortunate
brother: the rules of the service are so strict, that
prisoners are not permitted to have any communication with female relations; thus even the sight
of, and conversation with, so truly affectionate a
sister is for the present denied me! The happiness of such an interview let us defer till a time

o

(which, please God, will arrive) when it can be enjoyed with more freedom, and unobserved by the gazing eyes of an inquisitive world, which in my present place of confinement would of course not be the case.

' I am very happy to hear that poor old Birket is still alive; remember me to her, and tell her not to *heave aback*, until God grants me the pleasure of seeing her.

'And now, my dear Nessy, cease to anticipate the happiness of personal communication with your poor, but resigned brother, until wished-for freedom removes the indignant shackles I now bear, from the feet of your fond and most affectionate brother,

' P. H.'

In a subsequent letter to his sister, he says, ' Let us at present be resigned to our fate, contented with this sort of communication, and be thankful to God for having even allowed us that happiness —for be assured the present confinement is *liberty*, compared with what it has been for the fifteen months last past.' On the 15th July, Commodore Pasley addresses the following business-like letter to Miss Heywood.

' I received your letter, my dearest Nessy, with the enclosure, [her brother's narrative,] but did not choose to answer it until I had made a thorough investigation; that is, seen personally all the principal evidences, which has ever since occupied my whole thoughts and time. I have also had some letters from himself; and notwithstanding he must still continue in confinement, every attention and indulgence possible is granted him by Captain Montague of the Hector, who is my particular friend. I have no doubt of the truth of your brother's narrative; the master, boatswain, gunner, and carpenter, late of the Bounty, I have seen, and have the pleasure to assure you that they are all favourable, and corroborate what he says. That *fellow*, Captain Edwards, whose inhuman rigour of confinement I shall never forget, I have likewise seen; he cannot deny that Peter avowed himself late of the Bounty when he came voluntarily aboard; this is a favourable circumstance. I have been at the Admiralty, and read over all the depositions taken and sent home by Bligh and his officers from Batavia, likewise the court-martial on himself; in none of which appears anything against Peter. As soon as Lieutenant Hayward arrives with the remainder of the Pandora's crew, the court-martial is to take place. I shall certainly attend, and we must have an able counsellor to assist, for I will not deceive you, my dear Nessy, however favourable circumstances may appear, our martial law is severe; by the tenor of it, the man who stands neuter is equally guilty with him who lifts his arm against his captain in such cases. His extreme youth and his delivering himself up, are the strong points of his defence. Adieu! my dearest Nessy; present my love to your mother and sisters, and rest assured of my utmost exertions to extricate your brother,

'Your affectionate uncle,

'T. Pasley.'

o 2

This excellent man did not stop here : knowing that sea-officers have a great aversion from counsel, he writes to say, ' A friend of mine, Mr. Graham, who has been secretary to the different Admirals on the Newfoundland station for these twelve years, and consequently has acted as judge-advocate at courts-martial all that time, has offered me to attend you; he has a thorough knowledge of the service, uncommon abilities, and is a very good lawyer. He has already had most of the evidences with him. Adieu! my young friend ; keep up your spirits, and rest assured I shall be watchful for your good. My heart will be more at ease, if I can get my friend Graham to go down, than if you were attended by the first counsel in England *.'. Mr. Graham accordingly attended, and was of the greatest service at the trial.

Nessy Heywood † having in one of her letters

* The late Aaron Graham, Esq., the highly respected police magistrate in London.

† Till the moment of the trial, it will readily be supposed that every thought of this amiable young lady was absorbed in her brother's fate. In this interval the following lines appear to have been written :—

On receiving information by a letter from my ever dearly loved brother Peter Heywood, that his trial was soon to take place.

> Oh! gentle Hope! with eye serene,
>   And aspect, ever sweetly mild ;
> Who deck'st with gayest flow'rs each scene,
>   In sportive, rich luxuriance wild.

> Thou—soother of corroding care,
>   When sharp affliction's pangs we feel,

enquired of her brother how tall he was, and
having received information on this point, expressed
some surprise that he was not taller.   ' And so,'
he replies, 'you are surprised I am not taller!—
Ah, Nessy! let me ask you this—suppose the two

> Teachest with fortitude to bear,
>   And know'st deep sorrow's wounds to heal.
>
> Thy timid vot'ry now inspire,
>   Thy influence, in pity, lend;
> With confidence this bosom fire,
>   Till anxious, dread suspense shall end.
>
> Let not fear invade my breast,
>   My Lycidas no terror knows;
> With conscious innocence he's blest,
>   And soon will triumph o'er his foes.
>
> Watch him, sweet Pow'r, with looks benign,
>   Possession of his bosom keep;
> While waking, make each moment shine,
>   With fancy gild his hours of sleep.
>
> Protect him still, nor let him dread
>   The awful, the approaching hour,
> When on his poor devoted head
>   Fell slander falls with cruel power.
>
> Yet, gentle Hope, deceive me not,
>   Nor with deluding smiles betray;
> Be honour's recompense his lot,
>   And glory crown each future day!
>
> And oh! support this fainting heart
>   With courage, till that hour is past,
> When, freed from envy's fatal dart,
>   His innocence shines forth at last :
>
> Then, my loved Lycidas, we'll meet,
>   Thy miseries and trials o'er;
> With soft delight thy heart shall beat,
>   And hail with joy thy native shore!
>
> Then will each hour with rapture fly,
>   Then sorrow's plaintive voice will cease;

last years of *your* growth had been retarded by close confinement,—nearly deprived of all kinds of necessary aliment—shut up from the all-cheering light of the sun for the space of five months, and never suffered to breathe the fresh air (an enjoyment which Providence denies to none of his creatures) during all that time—and without any kind of exercise to stretch and supple your limbs —besides many other inconveniences which I will not pain you by mentioning—how tall should you have been, my dear sister?—answer, four feet nothing : but enough of nonsense.'

Nessy Heywood had expressed a strong desire to see her brother, but was told the rules of the service would not allow it; also, that it would agitate him, when he ought to be cool and collected, to meet his approaching trial. This was quite enough: —' But as for myself,' she says, ' no danger, no fatigue, no difficulties, would deter me—I have youth, and health, and excellent natural spirits— these and the strength of my affection would support me through it all; if I were not allowed to see you, yet being in the same place which contains you, would be joy inexpressible! I will not, however, any longer desire it, but will learn to imitate your fortitude and patience.'

Mr. Heywood of Maristow, and his daughter,

> No care shall cause the heaving sigh,
>   But all our days be crown'd with peace.
>
> With love and fond affection blest,
>   No more shall grief our bliss destroy ;
> No pain disturb each faithful breast,
>   But rapture all and endless joy !

Isle of Man, August 22, 1792.   NESSY HEYWOOD.

Mrs. Bertie, had intimated the same thing. These excellent people, from the moment of young Heywood's arrival, had shown him every kindness, supplied him with money, and what was better, with friends, who could give him the best advice. To this worthy lady, Miss Nessy Heywood thus addresses herself.

' Overwhelmed with sensations of gratitude and pleasure, which she is too much agitated to express, permit me, dearest Madam, at my mama's request, to offer you hers and our most sincere acknowledgments for your invaluable letter, which, from the detention of the packet, she did not receive till yesterday. By a letter from my beloved brother, of the same date, we are informed that Mr. Larkham (who I suppose to be the gentleman you mention having sent to see him) has been on board the Hector, and has kindly offered him the most salutary advice relative to his present situation, for which allow me to request you will present him our best thanks. He also speaks with every expression a grateful heart can dictate of your excellent father's goodness in providing for all his wants, even before he could have received any letters from us to that purpose.

' Ah! my dear Madam, how truly characteristic is this of the kind friendship with which he has ever honoured our family! But my beloved Peter does not know that Mr. Heywood has a daughter, whose generosity is equal to his own, and whose amiable compassion for his sufferings it will be as impossible for us to forget, as it is to express the admiration and gratitude it has inspired. It would, I am convinced, be unnecessary, as well as a very

bad compliment to you, Madam, were I to presume to point out anything particular to be done
for our poor boy, as I have not the least doubt your
goodness and kind intention have long ago rendered every care of that sort on our part unnecessary. I shall only add, that my mama begs every
wish he forms may be granted, and sure I am, he
will not desire a single gratification that can be
deemed in the smallest degree improper.

' In one of my brother's letters, dated the 23rd, he
hints that he shall not be permitted to see any of
his relations till his trial is over, and that he therefore does not expect us. I have, however, written
to Mr. Heywood (without whose approbation I
would by no means take any step) for permission
to go to him. If it is absolutely impossible for
me to see him (though in the presence of witnesses),
yet even that prohibition, cruel as it is, I could
bear with patience, provided I might be near him,
to see the ship in which he at present exists—to
behold those objects, which, perhaps, at the same
moment, attract his notice—to breathe the same air
which he breathes.—Ah! my dearest Madam, these
are inestimable gratifications, and would convey
sensations of rapture and delight to the fond
bosom of a sister, which it is far, very far beyond
my power to describe. Besides, the anxiety and
impatience produced by the immense distance
which now separates us from him, and the uncertainty attending the packet, render it difficult
and sometimes impossible to hear of him so often
as we would wish—and, may I not add (though
Heaven in its mercy forbid it—for alas! the bare
idea is too dreadful, yet it is in the scale of possi-

bility,) that some accident might happen to deprive
us of my dearest brother : how insupportably bitter
would then be our reflexions, for having omitted
the opportunity, when it was in our power, of ad-
ministering comfort and consolation to him in
person.   For these reasons, I earnestly hope Mr.
Heywood will not judge it improper to comply with
my request, and shall wait with eager impatience
the arrival of his next letter.   Think not, my dear
Madam, that it is want of confidence in your care
and attention which makes me solicitous to be
with my beloved brother.   Be assured we are all
as perfectly easy in that respect as if we were on
the spot ; but I am convinced you will pardon the
dictates of an affection which an absence of five
years, rendered still more painful by his sufferings,
has heightened almost to a degree of adoration.   I
shall, with your permission, take the liberty of
enclosing a letter to my brother, which I leave
open for perusal, and at the same time request
your pardon for mentioning you to him in such
terms as I am apprehensive will wound the delicacy which ever accompanies generosity like
yours ; but indeed, my dearest Madam, I cannot,
must not, suffer my beloved boy to remain in
ignorance of that worth and excellence which has
prompted you to become his kind protectress.

' I have the honour to be, with every sentiment
of gratitude, &c. &c. &c.,

' NESSY HEYWOOD.'

Among the numerous friends that interested
themselves in the fate of this unhappy youth, was
his uncle, Colonel Holwell. The testimony he

bears to his excellent character is corroborated by all who knew him while a boy at home. About a fortnight before the trial he writes to him thus:—

'21st *August*, 1792.

'My very dear Peter,

'I have this day received yours of the 18th, and am happy to find by its contents that, notwithstanding your long and cruel confinement, you still preserve your health, and write in good spirits. Preserve it, my dear boy, awful as the approaching period must be, even to the most innocent, but from which all who know you have not a doubt of your rising as immaculate as a new-born infant. I have known you from your cradle, and have often marked with pleasure and surprise the many assiduous instances (far beyond your years) you have given of filial duty and paternal affection to the best of parents, and to brothers and sisters who doated on you. Your education has been the best; and from these considerations alone, without the very clear evidence of your own testimony, I would as soon believe the Archbishop of Canterbury would set fire to the city of London as suppose you could, directly or indirectly, join in such a d—d absurd piece of business. Truly sorry am I that my state of health will not permit me to go down to Portsmouth to give this testimony publicly before that respectable tribunal where your country's laws have justly ordained you must appear; but consider this as the *touchstone*, my dear boy, by which your worth must be known. Six years in the navy myself, and twenty-eight years a soldier, I

flatter myself my judgment will not prove erroneous. That Power, my dear Peter, of whose
grace and mercy you seem to have so just a sense,
will not now forsake you. Your dear aunt is as
must be expected in such a trying situation, but
more from your present sufferings than any apprehension of what is to follow,' &c.

With similar testimonies and most favourable
auguries from Commodore Pasley, the Rev. Dr.
Scott, of the Isle of Man, and others, young
Heywood went to his long and anxiously expected trial, which took place on the 12th September, and continued to the 18th of that month.
Mrs. Heywood had been anxious that Erskine and
Mingay should be employed as counsel, but Mr.
Graham, whom Commodore Pasley had so highly
recommended, gave his best assistance; as did
also Mr. Const, who had been retained, for which
the Commodore expresses his sorrow, as sea officers, he says, have a great aversion to lawyers.
Mr. Peter Heywood assigns a better reason; in a
letter to his sister Mary he says, that ' Counsel
to a naval prisoner is of no effect, and as they are
not allowed to speak, their eloquence is not of the
least efficacy; I request, therefore, you will desire my dear mother to revoke the letter she has
been so good to write to retain Mr. Erskine and
Mr. Mingay, and to forbear putting herself to so
great and needless an expense, from which no
good can accrue. No, no! Mary—it is not the
same as a trial on shore; it would then be highly
requisite; but, in this case, *I* alone must fight my
own battle; and I think my telling the truth
undisguised, in a plain, short, and concise manner,

is as likely to be deserving the victory, as the most elaborate eloquence of a Cicero upon the same subject.'

At this anxious moment many painfully interesting letters passed to and from the family in the Isle of Man : the last letter from his beloved Nessy previous to the awful event thus concludes :—' May that Almighty Providence whose tender care has hitherto preserved you be still your powerful protector! may he instil into the hearts of your judges every sentiment of justice, generosity, and compassion! may hope, innocence, and integrity be your firm support! and liberty, glory, and honour your just reward! may all good angels guard you from even the appearance of danger! and may you at length be restored to us, the delight, the pride of your adoring friends, and the sole happiness and felicity of that fond heart which animates the bosom of my dear Peter's most faithful and truly affectionate sister,

' N. H.'

CHAPTER VI.

THE COURT-MARTIAL.

'If any person in or belonging to the fleet shall make, or endeavour to make, any mutinous assembly, upon any pretence whatsoever, every person offending herein, and being convicted thereof, by the sentence of the Court-martial, shall suffer DEATH.'

Naval Articles of War, Art. 19.

THE Court assembled to try the prisoners on board his Majesty's ship Duke, on the 12th September, 1792, and continued by adjournment from day to day (Sunday excepted) until the 18th of the same month *

PRESENT,

Vice-Admiral Lord Hood, *President.*

Capt. Sir Andrew Snape Hamond, Bart.,
    ,,   John Colpoys,
    ,,   Sir George Montagu,
    ,,   Sir Roger Curtis,
    ,,   John Bazeley,
    ,,   Sir Andrew Snape Douglas,
    ,,   John Thomas Duckworth,
    ,,   John Nicholson Inglefield,
    ,,   John Knight,
    ,,   Albemarle Bertie,
    ,,   Richard Goodwin Keats.

The charges set forth that Fletcher Christian, who was mate of the Bounty, assisted by others

* The minutes being very long, a brief abstract only, containing the principal points of evidence, is here given.

of the inferior officers and men, armed with muskets and bayonets, had violently and forcibly taken
that ship from her commander, Lieutenant Bligh;
and that he, together with the master, boatswain,
gunner, and carpenter, and other persons, (being
nineteen in number,) were forced into the launch
and cast adrift;—that Captain Edwards, in the
Pandora, was directed to proceed to Otaheite, and
other islands in the South Seas, and to use his best
endeavours to recover the said vessel, and to bring
in confinement to England the said Fletcher
Christian and his associates, or as many of them
as he might be able to apprehend, in order that
they might be brought to condign punishment, &c.
That Peter Heywood, James Morrison, Charles
Norman, Joseph Coleman, Thomas Ellison,
Thomas M'Intosh, Thomas Burkitt, John Millward, William Muspratt, and Michael Byrne, had
been brought to England, &c., and were now put
on their trial.

Mr. Fryer, the master of the Bounty, being first
sworn, deposed—

That he had the first watch; that between ten
and eleven o'clock Mr. Bligh came on deck, according to custom, and after a short conversation,
and having given his orders for the night, left the
deck; that at twelve he was relieved by the gunner, and retired, leaving all quiet; that at dawn of
day he was greatly alarmed by an unusual noise;
and that, on attempting to jump up, John Sumner
and Matthew Quintal laid their hands upon his
breast and desired him to lie still, saying he was
their prisoner; that on expostulating with them,
he was told, ' Hold your tongue, or you are a dead

man, but if you remain quiet there is none on board
will hurt a hair of your head ; ' he further deposes,
that on raising himself on the locker, he saw on
the ladder, going upon deck, Mr. Bligh in his
shirt, with his hands tied behind him, and Christian
holding him by the cord; that the master-at-
arms, Churchill, then came to his cabin and took
a brace of pistols and a hanger, saying, ' I will
take care of these, Mr. Fryer ; ' that he asked, on
seeing Mr. Bligh bound, what they were going to
do with the captain ; that Sumner replied, ' D—n
his eyes, put him into the boat, and let the ——
see if he can live upon three-fourths of a pound of
yams a day ; ' that he remonstrated with such conduct, but in vain. They said he must go in the small
cutter.   ' The small cutter ! ' Mr. Fryer exclaimed;
' why her bottom is almost out, and very much
eaten by the worms ! ' to which Sumner and Quintal
both said, ' D—n his eyes, the boat is too good
for him ; ' that after much entreaty he prevailed
on them to ask Christian if he might be allowed to
go on deck, which, after some hesitation, was
granted.   When I came on deck, says Mr
Fryer, Mr. Bligh was standing by the mizen
mast, with his hands tied behind him, and Christian
holding the cord with one hand, and a bayonet
in the other.   I said, ' Christian, consider what you
are about.'   ' Hold your tongue, Sir,' he said ; ' I
have been in hell for weeks past; Captain Bligh
has brought all this on himself.'   I told him that
Mr. Bligh and he not agreeing was no reason
for taking the ship.   ' Hold your tongue, Sir,' he
said.   I said,—Mr. Christian, you and I have
been on friendly terms during the voyage, there-

fore give me leave to speak,—let Mr. Bligh go
down to his cabin, and I make no doubt we shall
all be friends again;—he then repeated, ' Hold
your tongue, Sir ; it is too late ;' and threatening
me if I said anything more.   Mr. Fryer then
asked him to give a better boat than the cutter;
he said, ' No, that boat is good enough.'   Bligh
now said to the master, that the man behind the
hencoops (Isaac Martin) was his friend, and desired him (the master) to knock Christian down,
which Christian must have heard, but took no
notice ; that Fryer then attempted to get past
Christian to speak to Martin, but he put his bayonet to his breast, saying, ' Sir, if you advance an
inch farther, I will run you through,' and ordered
two armed men to take him down to his cabin.
Shortly afterwards he was desired to go on deck,
when Christian ordered him into the boat: he
said, ' I will stay with you, if you will give me
leave.'   ' No, Sir,' he replied, ' go directly into the
boat.'   Bligh, then on the gangway, said, ' Mr.
Fryer, stay in the ship.'   ' No, by G——d, Sir,'
Christian said, ' go into the boat, or I will run
you through.'   Mr. Fryer states, that during this
time very bad language was used by the people
towards Mr. Bligh ; that with great difficulty they
prevailed on Christian to suffer a few articles to be
put into the boat ; that after the persons were ordered
into the boat to the number of nineteen, such opprobrious language continued to be used, several
of the men calling out ' Shoot the ——,' that
Cole, the boatswain, advised they should cast off
and take their chance, as the mutineers would certainly do them a mischief if they stayed much

longer. Mr. Fryer then states the names of those who were under arms; and that Joseph Coleman, Thomas M'Intosh, Charles Norman, and Michael Byrne, (prisoners,) wished to come into the boat, declaring they had nothing to do in the business; that he did not perceive Mr. Peter Heywood on deck at the seizure of the ship.

On being asked what he supposed Christian meant when he said he had been in hell for a fortnight? he said, from the frequent quarrels that they had, and the abuse he had received from Mr. Bligh, and that the day before the mutiny Mr. Bligh had challenged all the young gentlemen and people with stealing his cocoa-nuts.

Mr. Cole, the boatswain, deposes,—that he had the middle watch; was awakened out of his sleep in the morning, and heard a man calling out to the carpenter, that they had mutinied and taken the ship; that Christian had the command, and that the captain was a prisoner on the quarter-deck; that he went up the hatchway, having seen Mr. Heywood and Mr. Young in the opposite berth; that coming on deck he saw the captain with his hands tied behind him, and four sentinels standing over him, two of which were Ellison and Burkitt, the prisoners; that he asked Mr. Christian what he meant to do, and was answered by his ordering him to hoist the boat out, and shook the bayonet, threatening him and damning him if he did not take care ; that when he found the captain was to be sent out of the ship, he again went aft with the carpenter to ask for the long-boat; that they asked three or four times before he granted it ; that he saw Mr. Peter Heywood,

P

one of the prisoners, lending a hand to get the fore-stayfall along, and when the boat was hooked on, spoke something to him, but what it was does not know, as Christian was threatening him at the time; that Heywood then went below, and does not remember seeing him afterwards; that after the few things were got into the boat, and most of the people in her, they were trying for the carpenter's tool-chest, when Quintal said, ' D—n them, if we let them have these things they will build a vessel in a month;' but when all were in the boat she was veered astern, when Coleman, Norman, and M'Intosh, prisoners, were crying at the gangway, wishing to go in the boat; and Byrne in the cutter alongside was also crying; that he advised Mr. Bligh to cast off, as he feared they would fire into the boat.

The Court asked if he had any reason to believe that any other of the prisoners than those named were detained contrary to their inclinations? Answer—' I believe Mr. Heywood was; I thought all along he was intending to come away; he had no arms, and he assisted to get the boat out, and then went below; I heard Churchill call out, ' Keep them below.' *The Court*—' Do you think he meant Heywood?' ' I have no reason to think any other.'

Mr. Peckover the gunner's evidence is similar to that of Mr. Cole's, and need not be detailed.

Mr. Purcell, the carpenter, corroborated, generally, the testimony of the three who had been examined. *The Court* asked, ' Did you see Mr. Heywood standing upon the booms?' ' Yes; he was leaning the flat part of his hand on a cutlass, when I exclaimed, In the name of God, Peter, what do you with that? when he instantly dropped it, and assisted in hoisting the launch out, and handing the things into the boat, and then went down below, when I heard Churchill call to Thompson to keep them below, but could not tell whom he meant; I did not see Mr. Heywood after that.' *The Court*—' In what light did you look upon Mr. Heywood, at the time you say he dropped the cutlass on your speaking to him?'   *Witness*— ' I looked upon him as a person confused, and that he did not know he had the weapon in his hand, or his hand being on it, for it was not in his hand; I considered him to be confused, by his instantly dropping it, and assisting in hoisting the boat out, which convinced me in my own mind that he had no hand in the conspiracy; that after this he went below, as I think, on his own account, in order to collect some of his things to put into the boat.' *The Court*—' Do you, upon the solemn oath you have taken, believe that Mr. Heywood, by being armed with a cutlass at the time you have mentioned, by anything that you could collect from his gestures or speeches, had any intention of opposing, or joining others that might oppose, to stop the progress of the mutiny?' *Witness*—' No.' *The Court*—' In the time that Mr. Heywood was assisting you to get the things into the boat, did he, in any degree whatever, manifest a disposition to assist in the mutiny?' *Witness*—' No.' *The Court*—' Was he, during that time, deliberate or frightened, and in what manner did he behave himself?' *Witness*—' I had not an opportunity of observing his every action, being myself at that time engaged in getting several things into the boat, so that I cannot tell.' *The Court*—' Putting every circumstance together, declare to this court, upon the oath you have taken, how you considered his behaviour, whether as a person joined in the mutiny, or as a person wishing well to Captain Bligh?' *Witness*— ' I by no means considered him as a person concerned in the mutiny or conspiracy.'

Lieutenant Thomas Hayward, late third lieutenant of the Pandora, and formerly midshipman of the Bounty, deposes, that he had the morning watch; that at four o'clock Fletcher Christian relieved the watch as usual ; that at five he ordered him, as master's mate of his watch, to look out, while he went down to lash his hammock up ; that while looking at a shark a-stern of the ship, to his unutterable surprise, he saw Fletcher Christian, Charles Churchill, Thomas Burkitt, (the prisoner,) John Sumner, Matthew Quintal, William M'Koy, Isaac Martin, Henry Hillbrandt, and Alexander Smith, coming aft, armed with muskets and bayonets ; that on going forward, he asked Christian the cause of such an act, who told him to hold his tongue instantly ; and leaving Isaac Martin as a sentinel on deck, he proceeded with the rest of his party below to Lieutenant Bligh's cabin ; that the people on deck were Mr. John Hallet, myself, Robert Lamb, Butcher, Thomas Ellison (prisoner) at the helm, and John Mills at the conn ; that he asked Mills if he knew any thing of the matter, who pleaded total ignorance, and Thomas Ellison quitted the helm and armed himself with a bayonet; that the decks now became thronged with armed men; that Peter Heywood, James Morrison, (two of the prisoners,) and George Stewart, were unarmed on the booms; that Fletcher Christian and his gang had not been down long before he heard the cry of murder from Lieutenant Bligh, and Churchill calling out for a rope, on which Mills, contrary to all orders and entreaties, cut the deep-sea line and carried a piece of it to their assistance; that soon after Lieutenant Bligh was brought upon the quarter-deck with his hands bound behind him, and was surrounded by most of those who came last on deck.

This witness then states, that on the arrival of the Pandora at Matavai Bay, Joseph Coleman was the first that came on board; that he was upset in a canoe and assisted by the natives; that as soon as the ship was at anchor, George Stewart and Peter Heywood came on board; that they made themselves known to Captain Edwards, and expressed their happiness that he was arrived; that he asked them how they came to go away with his Majesty's ship the Bounty, when George Stewart said, when called upon hereafter, he would answer all particulars; that he was prevented by Captain Edwards from answering further questions, and they were sent out of the cabin to be confined. He then describes the manner in which the rest of the mutineers were taken on the island. Having stated that when he went below to get some things he saw Peter Heywood in his berth, and told him to go into the boat, he was asked by *the Court* if Heywood was prevented by any force from going upon deck, he answered ' No.' *The Court*—' Did you, from his behaviour, con-

sider him as a person attached to his duty, or to
the party of the mutineers?' *Witness*—'I should
rather suppose, after my having told him to go
into the boat, and he not joining us, to be on the
side of the mutineers; but that must be understood
only as an opinion, as he was not in the least
employed during the active part of it.' *The Court*
—' Did you observe any marks of joy or sorrow
on his countenance or behaviour?' *Witness*—
' Sorrow.'

Lieutenant Hallet, late midshipman of the
Bounty, states,—that he had the morning-watch;
that he heard Lieutenant Bligh call out murder,
and presently after saw him brought upon deck
naked, excepting his shirt, with his hands tied
behind him, and Christian holding the end of the
cord which tied them in one hand, and either a
bayonet or a cutlass in the other; that the cutter
was hoisted out, and Mr. Samuel, Mr. Hayward,
and myself ordered to go into her; but the boatswain and carpenter going aft, and telling Christian they wished to go with the captain rather
than stay in the ship, and asking to have the
launch, it was granted. On being asked if he
saw Peter Heywood on that day, he replied, once,
on the platform, standing still and looking atten-
tively towards Captain Bligh; never saw him
under arms nor spoke to him; does not know
if he offered to go in the boat, nor did he hear
any one propose to him to go in the boat; that
when standing on the platform, Captain Bligh
said something to him, but what he did not hear,
upon which Heywood laughed, turned round, and
walked away.

Captain Edwards being then called and sworn, was desired by the Court to state the conversation that passed between him and Coleman, Peter Heywood, and George Stewart, when they came on board the Pandora.

Edwards — ' Joseph Coleman attempted to come on board before the ship came to an anchor at Otaheite; he was soon afterwards taken up by canoes and came on board before the ship came to an anchor; I began to make inquiries of him after the Bounty and her people. The next who came on board were Stewart and Peter Heywood; they came after the ship was at anchor, but before any boat was on shore. I did not see them come alongside. I desired Lieutenant Larkin to bring them down to the cabin. I asked them what news; Peter Heywood, I think, said he supposed I had heard of the affair of the Bounty. I don't recollect all the conversation that passed between us; he sometimes interrupted me by asking for Mr. Hayward, the lieutenant of the Pandora, whether he was on board or not—he had heard that he was; at last I acknowledged that he was, and I desired him to come out of my stateroom, where I had desired him to go into, as he happened to be with me at the time. Lieutenant Hayward treated him with a sort of contemptuous look, and began to enter into conversation with him respecting the Bounty, but I called the sentinel in to take them into custody, and ordered Lieutenant Hayward to desist, and I ordered them to be put into irons : some words passed, and Peter Heywood said he should be able to vindicate his conduct.

Lieutenant Corner, of the Pandora, merely states his being sent to bring the rest of the mutineers on board, who were at some distance from Matavai Bay.

The prisoners being called on for their defence, the witnesses were again separately called and examined on the part of the prisoners.

Mr. Fryer, the master, called in and examined by Mr. Heywood.—' If you had been permitted, would you have stayed in the ship in preference to going into the boat?' *Witness*—'Yes.' *Prisoner*— ' Had you stayed in the ship in expectation of retaking her, was my conduct such, from the first moment you knew me to this, as would have induced you to intrust me with your design ; and do you believe I would have favoured it, and given you all the assistance in my power?' *Witness*—' I believe he would : I should not have hesitated a moment in asking of him when I had had an opportunity of opening my mind to him.'

The same question being put to *Mr. Cole*, the boatswain, *Mr. Peckover*, the gunner, and *Mr. Purcell*, the carpenter, they all answered in the affirmative.

Mr. Heywood asked, ' What was my general conduct, temper, and disposition on board the ship?' *Witness*—' Beloved by everybody, to the best of my recollection.' To the same question, *Mr. Cole* answers, ' Always a very good character.' *Mr. Peckover*—' The most amiable, and deserving of every one's esteem. *Mr. Purcell*— ' In every respect becoming the character of a gentleman, and such as merited the esteem of everybody.'

Mr. Cole being examined, gave his testimony, —that he never saw Mr. Heywood armed ; that he did not consider him of the mutineers' party ; that he saw nothing of levity or apparent merriment in his conduct ; that when he was below with Stewart, he heard Churchill call out, ' Keep them below,' and that he believes Heywood was one of the persons meant—has no doubt of it at all ; that Bligh could not have spoken to him, when on the booms, loud enough to be heard ; that Hayward was alarmed, and Hallet alarmed ; that he by no means considers Heywood or Morrison as mutineers.

Mr. Purcell being examined, states,—that, respecting the cutlass on which he saw Mr. Heywood's hand resting, he does not consider him as being an armed man ; that he never thought him as of the mutineers' party ; that he never heard Captain Bligh speak to him ; that he thinks, from his situation, he could not have heard him ; that he was by no means guilty of levity or apparent merriment ; that he heard the master-at-arms call out to keep them below ; that Mr. Hallet appeared to him to be very much confused ; and that Mr. Hayward likewise appeared to be very much confused.

The Court asked,—' As you say you did not look upon the prisoner as a person armed, to what did you allude when you exclaimed, " Good God, Peter, what do you do with that ? " *Witness*—' I look upon it as an accidental thing.'

Captain Edwards, being asked by Heywood— ' Did I surrender myself to you upon the arrival of the Pandora at Otaheite ? ' *Witness*—'Not to

me, to the Lieutenant. I apprehend he put liim-
self in my power. I always understood he came
voluntarily; our boats were not in the water.'
Prisoner—' Did I give you such information respecting myself and the Bounty as afterwards
proved true?' *Witness*—' He gave me some information respecting the people on the island, that
corroborated with Coleman's. I do not recollect
the particular conversation, but in general it
agreed with the account given by Coleman.' *Prisoner*—' When I told you that I went away the
first time from Otaheite with the pirates, did I not at
the same time inform you that it was not possible
for me to separate myself from Christian, who
would not permit any man of the party to leave
him at that time, lest, by giving intelligence, they
might have been discovered whenever a ship
should arrive?' *Witness*—' Yes, but I do not
recollect the latter part of it, respecting giving
intelligence.'

Mr. Fryer again called in and examined by Mr.
Morrison.— Mr. Fryer states, he saw him assist
in hoisting out the boats; that he said to him
(Fryer), ' Go down below.' *The Court* asked,
' Whether it might not have been from a laudable
motive, as supposing your assistance at that time
might have prevented a more advantageous effort?'
Witness—' Probably it might: had I stayed in the
ship, he would have been one of the first that I
should have opened my mind to, from his good
behaviour in the former part of the voyage:' states
his belief, that he addressed him as advice; and
that, in hoisting out the boat, he was assisting
Captain Bligh.

Mr. Cole, the boatswain, states, that he ordered Morrison to go and help them with the cutter; that he told him the boat was overloaded; that Captain Bligh had begged that no more people should go in her, and said he would take his chance in the ship; that he shook Morrison by the hand, and said he would do him justice in England; that he had no reason to suppose him concerned in the mutiny.

Lieutenant Thomas Hayward states, that Morrison appeared joyful, and supposed him to be one of the mutineers; on being asked by Morrison if he could declare before God and the Court that what he stated was not the result of a private pique? *Witness*—' Not the result of any private pique, but an opinion formed after quitting the ship, from his not coming with us, there being more boats than one; cannot say they might have had the cutter.' This witness was pleased to remember nothing that was in favour of the prisoner.

Lieutenant Hallet states, he saw Morrison under arms; being asked in what part of the ship, he says, ' I did not see him under arms till the boat was veered astern, and he was then looking over the taffrail, and called out, in a jeering manner, " If my friends inquire after me, tell them I am somewhere in the South Seas." '

Captain Edwards bore testimony that Morrison voluntarily surrendered himself.

Mr. Fryer did not see Morrison armed; he was in his watch, and he considered him a steady, sober, attentive, good man; and acknowledged, that if he had remained in the ship, with the view of retaking her, Morrison would have been one of the first he should have called to his assistance.

Mr. Cole gave testimony to his being a man of good character, attentive to his duty, and he never knew any harm of him.

Mr. Purcell bore witness to his good character, being always diligent and attentive; did not see him under arms on the taffrail; never heard him use any jeering speeches.

Respecting the prisoner *Muspratt,* Mr. *Cole's* evidence proves that he had a musket in his hands, but not till the latter part of the business; it is also proved that he assisted in getting things into the launch. *Mr. Peckover* saw him standing on the forecastle doing nothing—he was not armed.

Lieutenant Hayward saw Muspratt among the armed men : was asked, when Captain Bligh used the words, ' Don't let the boat be overloaded, my lads '—' I'll do you justice ;' do you understand the latter words, ' My lads, I'll do you justice,' to apply to clothes or to men, whom he apprehended might go into the boat? *Witness*—' If Captain Bligh made use of the words " my lads," it was to the people already in the boat, and not to those in the ship.' *The Court*—' To whom do you imagine Captain Bligh alluded : was it, in your opinion, to the men in the boat with him, or to any persons then remaining in the ship?' *Witness*—' To persons remaining in the ship.'

Against the prisoners Ellison, Burkitt, and Millward, the evidence given by all the witnesses so clearly and distinctly proved they were under arms the whole time, and actively employed against

Bligh, that it is unnecessary to go into any detail as far as they are concerned.

The Court having called on the prisoners, each separately, for his defence, Mr. Heywood delivered his as follows :—

'My lords and gentlemen of this honourable Court,—Your attention has already been sufficiently exercised in the painful narrative of this trial; it is therefore my duty to trespass further on it as little as possible.

'The crime of mutiny, for which I am now arraigned, is so seriously pregnant with every danger and mischief, that it makes the person so accused, in the eyes, not only of military men of every description, but of every nation, appear at once the object of unpardonable guilt and exemplary vengeance.

'In such a character it is my misfortune to appear before this tribunal, and no doubt I must have been gazed at with all that horror and indignation which the conspirators of such a mutiny as that in Captain Bligh's ship so immediately provoke; hard, then, indeed is my fate, that circumstances should so occur to point me out as one of them.

'Appearances, probably, are against me, but they are appearances only; for unless I may be deemed guilty for feeling a repugnance at embracing death unnecessarily, I declare before this Court and the tribunal of Almighty God, I am innocent of the charge.

'I chose rather to defer asking any questions of the witnesses until I heard the whole of the evidence; as the charge itself, although I knew it

generally, was not in its full extent, nor in parti-
lar points, made known to me before I heard it read
by the Judge Advocate at the beginning of the
trial; and I feel myself relieved by having adopted
such a mode, as it enables me to set right a few
particulars of a narrative which I had the honour
to transmit to the Earl of Chatham, containing an
account of all that passed on the fatal morning of
the 28th of April, 1789, but which, from the confusion the ship was in during the mutiny, I might
have mistaken, or from the errors of an imperfect
recollection I might have misstated; the difference, however, will now be open to correction; and
I have great satisfaction in observing, that the
mistakes but very slightly respect my part of the
transaction, and I shall consequently escape the
imputation of endeavouring to save myself by
imposing on my judges.

' When first this sad event took place I was
sleeping in my hammock; nor, till the very moment of being awakened from it, had I the least
intimation of what was going on. The spectacle
was as sudden to my eyes, as it was unknown to
my heart; and both were convulsed at the scene.

' Matthew Thompson was the first that claimed
my attention upon waking: he was sitting as a
sentinel over the arm-chest and my berth, and informed me that the captain was a prisoner, and
Christian had taken the command of the ship. I
entreated for permission to go upon deck; and
soon after the boatswain and carpenter had seen
me in my berth, as they were going up the fore-
hatchway, I followed them, as is stated in their
evidence. It is not in my power to describe my

feelings upon seeing the captain as I did, who, with his hands tied behind him, was standing on the quarter-deck, a little abaft the mizen-mast, and Christian by his side. My faculties were be- numbed, and I did not recover the power of recol- lection until called to by somebody to take hold of the tackle-fall, and assist to get out the launch, which I found was to be given to the captain in- stead of the large cutter, already in the water alongside the ship. It were in vain to say what things I put into the boat, but many were handed in by me; and in doing this it was that my hand touched the cutlass (for I will not attempt to deny what the carpenter has deposed), though, on my conscience, I am persuaded it was of momen- tary duration, and innocent as to intention. The former is evident, from its being unobserved by every witness who saw me upon deck, some of whom must have noticed it had it continued a single minute; and the latter is proved by the only person who took notice of the circumstance, and has also deposed that, at the moment he beheld me, I was apparently in a state of absolute stupor. The poison, therefore, carries with it its antidote; and it seems needless to make any further com- ment on the subject, for no man can be weak enough to suppose, that if I had been armed for the purpose of assisting in the mutiny, that I should have resumed a weapon in the moment of triumph, and when the ship was so completely in the possession of the party, that (as more than one witness has emphatically expressed it) all attempts at recovering her would have been im- practicable.

' The boat and ship, it is true, presented themselves to me without its once occurring that I was at liberty to choose, much less that the choice I should make would be afterwards deemed criminal; and I bitterly deplore that my extreme youth and inexperience concurred in torturing me with apprehensions, and prevented me from preferring the former ; for as things have turned out, it would have saved me from the disgrace of appearing before you as I do at this day—it would have spared the sharp conflicts of my own mind ever since, and the agonizing tears of a tender mother and my much-beloved sisters.

'Add to my youth and inexperience, that I was influenced in my conduct by the example of my messmates, Mr. Hallet and Mr. Hayward, the former of whom was very much agitated, and the latter, though he had been many years at sea, yet, when Christian ordered him into the boat, he was evidently alarmed at the perilous situation, and so much overcome by the harsh command, that he actually shed tears.

' My own apprehensions were far from being lessened at such a circumstance as this, and I fearfully beheld the preparations for the captain's departure as the preliminaries of inevitable destruction, which, although I did not think could be more certain, yet I feared would be more speedy, by the least addition to their number.

' To show that I have no disposition to impose upon this Court, by endeavouring to paint the situation of the boat to be worse than it really was, I need only refer to the captain's own narrative, wherein he says that she would have sunk with them on the evening of the 3rd May, had it not been for his timely caution of throwing out some of the stores, and all the clothes belonging to the people, excepting two suits for each.

'Now what clothes or stores could they have spared which in weight would have been equal to that of two men? (for if I had been in her, and the poor fellow, Norton, had not been murdered at Tofoa, she would have been encumbered with our additional weight), and if it be true that she was saved by those means, which the captain says she was, it must follow that if Norton and myself had been in her (to say nothing of Coleman, M'Intosh, Norman, and Byrne, who, 'tis confessed, were desirous of leaving the ship), she must either have gone down with us, or, to prevent it, we must have lightened her of the provisions and other necessary articles, and thereby have perished for want—dreadful alternative!

'A choice of deaths to those who are certain of dying may be a matter of indifference; but where, on one hand, death appears inevitable, and the means of salvation present themselves on the other, however imprudent it might be to resort to those means in any other less trying situation, I think (and hope even at my present time of life) that I shall not be suspected of a want of courage for saying, few would hesitate to embrace the latter.

'Such, then, was exactly my situation on board the Bounty; to be starved to death, or drowned, appeared to be inevitable if I went in the boat; and surely it is not to be wondered at, if, at the age of sixteen years, with no one to advise with, and so ignorant of the discipline of the service

Q

(having never been at sea before) as not to
know or even suppose it was possible that what I
should determine upon might afterwards be alleged against me as a crime—I say, under such
circumstances, in so trying a situation, can it be
wondered at, if I suffered the preservation of my
life to be the first, and to supersede every other,
consideration.

' Besides, through the medium of the master, the
captain had directed the rest of the officers to
remain on board, in hopes of re-taking the ship.
Such is the master's assertion, and such the report
on board, and as it accorded with my own wishes
for the preservation of my life, I felt myself
doubly justified in staying on board, not only as
it appeared to be safer than going in the boat, but
from a consideration also of being in the way to
be useful in assisting to accomplish so desirable a
wish of the captain.

' Let it not—for God's sake—let it not be
argued that my fears were groundless, and that
the arrival of the boat at Timor is a proof that
my conduct was wrong. This would be judging
from the event, and I think I have plainly shewn
that, but for the death of Norton at Tofoa, and
the prudent order of the captain not to overload
the boat, neither himself nor any of the people
who were saved with him, would at this moment
have been alive to have preferred any charge
against me, or given evidence at this trial.

' If deliberate guilt be necessarily affixed to all
who continued on board the ship, and that in consequence they must be numbered with Christian's
party—in such a strict view of matters it must

irrevocably impeach the armourer and two carpenter's mates, as well as Martin and Byrne, who certainly wished to quit the ship. And if Christian's first intention of sending away the captain, with a few persons only, in the small cutter, had not been given up, or if even the large cutter had not been exchanged for the launch, more than half of those who did go with him would have been obliged to stay with me. Forgetful for a moment of my own misfortunes, I cannot help being agitated at the bare thought of their narrow escape.

' Every body must, and I am sure that this court will, allow that my case is a peculiarly hard one, inasmuch as the running away with the ship is a proof of the mutiny having been committed. The innocent and the guilty are upon exactly the same footing—had the former been confined by sickness, without a leg to stand on, or an arm to assist them in opposing the mutineers, they must have been put upon their trial, and instead of the captain being obliged to prove their guilt, it would have been incumbent upon them to have proved themselves innocent. How can this be done but negatively ? If all who wished it could not accompany the captain, they were necessarily compelled to stay with Christian ; and being with him, were dependent on him, subject to his orders, however disinclined to obey them, for force in such a state is paramount to every thing. But when, on the contrary, instead of being in arms, or obeying any orders of the mutineers, I did every thing in my power to assist the captain, and those who went with him, and by all my actions (except in neglecting to do what, if I had done, must have endangered the lives of those who were so fortunate as to quit the ship) I shewed myself faithful to the last moment of the captain's stay, what is there to leave a doubt in the minds of impartial and dispassionate men of my being perfectly innocent? Happy indeed should I have been if the master had stayed on board, which he probably would have done, if his reasons for wishing to do so had not been over-heard by the man who was in the bread-room.

'Captain Bligh in his narrative acknowledges that he had left some friends on board the Bounty, and no part of my conduct could have induced him to believe that I ought not to be reckoned of the number. Indeed from his attention to and very kind treatment of me personally, I should have been a monster of depravity to have betrayed him. The idea alone is sufficient to disturb a mind where humanity and gratitude have, I hope, ever been noticed as its characteristic features; and yet Mr. Hallet has said that he saw me laugh at a time when, Heaven knows, the conflict in my own mind, independent of the captain's situation, rendered such a want of decency impos-sible. The charge in its nature is dreadful, but I boldly declare, notwithstanding an internal con-viction of my innocence has enabled me to en-dure my sufferings for the last sixteen months, could I have laid to my heart so heavy an accu-sation, I should not have lived to defend myself from it. And this brings to my recollection an-other part of Captain Bligh's narrative, in which he says, " I was kept apart from every one, and all I could do was by speaking to them in general, but my endeavours were of no avail, for I was kept securely bound, and no one but the guard was suffered to come near me."

' If the captain, whose narrative we may suppose to have been a detail of every thing which happened, could only recollect that he had spoken generally to the people, I trust it will hardly be believed that Mr. Hallet, without notes, at so distant a period as this, should be capable of recollecting that he heard him speak to any one in particular; and here it may not be improper to observe that, at the time to which I allude, Mr. Hallet (if I am rightly informed) could not have been more than fifteen years of age. I mean not to impeach his courage, but I think if circumstances be considered, and an adequate idea of the confused state of the ship can be formed by this Court, it will not appear probable that this young gentleman should have been so perfectly unembarrassed as to have been able to particularize the muscles of a man's countenance, even at a considerable distance from him; and what is still more extraordinary is, that he heard the captain call to me from abaft the mizen to the platform where I was standing, which required an exertion of voice, and must have been heard and noticed by all who were present, as the captain and Christian were at that awful moment the objects of every one's peculiar attention; yet he who was standing between us, and noticing the transactions of us both, could not hear what was said.

' To me it has ever occurred that diffidence is very becoming, and of all human attainments a

knowledge of ourselves is the most difficult ; and
if, in the ordinary course of life, it is not an easy
matter precisely to account for our own actions,
how much more difficult and hazardous must it be,
in new and momentous scenes, when the mind is
hurried and distressed by conflicting passions, to
judge of another's conduct ; and yet here are two
young men, who, after a lapse of near four years
(in which period one of them, like myself, has
grown from a boy to be a man), without hesitation, in a matter on which my life is depending,
undertake to account for some of my actions, at
a time, too, when some of the most experienced
officers in the ship are not ashamed to acknowledge they were overcome by the confusion which
the mutiny occasioned, and are incapable of recollecting a number of their own transactions on
that day.

' I can only oppose to such open boldness the
calm suggestions of reason, and would willingly
be persuaded that the impression under which this
evidence has been given is not in any degree
open to suspicion.   I would be understood, at the
same time, not to mean anything injurious to the
character of Mr. Hallet ; and for Mr. Hayward, I
ever loved him, and must do him the justice to
declare, that whatever cause I may have to deplore the effect of his evidence, or rather his opinion, for he has deposed no fact against me, yet
I am convinced it was given conscientiously, and
with a tenderness and feeling becoming a man of
honour.

' But may they not both be mistaken ?   Let it
be remembered that their long intimacy with Cap-

tain Bligh, in whose distresses they were parta-
kers, and whose sufferings were severely felt by
them, naturally begot an abhorrence towards
those whom they thought the authors of their
misery,—might they not forget that the story had
been told to them, and by first of all believing,
then constantly thinking of it, be persuaded at
last it was a fact within the compass of their own
knowledge.

'It is the more natural to believe it is so, from
Mr. Hallet's forgetting what the captain said upon
the occasion, which, had he been so collected as he
pretends to have been, he certainly must have
heard. Mr. Hayward, also, it is evident, has
made a mistake in point of time as to the seeing
me with Morrison and Millward upon the booms;
for the boatswain and carpenter in their evidence
have said, and the concurring testimony of every
one supports the fact, that the mutiny had taken
place, and the captain was on deck, before they
came up, and it was not till after that time that
the boatswain called Morrison and Millward out of
their hammocks; therefore to have seen me at all
upon the booms with those two men, it must
have been long after the time that Mr. Hayward
has said it was. Again, Mr. Hayward has said
that he could not recollect the day nor even the
month when the Pandora arrived at Otaheite.
Neither did Captain Edwards recollect when, on
his return, he wrote to the Admiralty, that Michael Byrne had surrendered himself as one of the
Bounty's people, but in that letter he reported him
as having been apprehended, which plainly shews
that the memory is fallible to a very great degree;

and it is a fair conclusion to draw that, if when
the mind is at rest, which must have been the case
with Mr. Hayward in the Pandora, and things of
a few months' date are difficult to be remembered,.
it is next to impossible, in the state which every
body was on board the Bounty, to remember their
particular actions at the distance of three years
and a half after they were observed.

' As to the advice he says he gave me, to go
into the boat, I can only say, I have a faint recollection of a short conversation with somebody,—
I thought it was Mr. Stewart—but be that as it
may, I think I may take upon me to say it was
on deck and not below, for on hearing it suggested that I should be deemed guilty if I stayed
in the ship, I went down directly, and in passing
Mr. Cole, told him, in a low tone of voice, that I
would fetch a few necessaries in a bag and follow
him into the boat, which at that time I meant to
do, but was afterwards prevented.

' Surely I shall not be deemed criminal that I
hesitated at getting into a boat whose gunnel,
when she left the ship, was, not quite eight inches
above the surface of the water. And if, in the
moment of unexpected trial, fear and confusion
assailed my untaught judgment, and that by remaining in the ship I appeared to deny my commander, it was in appearance only—it was the
sin of my head—for I solemnly assure you before
God, that it was not the vileness of my heart.

' I was surprised into my error by a mixture of
ignorance, apprehension, and the prevalence of
example; and, alarmed as I was from my sleep,
there was little opportunity and less time for

better recollection. The captain, I am persuaded, did not see me during the mutiny, for I retired, as it were, in sorrowful suspense, alternately agitated between hope and fear, not knowing what to do. The dread of being asked by him, or of being ordered by Christian, to go into the boat,—or, which appeared to me worse than either—of being desired by the latter to join his party, induced me to keep out of the sight of both, until I was a second time confined in my berth by Thompson, when the determination I had made was too late to be useful.

' One instance of my conduct I had nearly forgot, which, with much anxiety and great astonishment, I have heard observed upon and considered as a fault, though I had imagined it blameless, if not laudable—I mean the assistance I gave in hoisting out the launch, which, by a mode of expression of the boatswain's, who says I did it voluntarily (meaning that I did not refuse my assistance when he asked me to give it), the Court, I am afraid, has considered it as giving assistance to the mutineers, and not done with a view to help the captain ; of which, however, I have no doubt of being able to give a satisfactory explanation in evidence.

' Observations on matters of opinion I will endeavour to forbear where they appear to have been formed from the impulse of the moment ; but I shall be pardoned for remembering Mr. Hayward's (given I will allow with great deliberation, and after long weighing the question which called for it), which cannot be reckoned of that description, for although he says he rather considered me as a friend to Christian's party, he states that his last words to me were, " Peter, go into the boat," which words could not have been addressed to one who was of the party of the mutineers. And I am sure, if the countenance is at all an index to the heart, mine must have betrayed the sorrow and distress he has so accurately described.

' It were trespassing unnecessarily upon the patience of the Court, to be giving a tedious history of what happened in consequence of the mutiny, and how, through one very imprudent step, I was unavoidably led into others.

' But, amidst all this pilgrimage of distress, I had a conscience, thank heaven, which lulled away the pain of personal difficulties, dangers, and distress. It was this conscious principle which determined me not to hide myself as if guilty. No —I welcomed the arrival of the Pandora at Otaheite, and embraced the earliest opportunity of freely surrendering myself to the captain of that ship.

' By his order I was chained and punished with incredible severity, though the ship was threatened with instant destruction : when fear and trembling came on every man on board, in vain, for a long time, were my earnest repeated cries, that the galling irons might not, in that moment of affrighting consternation, prevent my hands from being lifted up to heaven for mercy.

' But though it cannot fail deeply to interest the humanity of this Court, and kindle in the breast of every member of it compassion for my sufferings, yet as it is not relative to the point, and as I cannot for a moment believe that it proceeded

from any improper motive on the part of Captain
Edwards, whose character in the navy stands high
in estimation both as an officer and a man of
humanity, but rather that he was actuated in his
conduct towards me by the imperious dictates of
the laws of the service, I shall, therefore, waive
it, and say no more upon the subject.

' Believe me, again I entreat you will believe
me, when, in the name of the tremendous judge of
heaven and earth (before whose vindictive Majesty
I may be destined soon to appear), I now assert
my innocence of plotting, abetting, or assisting,
either by word or deed, the mutiny for which I am
tried—for, young as I am, I am still younger in
the school of art and such matured infamy.

' My parents (but I have only one left, a solitary and mournful mother, who is at home weeping and trembling for the event of this day),
thanks to their fostering care, taught me betimes
to reverence God, to honour the king, and be
obedient to his laws; and at no one time have I
resolutely or designedly been an apostate to
either.

' To this honourable Court, then, I now commit
myself.

' My character and my life are at your disposal;
and as the former is as sacred to me as the latter
is precious, the consolation or settled misery of a
dear mother and two sisters, who mingle their
tears together, and are all but frantic for my situation—pause for your verdict.

' If I am found worthy of life, it shall be im-
proved by past experience, and especially taught
from the serious lesson of what has lately hap-

pened; but if nothing but death itself can atone
for my pitiable indiscretion, I bow with submission
and all due respect to your impartial decision.

' Not with sullen indifference shall I then me-
ditate on my doom as not deserving it—no, such
behaviour would be an insult to God and an
affront to man, and the attentive and candid deportment of my judges in this place requires more
becoming manners in me.

' Yet, if I am found guilty this day, they will not
construe it, I trust, as the least disrespect offered
to their discernment and opinion, if I solemnly
declare that my heart will rely with confidence in
its own innocence, until that awful period when
my spirit shall be about to be separated from
my body to take its everlasting flight, and be
ushered into the presence of that unerring Judge,
before whom all hearts are open and from whom
no secrets are hid.   ' P. HEYWOOD.'

His witnesses fully established the facts which
he assumed in this defence. He then delivered
to the president a paper, of which the following is
a copy :—

' My Lord,—the Court having heard the witnesses I have been enabled to call, it will be unnecessary to add anything to their testimony in
point of fact, or to observe upon it by way of
illustration. It is, I trust, sufficient to do away
any suspicion which may have fallen upon me,
and to remove every implication of guilt which,
while unexplained, might by possibility have attached to me. It is true I have, by the absence
of Captain Bligh, Simpson, and Tinkler, been

deprived of the opportunity of laying before the
Court much that would at least have been grateful to my feelings, though I hope not necessary
to my defence; as the former must have exculpa-
ted me from the least disrespect, and the two last
would have proved past all contradiction that I
was unjustly accused.   I might regret that in
their absence I have been arraigned, but, thank
heaven, I have been enabled, by the very witnesses who were called to criminate me, to oppose
facts to opinions, and give explanation to circumstances of suspicion.

' It has been proved that I was asleep at the
time of the mutiny, and waked only to confusion
and dismay.   It has been proved, it is true, that I
continued on board the ship, but it has been also
proved I was detained by force; and to this I
must add, I left the society of those with whom I
was for a time obliged to associate, as soon as
possible, and with unbounded satisfaction resigned
myself to the Captain of the Pandora, to whom
I gave myself up, to whom I also delivered my
journal * (faithfully brought up to the preceding
day), and to whom I also gave every information
in my power.   I could do no more; for at the
first time we were at Otaheite it was impossible
for me, watched and suspected as I was, to separate from the ship.   My information to Captain
Edwards was open, sincere, and unqualified, and I
had many opportunities given me at different
times of repeating it.   Had a track been open to
my native country, I should have followed it; had

* This Journal, it is presumed, must have been lost
when the Pandora was wrecked.

a vessel arrived earlier, I should earlier with the
same eagerness have embraced the opportunity,
for I dreaded not an inquiry in which I foresaw no
discredit.   But Providence ordained it otherwise.
I have been the victim of suspicion, and had nearly
fallen a sacrifice to misapprehension.   I have,
however, hitherto surmounted it, and it only remains with this Court to say, if my sufferings
have not been equal to my indiscretion.

' The decision will be the voice of honour, and
to that I must implicitly resign myself.

' P. HEYWOOD.'

Mr. Morrison's Defence

Sets out by stating that he was waked at daylight
by Mr. Cole the boatswain, who told him that the
ship was taken by Christian ; that he assisted in
clearing out the boat at Mr. Cole's desire, and
says, ' While I was thus employed Mr. Fryer came
to me and asked if I had any hand in the mutiny ;
I told him No.   He then desired me to see who
I could find to assist me, and try to rescue the
ship ; I told him I feared it was then too late,
but would do my endeavour ; when John Milward,
who stood by me, and heard what Mr. Fryer said,
swore he would stand by me if an opportunity
offered.   Mr. Fryer was about to speak again, but
was prevented by Matthew Quintal, who, with a
pistol in one hand, collared him with the other,
saying, "Come, Mr. Fryer, you must go down into
your cabin;" and hauled him away. Churchill then
came, and shaking his cutlass at me, demanded
what Mr. Fryer said.   I told him that he only
asked me if they were going to have the long-

boat, upon which Alexander Smith (Adams), who stood on the opposite side of the boat, said, "It's a d—d lie, Charley, for I saw him and Milward shake hands when the master spoke to them." Churchill then said to me, "I would have you mind how you come on, for I have an eye upon you." Smith at the same time called out, "Stand to your arms, for they intend to make a rush." This, as it was intended, put the mutineers on their guard, and I found it necessary to be very cautious how I acted; and I heard Captain Bligh say to Smith, "I did not expect you would be against me, Smith;" but I could not hear what answer he made.'

He says that, while clearing the boat, he heard Christian order Churchill to see that no arms were put into her; to keep Norman, M'Intosh, and Coleman in the ship, and get the officers into the boat as fast as possible; that Mr. Fryer begged permission to stay, but to no purpose. 'On seeing Mr. Fryer and most of the officers going into the boat, without the least appearance of an effort to rescue the ship, I began to reflect on my own situation; and seeing the situation of the boat, and considering that she was at least a thousand leagues from any friendly settlement, and judging, from what I had seen of the Friendly Islanders but a few days before, that nothing could be expected from them but to be plundered or killed, and seeing no choice but of one evil, I chose, as I thought the least, to stay in the ship, especially as I considered it as obeying Captain Bligh's orders, and depending on his promise to do justice to those who remained. I informed Mr. Cole of

my intention, who made me the like promise,
taking me by the hand and saying, " God bless
you, my boy ; I will do you justice if ever I reach
England."

' I also informed Mr. Hayward of my intention ;
and on his dropping a hint to me that he intended
to knock Churchill down, I told him I would
second him, pointing to some of the Friendly
Island clubs which were sticking in the booms,
and saying, " There were tools enough:" but
(he adds) I was suddenly damped to find that he
went into the boat without making the attempt he
had proposed.'

He then appeals to the members of the Court,
as to the alternative they would themselves have
taken : — ' A boat alongside, already crowded ;
those who were in her crying out she would sink ;
and Captain Bligh desiring no more might go in
—with a slender stock of provisions,—what hope
could there be to reach any friendly shore, or with-
stand the hostile attacks of the boisterous ele-
ments ? The perils those underwent who reached
the island of Timor, and whom nothing but the
apparent interference of Divine Providence could
have saved, fully justify my fears, and prove beyond a doubt that they rested on a solid foundation ; for by staying in the ship, an opportunity
might offer of escaping, but by going in the boat
nothing but death appeared, either from the lingering torments of hunger and thirst, or from the
murderous weapons of cruel savages, or being
swallowed up by the deep.

' I have endeavoured,' he says, ' to recall to
Mr. Hayward's remembrance a proposal he at

one time made, by words, of attacking the mutineers, and of my encouraging him to the attempt, promising to back him. He says he has but a faint recollection of the business—so faint indeed that he cannot recall to his memory the particulars, but owns there was something passed to that effect. Faint, however, as his remembrance is (which for me is the more unfortunate), ought it not to do away all doubt with respect to the motives by which I was then influenced?' And, in conclusion, he says, ' I beg leave most humbly to remind the members of this honourable Court, that I did freely, and of my own accord, deliver myself up to Lieutenant Robert Corner, of H.M.S. Pandora, on the first certain notice of her arrival.'

William Muspratt's Defence

Declares his innocence of any participation in the mutiny ; admits he assisted in hoisting out the boat, and in putting several articles into her ; after which he sat down on the booms, when Millward came and mentioned to him Mr. Fryer's intention to rescue the ship, when he said he would stand by Mr. Fryer as far as he could ; and with that intention, and for that purpose only, he took up a musket which one of the people had laid down, and which he quitted the moment he saw Bligh's people get into the boat. Solemnly denies the charge of Mr. Purcell against him, of handing liquor to the ship's company. Mr. Hayward's evidence, he trusts, must stand so impeached before the Court, as not to receive the least attention, when the lives of so many men are to be affected by it—for, he observes, he swears that

R

Morrison was a mutineer, because he assisted in hoisting out the boats; and that M'Intosh was not a mutineer, notwithstanding he was precisely employed on the same business—that he criminated Morrison from the appearance of his countenance—that he had only a faint remembrance of that material and striking circumstance of Morrison offering to join him to retake the ship—that, in answer to his (Muspratt's) question respecting Captain Bligh's words, ' My lads, I'll do you justice,' he considered them applied to the people in the boat, and not to those in the ship—to the same question put by the Court, he said they applied to persons remaining in the ship. And he notices some other instances which he thinks most materially affect Mr. Hayward's credit; and says, that if he had been under arms when Hayward swore he was, he humbly submits Mr. Hallet must have seen him. And he concludes with asserting (what indeed was a very general opinion), ' that the great misfortune attending this unhappy business is, that no one ever attempted to rescue the ship ; that it might have been done, Thompson being the only sentinel over the arm-chest.'

Michael Byrne's Defence

was very short. He says, ' It has pleased the Almighty, among the events of his unsearchable providence, nearly to deprive me of sight, which often puts it out of my power to carry the intentions of my mind into execution.

' I make no doubt but it appears to this honourable Court, that on the 28th of April, 1789, my intention was to quit his Majesty's ship Bounty with the officers and men who went away, and that the sorrow I expressed at being detained was real and unfeigned.

' I do not know whether I may be able to repeat the exact words that were spoken on the occasion, but some said, " We must not part with our fiddler ;" and Charles Churchill threatened to send me to the shades if I attempted to quit the cutter, into which I had gone for the purpose of attending Lieutenant Bligh :' and, without further trespassing on the time of the Court, he submits his case to its judgment and mercy.

It is not necessary to notice any parts of the defence made by Coleman, Norman, and M'Intosh, as it is clear, from the whole evidence and from Bligh's certificates, that those men were anxious to go in the boat, but were kept in the ship by force.

It is equally clear, that Ellison, Millward, and Burkitt, were concerned in every stage of the mutiny, and had little to offer in their defence in exculpation of the crime of which they were accused.

On the sixth day, namely, on the 18th of September, 1792, the Court met,—the prisoners were brought in, audience admitted, when the president, having asked the prisoners if they or any of them had anything more to offer in their defence, the Court was cleared, and agreed,—

' That the charges had been proved against the said Peter Heywood, James Morrison, Thomas Ellison, Thomas Burkitt, John Millward, and William Muspratt ; and did adjudge them, and each

R 2

of them, to suffer death, by being hanged by the
neck, on board such of his Majesty's ship or ships of
war, and at such time or times, and at such place
or places, as the commissioners for executing the
office of Lord High Admiral of Great Britain and
Ireland, &c., or any three of them, for the time
being, should, in writing, under their hands, direct;
but the Court, in consideration of various circumstances, did humbly and most earnestly recommend the said Peter Heywood and James Morrison
to his Majesty's mercy; and the Court further
agreed, that the charges had not been proved
against the said Charles Norman, Joseph Coleman, Thomas M'Intosh, and Michael Byrne, and
did adjudge them, and each of them, to be acquitted.'

The Court was then opened and audience admitted, and sentence passed accordingly.

CHAPTER VII.

THE KING'S WARRANT.

' Well, believe this—
No ceremony that to great ones 'longs,
Not the king's crown, nor the deputed sword,
The marshal's truncheon, nor the judge's robe,
Become them with one half so good a grace,
As mercy does.'

IT was a very common feeling that Heywood and Morrison, the former in particular, had been hardly dealt with by the Court in passing upon them a sentence of death, tempered as it was with the recommendation to the king's mercy. It should, however, have been recollected, that the Court had no discretional power to pass any other sentence but that, or a full acquittal. But earnestly, no doubt, as the Court was disposed towards the latter alternative, it could not, consistently with the rules and feelings of the service, be adopted. It is not enough in cases of mutiny (and this case was aggravated by the piratical seizure of a king's ship) that the officers and men in his Majesty's naval service should take no active part;—to be neutral or passive is considered as tantamount to aiding and abetting. Besides, in the present case, the remaining in the ship along with the mutineers, without having recourse to such means as offered of leaving her, presumes a voluntary adhesion to the criminal party. The only fault of Heywood, and a pardonable one on account of his youth and inexperience, was his not asking Christian to be allowed to go with his captain,—his not *trying* to go in time. M'Intosh, Norman, Byrne, and Coleman were acquitted because they expressed a strong desire to go, but were forced to remain. This was not only clearly proved, but they were in possession of written testimonies from Bligh to that effect; and so would Heywood have had, but for some prejudice Bligh had taken against him, in the course of the boat-voyage home, for it will be shewn that he knew he was confined to his berth below.

In favour of three of the four men condemned without a recommendation, there were unhappily no palliating circumstances. Millward, Burkitt, and Ellison were under arms from first to last; and Ellison not only left the helm to take up arms, but, rushing aft towards Bligh, called out, 'D—n him, I'll be sentry over him.' The fourth man, Muspratt, was condemned on the evidence of Lieutenant Hayward, which, however, appears to have been duly appreciated by the Lords Commissioners of the Admiralty, and in consequence of which the poor man escaped an ignominious death.

The family of young Heywood in the Isle of Man had been buoyed up, from various quarters, with the almost certainty of his full acquittal. From the 12th September, when the court-martial first sat, till the 24th of that month, they were prevented, by the strong and contrary winds which cut off all communication with England, from receiving any tidings whatever. But while Mrs. Heywood and her daughters were fondly flattering themselves with everything being most happily concluded, one evening, as they were indulging these pleasing hopes, a little boy, the son of one of their particular friends, ran into the room and told them, in the most abrupt manner, that the trial was over and all the prisoners condemned, but that Peter Heywood was recommended to mercy; he added that a man whose name he mentioned had told him this. The man was sent for, questioned, and replied he had seen it in a newspaper at Liverpool, from which place he was just arrived in a small fishing-boat, but had forgotten to bring the paper with him. In this state of doubtful uncertainty this wretched family remained another whole week, harassed by the most cruel agony of mind, which no language can express*. The affectionate Nessy determined

* It was in this state of mind, while in momentary expectation of receiving an account of the termination of the court-martial, that Heywood's charming sister Nessy wrote the following lines:—

ANXIETY.

DOUBTING, dreading, fretful guest,
Quit, oh! quit this mortal breast.
Why wilt thou my peace invade,
And each brighter prospect shade?
Pain me not with needless Fear,
But let Hope my bosom cheer;
While I court her gentle charms,
Woo the flatterer to my arms;
While each moment she beguiles
With her sweet enliv'ning smiles,
While she softly whispers me,
'Lycidas again is free,'   While

at once to proceed to Liverpool, and so on to
London. She urges her brother James at Liverpool to hasten to Portsmouth : ' Don't wait for me,
I can go alone ; fear and even despair will support me through the journey ; think only of our
poor unfortunate and adored boy, bestow not one
thought on me.' And she adds, ' yet, if I could
listen to reason (which is indeed difficult), it is not
likely that anything serious has taken place, or
will do so, as we should then certainly have had
an express.' She had a tempestuous passage of
forty-nine hours, and to save two hours got into
an open fishing-boat at the mouth of the Mersey,
the sea running high and washing over her every
moment ; but, she observes, ' let me but be blessed
with the cheering influence of *hope*, and I have
spirit to undertake anything.' From Liverpool
she set off the same night in the mail for London ;
and arrived at Mr. Graham's on the 5th October,
who received her with the greatest kindness, and
desired her to make his house her home.

The suspense into which the afflicted family in
the Isle of Man had been thrown, by the delay of
the packet, was painfully relieved on its arrival in
the night of the 29th September, by the following
letter from Mr. Graham to the Rev. Dr. Scott,
which the latter carried to Mrs. Heywood's family the following morning.

> While I gaze on Pleasure's gleam,
> Say not thou "'Tis all a dream.'
> Hence—nor darken Joy's soft bloom
> With thy pale and sickly gloom :
> Nought have I to do with thee—
> Hence—begone—Anxiety.

Isle of Man, September 10th.   NESSY HEYWOOD.

' *Portsmouth, Tuesday*, 18*th September.*
' Sir,
' Although a stranger, I make no apology in
writing to you. I have attended and given my
assistance at Mr. Heywood's trial, which was
finished and the sentence passed about half an
hour ago. Before I tell you what that sentence
is, I must inform you that his life is safe, notwithstanding it is at present at the mercy of the
king, to which he is in the strongest terms recommended by the Court. That any unnecessary
fears may not be productive of misery to the
family, I must add, that the king's attorney-
general (who with Judge Ashurst attended the
trial) desired me to make myself perfectly easy,
for that my friend was as safe as if he had not
been condemned. I would have avoided making
use of this dreadful word, but it must have come
to your knowledge, and perhaps unaccompanied
by many others of a pleasing kind. To prevent
its being improperly communicated to Mrs. or the
Misses Heywood, whose distresses first engaged
me in the business, and could not fail to call forth
my best exertions upon the occasion, I send you
this by express. The mode of communication I
must leave to your discretion; and shall only add
that, although from a combination of circumstances, ill-nature, and mistaken friendship, the
sentence is in itself terrible, yet it is incumbent on
me to assure you that, from the same combination
of circumstances, everybody who attended the trial
is perfectly satisfied in his own mind that he was
*hardly guilty in appearance, in intention he was
perfectly innocent.* I shall of course write to

Commodore Pasley, whose mind, from my letter to him of yesterday, must be dreadfully agitated, and take his advice about what is to be done when Mr. Heywood is released. I shall stay here till then, and my intention is afterwards to take him to my house in town, where I think he had better stay till one of the family calls for him: for he will require a great deal of tender management after all his sufferings; and it would perhaps be a necessary preparation for seeing his mother, that one or both his sisters should be previously prepared to support her on so trying an occasion.'

On the following day Mr. Graham again writes to Dr. Scott, and among other things observes, 'It will be a great satisfaction to his family to learn, that the declarations of some of the other prisoners, since the trial, put it past all doubt that the evidence upon which he was convicted must have been (to say nothing worse of it) an unfortunate belief, on the part of the witness, of circumstances which either never had existence, or were applicable to one of the other gentlemen who remained in the ship, and not to Mr. Heywood *.'

On the 20th September Mr. Heywood addresses the first letter he wrote, after his conviction, to Dr. Scott.

' Honoured and dear Sir,
' On Wednesday the 12th instant the awful trial commenced, and on *that* day, *when in Court,*

* This is supposed to allude to the evidence given by Hallet.

I had the pleasure of receiving your most kind and parental letter*, in answer to which I now communicate to you the melancholy issue of it, which, as I desired my friend Mr. Graham to inform you of immediately, will be no dreadful news to you. The morning lowers, and all my hope of worldly joy is fled. On Tuesday morning the 18th the dreadful sentence of death was pronounced upon me, to which (being the just decree of that Divine Providence who first gave me breath) I bow my devoted head, with that fortitude, cheerfulness, and resignation, which is the duty of every member of the church of our blessed saviour and redeemer Christ Jesus. To Him alone I now look up for succour, in full hope that perhaps a few days more will open to the view of my astonished and fearful soul his kingdom of eternal and incomprehensible bliss, prepared only for the righteous of heart.

' I have not been found guilty of the slightest act connected with that detestable crime of mutiny, but am doomed to die for not being active in my endeavours to suppress it. Could the witnesses who appeared on the Court-martial be themselves tried, *they* would also suffer for the very same and only crime of which I have been found guilty. But I am to be the victim. Alas! my youthful inexperience, and not depravity of will, is the sole cause to which I can attribute my misfortunes. But so far from repining at my fate, I

---

* This refers to a very kind and encouraging letter written to him by the Rev. Dr. Scott, of the Isle of Man, who knew him from a boy, and had the highest opinion of his character.

receive it with a dreadful kind of joy, composure, and serenity of mind ; well assured that it has pleased God to point me out as a subject through which some greatly useful (though at present unsearchable) intention of the divine attributes may be carried into execution for the future benefit of my country. Then why should I repine at being made a sacrifice for the good, perhaps, of thousands of my fellow-creatures ; forbid it, Heaven! Why should I be sorry to leave a world in which I have met with nothing but misfortunes and all their concomitant evils? I shall on the contrary endeavour to divest myself of all wishes for the futile and sublunary enjoyments of it, and prepare my soul for its reception into the bosom of its Redeemer. For though the very strong recommendation I have had to his Majesty's mercy by all the members of the Court may meet with his approbation, yet that is but the balance of a straw, a mere uncertainty, upon which no hope can be built ; the other is a certainty that must one day happen to every mortal, and therefore the salvation of my soul requires my most prompt and powerful exertions during the short time I may have to remain on earth.

' As this is too tender a subject for me to inform my unhappy and distressed mother and sisters of, I trust, dear Sir, you will either shew them this letter, or make known to them the truly dreadful intelligence in such a manner as (assisted by your wholesome and paternal advice) may enable them to bear it with Christian fortitude. The only worldly feelings I am now possessed of are for their happiness and welfare; but even these,

in my present situation, I must endeavour, with
God's assistance, to eradicate from my heart, how
hard soever the task.   I must strive against che-
rishing any temporal affections.   But, my dear
Sir, endeavour to mitigate my distressed mother's
sorrow.   Give my everlasting duty to her, and
unabated love to my disconsolate brothers and
sisters, and all my other relations.   Encourage
them, by my example, to bear up with fortitude
and resignation to the Divine will, under their
load of misfortunes, almost too great for female
nature to support, and teach them to be fully persuaded that all hopes of happiness on earth are
vain.   On my own account I still enjoy the most
easy serenity of mind ; and am, dear Sir, for ever
your greatly indebted and most dutiful. but ill-
fated,   'PETER HEYWOOD.'

His next letter is to his dearly beloved Nessy.

    ' Had I not a strong idea that, ere this mourn-
ful epistle from your ill-fated brother can reach
the trembling hand of my ever dear and much
afflicted Nessy, she must have been informed of
the final issue of my trial on Wednesday morning,
by my honoured friend Dr. Scott, I would not
now add trouble to the afflicted by a confirmation
of it.   Though I have indeed fallen an early victim to the rigid rules of the service, and though
the jaws of death are once more opened upon me,
yet do I not now nor ever will bow to the tyranny
of base-born fear.   Conscious of having done
my duty to God and man, I feel not one moment's anxiety on my own account, but cherish a

full and sanguine hope that perhaps a few days
more will free me from the load of misfortune
which has ever been my portion in this transient
period of existence; and that I shall find an everlasting asylum in those blessed regions of eternal
bliss, where the galling yoke of tyranny and oppression is felt no more.

' If earthly Majesty, to whose mercy I have
been recommended by the Court, should refuse to
put forth its lenient hand and rescue me from
what is *fancifully* called an ignominious death,
there is a heavenly King and Redeemer ready to
receive the righteous penitent, on whose gracious
mercy alone I, as we all should, depend, with
that pious resignation which is the duty of every
Christian; well convinced that, without his express permission, not even a hair of our head can
fall to the ground.

' Oh! my sister, my heart yearns when I picture
to myself the affliction, indescribable affliction,
which this melancholy intelligence must have
caused in the mind of my much honoured mother.
But let it be your peculiar endeavour to watch
over her grief and mitigate her pain. I hope, indeed, this little advice from me will be unnecessary; for I know the holy precepts of that inspired religion, which, thank heaven! have been
implanted in the bosoms of us all, will point out
to you, and all my dear relatives, that fortitude
and resignation which are required of us in the
conflicts of human nature, and prevent you from
arraigning the wisdom of that omniscient Providence, of which we ought all to have the fullest
sense.

'I have had all my dear Nessy's letters; the one of the 17th this morning, but alas! what do they now avail? Their contents only serve to prove the instability of all human hopes and expectations; but, my dear sister, I begin to feel the pangs which you must suffer from the perusal of this melancholy paper, and will therefore desist, for I know it is more than your nature can support. The contrast between last week's correspondence and this is great indeed; but why? we had only hope then; and have we not the same now? certainly. Endeavour then, my love, to cherish that hope, and with faith rely upon the mercy of that God who does as to him seems best and most conducive to the general good of his miserable creatures.

'Bear it then with Christian patience, and instil into the mind of my dear and now sorrowful sisters, by your advice, the same disposition; and, for heaven's sake, let not despair touch the soul of my dear mother—for then all would be over. Let James also employ all his efforts to cheer her spirits under her weight of woe. I will write no more. Adieu, my dearest love! Write but little to me, and pray for your ever affectionate but ill-fated brother.

'P.S. I am in perfect spirits, therefore let not your sympathizing feelings for my sufferings hurt your own precious health, which is dearer to me than life itself. Adieu!—'

In a letter to his mother he assures her of the perfect tranquillity of his mind; advises her not to entertain too sanguine hopes, but at the same

time not to be uneasy ; and he adds, ' A minister
of the gospel, who now attends me, has advised me
not to say too much to any of my dear relations,
but now and then I cannot avoid it.' To his
dearest Nessy, who encourages him to take hope,
he says, ' Alas! it is but a broken stick which *I*
have leaned on, and it has pierced my soul in
such a manner that I will never more trust to it,
but wait with a contented mind and patience for
the final accomplishment of the Divine will. . . . .
Mrs. *Hope* is a faithless and ungrateful acquaintance, with whom I have now broken off all connexions, and in her stead have endeavoured to
cultivate a more sure friendship with *Resignation,*
in full trust of finding her more constant.' He
desires her to write through her brother James
who is with him; and says that the reason for his
having desired her not to write much was, lest she
might hurt herself by it; and he adds, '.from an
idea that your exalted sentiments upon so tender
a subject ought not to be known by an inquiring
world;' but, he continues, ' do just as you like
best: I am conscious that your good sense will
prompt you to nothing inconsistent with our present circumstances.' To this she replies, in the
true spirit of a character like her own. ' Yes! my
ever dearest brother, I *will* write to you, and I
know I need not add, that in *that* employment
(while thus deprived of your loved society) consists
my only happiness. But why not express my
sentiments to yourself ? I have nothing to say
which I should blush to have known to all the
world;—nothing to express in my letters to you but
love and affection, and shall I blush for this ? Or

can I have a wish to conceal sentiments of such a
nature for an object who I am so certain merits
all my regard, and in whom the admiration of
surrounding friends convinces me I am not mistaken. No, surely; 'tis my pride, my chiefest
glory, to love you; and when you think me worthy
of commendation, *that* praise, and *that* only, can
make me vain. I shall not therefore write to you,
my dearest brother, in a private manner, for it is
unnecessary, and I abhor all deceit; in which I
know you agree with me.'

To her sister Mary in the Isle of Man she says,
' With respect to that little wretch Hallet, his
intrepidity in court was astonishing ; and after
every evidence had spoken highly in Peter's favour,
and given testimony of his innocence, so strong
that not a doubt was entertained of his acquittal,
he declared, unasked, that while Bligh was upon
deck, he (Hallet) saw him look at and speak to
Peter. What he said to him Hallet could not
hear, (being at the distance of twenty feet from
Bligh, and Peter was twenty feet farther off,
consequently a distance of forty feet separated
Mr. Bligh and my brother;) but he added that
Peter, on *hearing* what Mr. Bligh said to him,
laughed and turned contemptuously away. No
other witness saw Peter laugh but Hallet; on
the contrary, all agreed he wore a countenance on
that day remarkably sorrowful ; yet the effect of
this cruel evidence was wonderful upon the minds
of the Court, and they concluded by pronouncing
the dreadful sentence, though at the same time
accompanied by the strongest recommendation to
mercy. Assure yourselves (I have it from Mr.

Graham's own mouth), that Peter's honour is and
will be as secure as his own; that every professional man, as well as every man of sense, of whatever denomination, does and will esteem him
highly; that my dear uncle Pasley (who was in
town the night before my arrival) is delighted
with his worth; and that, in short, we shall at
length be happy.'

From this time a daily correspondence passed
between Peter Heywood and his sister Nessy, the
latter indulging hope, even to a certainty, that she
will not be deceived,—the other preaching up patience and resignation, with a full reliance on his
innocence and integrity. ' Cheer up then,' says
he, ' my dear Nessy; cherish *your hope*, and I
will exercise *my patience.*' Indeed so perfectly
calm was this young man under his dreadful calamity, that in a very few days after condemnation his brother says, ' While I write this, Peter
is sitting by me making an Otaheitan Vocabulary,
and so happy and intent upon it, that I have
scarcely an opportunity of saying a word to him;
he is in excellent spirits, and I am convinced they
are better and better every day.'

This vocabulary is a very extraordinary per-
formance; it consists of one hundred full-written
folio pages, the words alphabetically arranged, and
all the syllables accented. It appears, from a
passage in the ' Voyage of the Duff,' that a copy
of this vocabulary was of great use to the missionaries who were first sent to Otaheite in this
ship.

During the delay which took place in carrying
the sentence into execution, Commodore Pasley,

Mr. Graham, and others, were indefatigable in
their inquiries and exertions to ascertain what progress had been made in bringing to a happy issue
the recommendation to the fountain of mercy:
not less so was Nessy Heywood: from Mr.
Graham she learnt what this excellent man considered to be the principal parts of the evidence
that led to the conviction of her unhappy brother,
which, having undersood to be the following, she
transmitted to her brother:—

First. That he assisted in hoisting out the
launch.

Second. That he was seen by the carpenter
resting his hand upon a cutlass.

Third. That on being called to by Lieutenant
Bligh, he laughed.

Fourth. That he remained in the Bounty, instead of accompanying Bligh in the launch.

On these points of the evidence, Mr. Heywood
made the following comments, which he sent from
Portsmouth to his sister in town.

' Peter Heywood's Remarks upon material points
  of the evidence which was given at his trial, on
  board the Duke, in Portsmouth Harbour.

  ' *First. That I assisted in hoisting out the
  launch.*—This boat was asked for by the captain
  and his officers, and whoever assisted in hoisting
  her out were their friends; for if the captain had
  been sent away in the cutter, (which was Christian's first intention,) he could not have taken
  with him more than nine or ten men, whereas the
  launch carried nineteen. The boatswain, the
  master, the gunner, and the carpenter say, in their

s 2

evidence, that they considered me as helping the captain on this occasion.

' *Second. That I was seen by the carpenter resting my hand on a cutlass.*—I was seen in this position by no other person than the carpenter— no other person therefore could be intimidated by my appearance.   Was the carpenter intimidated by it?—No. So far from being afraid of me, he did not even look upon me in the light of a person armed, but pointed out to me the danger there was of my being thought so, and I immediately took away my hand from the cutlass, upon which I had very innocently put it when I was in a state of stupor. The Court was particularly pointed in its inquiries into this circumstance; and the carpenter was pressed to declare, on the oath he had taken, and after maturely considering the matter, whether he did at the time he saw me so situated, or had since been inclined to believe, that, under all the circumstances of the case, I could be considered as an *armed man,* to which he unequivocally answered, No; and he gave some good reasons (which will be found in his evidence) for thinking that I had not a wish to be armed during the mutiny. The master, the boatswain, the gunner, Mr. Hayward, Mr. Hallet, and John Smith, (who, with the carpenter, were all the witnesses belonging to the Bounty,) say, in their evidence, that they did not, *any of them,* see me armed; and the boatswain and the carpenter further say, in the most pointed terms, that they considered me to be one of the captain's party, and *by no means* as belonging to the mutineers: and the master, the boatswain, the carpenter, the gunner, all declare

that, from what they observed on my conduct
during the mutiny, and from a recollection of my
behaviour previous thereto, they were convinced
I would have afforded them all the assistance in
my power, if an opportunity had offered to retake
the ship.

*Third. That, upon being called to by the cap-
tain, I laughed.*— If this was believed by the
Court, it must have had, I am afraid, a very great
effect upon its judgment; for, if viewed in too
serious a light, it would seem to bring together
and combine a number of trifling circumstances,
which by themselves could only be treated merely
as matters of suspicion. It was no doubt, therefore, received with caution, and considered with
the utmost candour. The countenance, I grant,
on some other occasions, may warrant an opinion
of good or evil existing in the mind; but on the
momentous events of life and death, it is surely
by much too indefinite and hazardous even to
listen to for a moment. The different ways of
expressing our various passions are, with many,
as variable as the features they wear. Tears have
often been, nay generally are, the relief of excessive joy, while misery and dejection have, many
a time, disguised themselves in a smile; and con-
vulsive laughs have betrayed the anguish of an
almost broken heart. To judge, therefore, the
principles of the heart, by the barometer of the
face, is as erroneous as it would be absurd and
unjust. This matter may likewise be considered
in another point of view. Mr. Hallet says I
laughed in consequence of being called to by the

captain, who was abaft the mizen-mast, while I was upon the platform near the fore hatchway, a distance of more than thirty feet: if the captain intended I should hear him, and there can be no doubt that he wished it; if he really called to me, he must have exerted his voice, and very considerably too, upon such an occasion and in such a situation; and yet Mr. Hallet himself, who, by being on the quarter-deck, could not have been half the distance from the captain that I was, even he, I say, could not hear what was said to me: how then, in the name of God, was it possible that I should have heard the captain at all, situated, as I must have been, in the midst of noisy confusion? And if I did not hear him, which I most solemnly aver to be the truth, even granting that I laughed, (which, however, in my present awful situation I declare I believe I did not,) it could not have been at what the captain said. Upon this ground, then, I hope I shall stand acquitted of this charge, for if the crime derives its guilt from the knowledge I had of the captain's speaking to me, it follows, of course, that if I did not hear him speak, there could be no crime in my laughing. It may, however, very fairly be asked, why Mr. Hallet did not make known that the captain was calling to me? His duty to the captain, if not his friendship for me, should have prompted him to it; and the peculiarity of our situation required this act of kindness at his hands*. I shall only observe further upon

* Captain Bligh states in his journal, that none of his officers were suffered to come near him while held a prisoner

this head, that the boatswain, the carpenter, and Mr. Hayward, who saw more of me than any other of the witnesses, did say in their evidence, that I had rather a sorrowful countenance on. the day of the mutiny.

' *Fourth. That I remained on board the ship, instead of going in the boat with the captain.*—That I was at first alarmed and afraid of going into the boat I will not pretend to deny ; but that afterwards I wished to accompany the captain, and should have done it, if I had not been prevented by Thompson, who confined me below by the order of Churchill, is clearly proved by the evidence of several of the witnesses. The boatswain says, that just before he left the ship I went below, and in passing him said something about a bag—(it was, that I would put a few things into a bag and follow him) ; the carpenter says he saw me go below at this time ; and both those wit-

by Christian; and Hallet was, no doubt, mistaken, but he had probably said it in the boat, and thought it right to be consistent on the trial.

It has been said that Hallet, when in the Penelope, in which frigate he died, expressed great regret at the evidence he had given at the court-martial, and frequently alluded to it, admitting that he might have been mistaken.—There can be very little doubt that he was so. But the Editor has ascertained, from personal inquiry of one of the most distinguished flag-officers in the service, who was then first lieutenant of the Penelope, that Hallet frequently expressed to him his deep contrition for having given in evidence what, on subsequent reflection, he was convinced to be incorrect; that he ascribed it to the state of confusion in which his mind was when under examination before the Court; and that he had since satisfied himself that, owing to the general alarm and confusion during the mutiny, he must have confounded Heywood with some other person.

nesses say, that they heard the master-at-arms call
to Thompson " *to keep them below.*" The point,
therefore, will be to prove to whom this order,
" *keep them below,*" would apply. The boatswain
and carpenter say, they have no doubt of its meaning me as one ; and that it must have been so, I
shall have very little difficulty in shewing, by the
following statement :—

'There remained on board the ship after the boat
put off, twenty-five men. Messrs. Hayward and
Hallet have proved that the following were under
arms :—Christian, Hillbrant, Millward, Burkitt,
Muspratt, Ellison, Sumner, Smith, Young, Skinner, Churchill, M'Koy, Quintal, Morrison, Williams, Thompson, Mills, and Brown, in all eighteen. The master (and upon this occasion I may
be allowed to quote from the captain's printed narrative) mentions Martin as one, which makes the
number of armed men nineteen, none of whom,
we may reasonably suppose, were ordered to be
kept below. Indeed, Mr. Hayward says, that
there were at the least eighteen of them upon deck,
when he went into the boat; and if Thompson,
the sentinel over the arm-chest, be added to them,
it exactly agrees with the number above-named ;
there remains then six, to whom Churchill's order,
" *keep them below,*" might apply, namely, Heywood, Stewart, Coleman, Norman, M'Intosh, and
Byrne.

' Could Byrne have been one of them? *No,* for
he was in the cutter alongside. Could Coleman
have been one of them ? *No,* for he was at the
gangway when the captain and officers went into
the launch, and aft upon the taffrail when the boat

was veered astern.   Could Norman have been one
of them? *No,* for he was speaking to the officers.
Could M'Intosh have been one of them? *No,* for
he was with Coleman and Norman, desiring the
captain and officers to take notice that they were
not concerned in the mutiny.   It could then have
applied to nobody but to Mr. Stewart and myself;
and by this order of Churchill, therefore, was I
prevented from going with the captain in the
boat.

' The foregoing appear to me the most material points of evidence on the part of the prosecu-
tion.   My defence being very full, and the body
of evidence in my favour too great to admit of
observation in this concise manner, I shall refer
for an opinion thereon to the minutes of the court-
martial.

(Signed)   ' P. HEYWOOD.

There is a note in Marshall's Naval Biography *,
furnished by Captain Heywood, which shews one
motive for keeping him and Stewart in the
ship.   It is as follows :—' Mr. Stewart was no
sooner released than he demanded of Christian the
reason of his detention; upon which the latter
denied having given any directions to that effect;
and his assertion was corroborated by Churchill,
who declared that he had kept both him and Mr.
Heywood below, knowing it was their intention
to go away with Bligh; " in which case," added
he, " what would become of us, if any thing should
happen to you; who is there but yourself and them
to depend upon in navigating the ship?" '   It
may be suspected, however, that neither Chris-

* Vol. ii., p. 778.

tian nor Churchill told the exact truth, and that
Mr. Heywood's case is, in point of fact, much
stronger than he ever could have imagined; and
that if Bligh had not acted the part of a preju-
diced and unfair man towards him, he would have
been acquitted by the court on the same ground
that Coleman, Norman, M'Intosh, and Byrne
were,—namely, that they were detained in the
ship against their will, as stated by Bligh in the
narrative on which they were tried, and also in his
printed report. It has before been observed, that
many things are set down in Bligh's original manuscript journal, that have not appeared in any published document; and on this part of the subject
there is, in the former, the following very important
admission. ' As for the officers, whose cabins
were in the cockpit, there was no relief for them ;
*they endeavoured to come to my assistance, but
were not allowed to put their heads above the
hatchway.*' To say, therefore, that in the suppression of this passage Bligh acted with prejudice and unfairness, is to make use of mild terms ;
it has more the appearance of a deliberate act of
malice, by which two innocent men might have
been condemned to suffer an ignominious death,
one of whom was actually brought into this predicament;—the other only escaped it by a premature
death. It may be asked, how did Bligh know that
Stewart and Heywood endeavoured, but were not
allowed, to come to his assistance ? Confined as he
was on the quarter-deck, how could he know what
was going on below ? The answer is, he must have
known it from Christian himself; Churchill, no
doubt, acted entirely by his leader's orders, and

the latter could give no orders that were not heard
by Bligh, whom he never left, but held the cord
by which his hands were fettered, till he was
forced into the boat. Churchill was quite right
as to the motive of keeping these young officers;
but Christian had no doubt another and a
stronger motive : he knew how necessary it was
to interpose a sort of barrier between himself
and his mutinous gang; he was too good an
adept not to know that seamen will always pay
a more ready and cheerful obedience to officers who are *gentlemen*, than to those who may
have risen to command from among themselves.
It is indeed a common observation in the service,
that officers who have risen from *before the mast*
are generally the greatest tyrants*. It was Bligh's
misfortune not to have been educated in the cockpit of a man of war, among young gentlemen,
which is to the navy what a public school is to
those who are to move in civil society. What
painful sufferings to the individual, and how much
misery to an affectionate family might have been
spared, had Bligh, instead of suppressing, only
suffered the passage to stand as originally written
in his journal!

The *remarks* of young Heywood above recited,
were received and transmitted by his sister Nessy

* Some few captains were in the habit of turning over a
delinquent to be tried by their messmates, and when found
guilty, it invariably happened that the punishment inflicted
was doubly severe to what it would have been in the ordinary way. This practice,—which, as giving a deliberative
voice to the ship's company, was highly reprehensible,—it is
to be hoped has entirely ceased.

in a letter to the Earl of Chatham, then first
Lord of the Admiralty, of which the following is
a copy.

' *Great Russell-Street*, 11*th Oct.* 1792.

' My Lord,
    ' To a nobleman of your lordship's known
humanity and excellence of heart, I dare hope
that the unfortunate cannot plead in vain. Deeply
impressed as I therefore am, with sentiments of
the most profound respect for a character which I
have been ever taught to revere, and alas ! nearly
interested as I must be in the subject of these
lines, may I request your lordship will generously
pardon a sorrowful and mourning sister, for presuming to offer the inclosed [remarks] for your
candid perusal. It contains a few observations
made by my most unfortunate and tenderly beloved
brother, Peter Heywood, endeavouring to elu-
cidate some parts of the evidence given at the
court-martial lately held at Portsmouth upon
himself and other prisoners of his Majesty's ship
Bounty. When I assure you, my lord, that he is
dearer and more precious to me than any object
on earth—nay, infinitely more valuable than life
itself—that, deprived of him, the word misery
would but ill express my complicated wretchedness
—and that, on his fate, my own, and (shall I not
add ?) that of a tender, fond, and alas ! widowed
mother, depends, I am persuaded you will not
wonder, nor be offended, that I am thus bold in
conjuring your lordship will consider, with your
usual candour and benevolence, the " Observa-

tions" I now offer you, as well as the painful situa-
tion of my dear and unhappy brother.
' I have the honour, &c.
' NESSY HEYWOOD.'

Whether this letter and its inclosure produced
any effect on the mind of Lord Chatham does not
appear; but no immediate steps were taken, nor
was any answer given; and this amiable young lady
and her friends were suffered to remain in the
most painful state of suspense for another fortnight. A day or two before the warrant was despatched, that excellent man, Mr. Graham, writes
thus to Mrs. Heywood.

' My dear Madam,
' If feeling for the distresses and rejoicing in
the happiness of others denote a heart which
entitles the owner of it to the confidence of the
good and virtuous, I would fain be persuaded that
mine has been so far interested in your misfortunes, and is now so pleased with the prospect of
your being made happy, as cannot fail to procure
me the friendship of your family, which, as it is
my ambition, it cannot cease to be my desire to
cultivate.
' Unused to the common rewards which are
sought after in this world, I will profess to anticipate more real pleasure and satisfaction from
the simple declaration of you and yours, that " we
accept of your services, and we thank you for
them," than it is in common minds to conceive;
but, fearful lest a too grateful sense should be entertained of the friendly offices I have been en-

gaged in, (which, however, I ought to confess, I
was prompted to, in the first place, by a remembrance of the many obligations I owed to Commodore Pasley,) I must beg you will recollect
that, by sending to me your charming Nessy, (and
if strong affection may plead such a privilege, I
may be allowed to call her *my* daughter also,)
you would have overpaid me if my trouble had
been ten times, and my uneasiness ten thousand
times greater than they were, upon what I once
thought the melancholy, but now deem the fortunate,
occasion which has given me the happiness of her
acquaintance.   Thus far, my dear Madam, I have
written to please myself.   Now, for what must
please you—and in which, too, I have my share of
satisfaction.

' The business, though not publicly known, is
most certainly finished, and what I had my doubts
about yesterday, I am satisfied of to-day.   Happy,
happy, happy family ! accept of my congratulations—not for what it is in the power of words to
express—but for what I know you will feel, upon
being told that your beloved Peter will soon be
restored to your bosom, with every virtue that
can adorn a man, and ensure to him an affectionate, a tender, and truly welcome reception.'

At the foot of this letter Nessy writes thus :—
' Now, my dearest mama, did you ever in all
your life read so charming a letter ? Be assured
it is exactly characteristic of the benevolent writer.
What would I give to be transported (though only
for a moment) to your elbow, that I might see
you read it ?   What will you feel, when you know
assuredly that you may with certainty believe its

contents ? Well may Mr. Graham call us happy!
for never felicity could equal ours ! Don't expect connected sentences from me at present, for
this joy makes me almost delirious.   Adieu ! love
to all—I need not say be happy and blessed as I
am at this dear hour, my beloved mother,

' Your most affectionate,

' N. H.'

On the 24th October, the king's warrant was
despatched from the Admiralty, granting a full
and free pardon to Heywood and Morrison, a
respite for Muspratt, which was followed by a pardon ; and for carrying the sentence of Ellison,
Burkitt, and Millward into execution, which was
done on the 29th, on board his Majesty's ship
Brunswick, in Portsmouth harbour.   On this melancholy occasion, Captain Hamond reports that
' the criminals behaved with great penitence and
decorum, acknowledged the justice of their sentence for the crime of which they had been found
guilty, and exhorted their fellow-sailors to take
warning by their untimely fate, and whatever
might be their hardships, never to forget their
obedience to their officers, as a duty they owed to
their king and country.'   The captain adds, ' A
party from each ship in the harbour, and at Spithead, attended the execution, and from the reports
I have received, the example seems to have made
a great impression upon the minds of all the
ships' companies present.'

The same warrant that carried with it affliction
to the friends of these unfortunate men, was the
harbinger of joy to the family and friends of young

Heywood. The happy intelligence was communi‑ cated to his affectionate Nessy on the 26th, who in‑ stantly despatched the joyful tidings to her anxious mother in the following characteristic note :—

' *Friday, 26th October, four o'clock.*

' Oh, blessed hour!—little did I think, my be‑ loved friends, when I closed my letter this morn‑ ing, that before night I should be out of my senses with joy!—this moment, this extatic moment, brought the inclosed*. I cannot speak my happi‑ ness; let it be sufficient to say, that in a very few hours our angel Peter will be FREE! Mr. Graham goes this night to Portsmouth, and to-morrow, or next day at farthest, I shall be—oh, heavens! what shall I be? I am already transported, even to pain; then how shall I bear to clasp him to the bosom of your happy, ah! how very happy, and affectionate   ' NESSY HEYWOOD.'

' I am too *mad* to write sense, but 'tis a plea‑ sure I would not forego to be the most reasonable being on earth. I asked Mr. Graham, who is at my elbow, if he would say anything to you, " Lord!" said he, " I can't say anything;" he is almost as mad as myself †.'

* Information that the pardon was gone down to Ports‑ mouth.

† She had received, previous to this, information of what the event would be, and thus gives vent to her feelings.

' *On receiving certain Intelligence that my most amiable and beloved Brother, Peter Heywood, would soon be restored to Freedom.*

' Oh, blissful hour!—oh moment of delight! Replete with happiness, with rapture bright!

Mr. Graham writes, ' I have however my senses sufficiently about me not to suffer this to go without begging leave to congratulate you upon, and to assure you that I most sincerely sympathize and participate in, the happiness which I am sure

An age of pain is sure repaid by this,
'Tis joy too great—'tis extasy of bliss !
Ye sweet sensations crowding on my soul,
Which following each other swiftly roll,—
Ye dear ideas which unceasing press,
And pain this bosom by your wild excess,
Ah ! kindly cease—for pity's sake subside,
Nor thus o'erwhelm me with joy's rapid tide :
My beating heart, oppress'd with woe and care,
Has yet to learn such happiness to bear:
From grief, distracting grief, thus high to soar,
To know dull pain and misery no more,
To hail each op'ning morn with new delight,
To rest in peace and joy each happy night,
To see my Lycidas from bondage free,
Restored to life, to pleasure, and to me,
To see him thus—adorn'd with virtue's charms,
To give him to a longing mother's arms,
To know him by surrounding friends caress'd,
Of honour, fame, of life's best gifts possess'd,
Oh, my full heart ! 'tis joy—'tis bliss supreme,
And though 'tis real—yet, how like a dream !
Teach me then, Heav'n, to bear it as I ought,
Inspire each rapt'rous, each transporting thought ;
Teach me to bend beneath thy bounteous hand,
With gratitude my willing heart expand :
To thy omnipotence I humbly bow,
Afflicted once—but ah ! how happy now !
Restored in peace, submissive to thy will,
Oh ! bless his days to come—protect him still ;
Prolong his life, thy goodness to adore,
And oh ! let sorrow's shafts ne'er wound him more.
                                        ' NESSY HEYWOOD.'

London, October 15th, 1792, Midnight.

T

the inclosed will convey to the mother and sisters of my charming and beloved Nessy.'

This ' charming' girl next writes to Mr. Const, who attended as counsel for her brother, to acquaint him with the joyful intelligence, and thus concludes. ' I flatter myself you will partake in the joy which, notwithstanding it is so excessive at this moment, as almost to deprive me of my faculties, leaves me however sufficiently collected to assure you of the eternal gratitude and esteem with which I am, &c.'

To which Mr. Const, after congratulations and thanks for her polite attention, observes, ' Give me leave, my dear Miss Heywood, to assure you that the intelligence has given me a degree of pleasure which I have not terms to express, and it is even increased by knowing what you must experience on the event. Nor is it an immaterial reflection, that although your brother was unfortunately involved in the general calamity which gave birth to the charge, he is uncontaminated by the crime, for there was not a credible testimony of the slightest fact against him that can make the strictest friend deplore anything that has passed, except his sufferings; and his uniform conduct under them only proved how little he deserved them.'

Mr. Graham's impatience and generous anxiety to give the finishing stroke to this joyful event would not permit him to delay one moment in setting out for Portsmouth, and bringing up to his house in town the innocent sufferer, where they arrived on the morning of the 29th October. Miss Heywood can best speak her own feelings.

'Great Russell Street, Monday Morning,
29th October, half past ten o'clock—
the brightest moment of my existence!

'My dearest Mama, I have seen him, clasped
him to my bosom, and my felicity is beyond expression! In person he is almost even now as I
could wish; in mind you know him an angel. I
can write no more, but to tell you, that the three
happiest beings at this moment on earth, are your
most dutiful and affectionate children,

'NESSY HEYWOOD.
'PETER HEYWOOD.
'JAMES HEYWOOD.
'· Love to and from all ten thousand times.'

The worthy Mr. Graham adds, 'If, my dearest
Madam, it were ever given for mortals to be su-
premely blest on earth, mine to be sure must be
the happy family. Heavens! with what unbounded extravagance have we been forming our
wishes! and yet how far beyond our most unbounded wishes we are blest! Nessy, Maria*, Peter
and James, I see, have all been endeavouring to
express their feelings. I will not fail in any such
attempt, for I will not attempt anything beyond
an assurance that the scene I have been witness of,
and in which I am happily so great a sharer, beg-
gars all description. Permit me however to offer
my most sincere congratulations upon the joyful
occasion.'

This amiable young lady, some of whose letters
have been introduced into this narrative, did not
long survive her brother's liberty. This impas-

Mr. Graham's daughter.

T 2

sioned and most affectionate of sisters, with an excess of sensibility, which acted too powerfully on her bodily frame, sunk, as is often the case with such susceptible minds, on the first attack of consumption. She died within the year of her brother's liberation. On this occasion the following note from her afflicted mother appears among the papers from which the letters and poetry are taken. ' My dearest Nessy was seized, while on a visit at Major Yorke's, at Bishop's Grove near Tonbridge Wells, with a violent cold, and not taking proper care of herself, it soon turned to inflammation on her lungs, which carried her off at Hastings, to which place she was taken on the 5th September, to try if the change of air, and being near the sea, would recover her ; but alas! it was too late for her to receive the wished for benefit, and she died there on the 25th of the same month 1793, and has left her only surviving parent a disconsolate mother, to lament, while ever she lives, with the most sincere and deep affliction, the irreparable loss of her most valuable, affectionate and darling daughter*.'

* Several elegiac stanzas were written on the death of this accomplished young lady. The following are dated from her native place, the Isle of Man, where her virtues and accomplishments could best be appreciated.

' How soon, sweet maid ! how like a fleeting dream
The winning graces, all thy virtues seem !
How soon arrested in thy early bloom
Has fate decreed thee to the joyless tomb !
Nor beauty, genius, nor the muse's care,
Nor aught could move the tyrant Death to spare :
Ah ! could their power revoke the stern decree,
The fatal shaft had past, unfelt by thee !

But to return to Mr. Heywood. When the king's full and free pardon had been read to this young officer by Captain Montagu, with a suitable admonition and congratulation, he addressed that officer in the following terms,—so suitably characteristic of his noble and manly conduct throughout the whole of the distressing business in which he was innocently involved :—

' Sir,—When the sentence of the law was passed upon me, I received it, I trust, as became a man ; and if it had been carried into execution, I should have met my fate, I hope, in a manner becoming a Christian. Your admonition cannot fail to make a lasting impression on my mind. I receive with gratitude my sovereign's mercy, for which my future life shall be faithfully devoted to his service*.'

> But vain thy wit, thy sentiment refined,
> Thy charms external, and accomplish'd mind;
> Thy artless smiles, that seized the willing heart,
> Thy converse, that could pure delight impart;
> The melting music of thy skilful tongue,
> While judgment listen'd, ravish'd with thy song:
> Not all the gifts that art and nature gave,
> Could save thee, lovely Nessy! from the grave.
>   Too early lost! from friendship's bosom torn,
> Oh might I tune *thy* lyre, and sweetly mourn
> In strains like thine, when beauteous Margaret's(a) fate
> Oppress'd thy friendly heart with sorrow's weight;
> Then should my numbers flow, and laurels bloom
> In endless spring around fair Nessy's tomb.

(a) Alluding to some elegant lines, by the deceased, on the death of a female friend.

* The following appears to have been written by Mr. P. Heywood on the day that the sentence of condemnation was passed on him.
                                        ' ———— Silence then
   The whispers of complaint,—low in the dust

And well did his future conduct fulfil that promise. Notwithstanding the inauspicious manner
in which the first five years of his servitude in the
navy had been passed, two of which were spent

> Dissatisfaction's dæmon's growl unheard.
> All—all is good, all excellent below;
> Pain is a blessing—sorrow leads to joy—
> Joy, permanent and solid! ev'ry ill,
> Grim death itself, in all its horrors clad,
> Is man's supremest privilege! it frees
> The soul from prison, from foul sin, from woe,
> And gives it back to glory, rest, and God!
> Cheerly, my friends,—oh, cheerly! look not thus
> With Pity's melting softness!—that alone
> Can shake my fortitude—all is not lost.
> Lo! I have gain'd on this important day
> A victory consummate o'er myself,
> And o'er this life a victory,—on this day,
> My birthday to eternity, I've gain'd
> Dismission from a world, where for a while,
> Like you, like all, a pilgrim, passing poor,
> A traveller, a stranger, I have met
> Still stranger treatment, rude and harsh! so much
> The dearer, more desired, the home I seek,
> Eternal of my Father, and my God!
> Then pious Resignation, meek-ey'd pow'r,
> Sustain me still!   Composure still be mine.
> Where rests it?   Oh, mysterious Providence!
> Silence the wild idea.—I have found
> No mercy yet—no mild humanity,
> With cruel, unrelenting rigour torn,
> And lost in prison—lost to all below!'

And the following appears to have been written on the
day of the king's pardon being received.

>   '———— Oh deem it not
> Presumptuous, that my soul grateful thus rates
> The present high deliv'rance it hath found;—
> Sole effort of thy wisdom, sov'reign Pow'r,
> Without whose knowledge, not a sparrow falls!
> Oh! may I cease to live, ere cease to bless

among mutineers and savages, and eighteen
months as a close prisoner in irons, in which condition he was shipwrecked, and within an ace of
perishing,— notwithstanding this unpromising
commencement, he re-entered the naval service
under the auspices of his uncle, Commodore
Pasley, and Lord Hood, who presided at his trial,
and who earnestly recommended him to embark
again as a midshipman without delay, offering to
take him into the Victory, under his own immediate patronage.   In the course of his service, to
qualify for the commission of lieutenant, he was
under the respective commands of three or four
distinguished officers, who had sat on his trial,
from all of whom he received the most flattering
proofs of esteem and approbation.   To the application of Sir Thomas Pasley to Lord Spencer, for
his promotion, that nobleman, with that due regard he was always known to pay to the honour
and interests of the navy, while individual claims
were never overlooked, gave the following reply,
which must have been highly gratifying to the
feelings of Mr. Heywood and his family.

Admiralty, Jan. 13th, 1797.
' Sir,
    ' I should have returned an earlier answer to
your letter of the 6th instant, if I had not been
desirous, before I answered it, to look over, with

That interposing hand, which turn'd aside—
Nay, to my life and preservation turn'd,—
The fatal blow precipitate, ordain'd
To level all my little hopes in dust,
And give me—to the grave.

as much attention as was in my power, the proceedings on the Court-Martial held in the year 1792, by which Court Mr. Peter Heywood was condemned for being concerned in the mutiny on board the Bounty. I felt this to be necessary, from having entertained a very strong opinion that it might be detrimental to the interests of his Majesty's service, if a person under such a predicament should be afterwards advanced to the higher and more conspicuous situations of the navy; but having, with great attention, perused the minutes of that Court-Martial, as far as they relate to Mr. Peter Heywood, I have now the satisfaction of being able to inform you, that I think his case was such an one, as, under all its circumstances, (though I do not mean to say that the Court were not justified in their sentence,) ought not to be considered as a bar to his further progress in his profession; more especially when the gallantry and propriety of his conduct, in his subsequent service, are taken into consideration. I shall, therefore, have no difficulty in mentioning him to the commander-in-chief on the station to which he belongs, as a person from whose promotion, on a proper opportunity, I shall derive much satisfaction, more particularly from his being so nearly connected with you.

'I have the honour to be, &c.

(Signed)   'SPENCER.'

It is not here intended to follow Mr. Heywood through his honourable career of service, during the long and arduous contest with France, and in the several commands with which he was entrusted.

In a note of his own writing it is stated, that on paying off the Montague, in July, 1816, he came on shore, after having been actively employed *at sea* twenty-seven years, six months, one week, and five days, out of a servitude in the navy of twenty-nine years, seven months, and one day. Having reached nearly the top of the list of captains, he died in this present year, leaving behind him a high and unblemished character in that service, of which he was a most honourable, intelligent, and distinguished member.

CHAPTER VIII.

THE LAST OF THE MUTINEERS.

Who by repentance is not satisfied,
Is nor of heaven nor earth; for these are pleased;
By penitence th' Eternal's wrath 's appeased.

TWENTY years had passed away, and the Bounty, and Fletcher Christian, and the piratical crew that he had carried off with him in that ship, had long ceased to occupy a thought in the public mind. Throughout the whole of that eventful period, the attention of all Europe had been absorbed in the contemplation of ' enterprizes of great pith and moment,'—of the revolutions of. empires— the bustle and business of warlike preparations —the movements of hostile armies—battles by sea and land, and of all ' the pomp and cir- cumstance of glorious war.' If the subject of the Bounty was accidentally mentioned, it was merely to express an opinion that this vessel, and those within her, had gone down to the bottom, or.that some savage islanders had inflicted on the mutineers that measure of retribution so justly due to their crime. It happened, however, some years before the conclusion of this war of unexampled duration, that an accidental discovery, as interesting as it was wholly unexpected, was brought to light, in consequence of an American trading vessel having by mere chance approached one of those numerous islands in the Pacific, against whose steep and iron-bound shores the surf almost everlastingly rolls with such tremendous violence, as to bid defiance to any attempt of boats to land, except at particular times and in very few places.

The first intimation of this extraordinary discovery was transmitted by Sir Sydney Smith from Rio de Janeiro, and received at the Admiralty, 14th May, 1809. It was conveyed to him from Valparaiso by Lieutenant Fitzmaurice, and was as follows :—

' Captain Folger, of the American ship Topaz, of Boston, relates that, upon landing on Pitcairn's Island, in lat. 25° 2' S., long. 130° W., he found there an Englishman of the name of Alexander Smith, the only person remaining of nine that escaped in his Majesty's late ship Bounty, Captain W. Bligh. Smith relates that, after putting Captain Bligh in the boat, Christian, the leader of the mutiny, took command of the ship and went to Otaheité, where great part of the crew left her, except Christian, Smith, and seven others, who each took wives, and six Otaheitean men-servants, and shortly after arrived at the said island (Pitcairn), where they ran the ship on shore, and broke her up; this event took place in the year 1790.

' About four years after their arrival (a great jealousy existing), the Otaheiteans secretly revolted, and killed every Englishman except himself, whom they severely wounded in the neck with a pistol ball. The same night, the widows of the deceased Englishmen arose and put to death the whole of the Otaheitans, leaving Smith the only man alive upon the island, with eight or nine women and several small children. On his recovery, he applied himself to tilling the ground, so that it now produces plenty of yams, cocoa-nuts, bananas and plantains; hogs and poultry in abundance. There are now some grown up men and women, children of the mutineers, on the island, the whole population amounting to about thirty-five, who acknowledge Smith as father and commander of them all; they all speak English, and have been educated by him (as Captain Folger represents) in a religious and moral way.

'The second mate of the Topaz asserts that Christian, the ringleader, became insane shortly after their arrival on the island, and threw him-self off the rocks into the sea; another died of a fever before the massacre of the remaining six took place. The island is badly supplied with water, sufficient only for the present inhabitants, and no anchorage.

'Smith gave to Captain Folger a chronometer made by Kendall, which was taken from him by the Governor of Juan Fernandez.

'Extracted from the log-book of the Topaz, 29th Sept. 1808.

(Signed)   'WM. FITZMAURICE, Lieut.
'Valparaiso, Oct. 10th, 1808.'

This narrative stated two facts that established its general authenticity—the name of Alexander

Smith, who was one of the mutineers, and the name of the maker of the chronometer, with which the Bounty was actually supplied. Interesting as this discovery was considered to be, it does not appear that any steps were taken in consequence of this authenticated information, the government being at that time probably too much engaged in the events of the war; nor was anything further heard of this interesting little society, until the latter part of 1814, when a letter was transmitted by Rear Admiral Hotham, then cruizing off the coast of America, from Mr. Folger himself, to the same effect as the preceding extract from his log, but dated March, 1813.

In the first-mentioned year (1814) we had two frigates cruizing in the Pacific,—the Briton, commanded by Sir Thomas Staines, and the Tagus, by Captain Pipon. The following letter from the former of these officers was received at the Admiralty early in the year 1815.

'*Briton, Valparaiso, 18th Oct.*, 1814.

' I have the honour to inform you that on my passage from the Marquesas islands to this port, on the morning of the 17th September, I fell in with an island where none is laid down in the Admiralty or other charts, according to the several chronometers of the Briton and Tagus. I therefore hove to, until day-light, and then closed to ascertain whether it was inhabited, which I soon discovered it to be, and, to my great astonishment, found that every individual on the island (forty in number), spoke very good English. They proved to be the descendants of the deluded crew of the

Bounty, who, from Otaheité, proceeded to the above-mentioned island, where the ship was burnt.

' Christian appeared to have been the leader and sole cause of the mutiny in that ship. A venerable old man, named John Adams, is the only surviving Englishman of those who last quitted Otaheité in her, and whose exemplary conduct, and fatherly care of the whole of the little colony, could not but command admiration. The pious manner in which all those born on the island have been reared, the correct sense of religion which has been instilled into their young minds by this old man, has given him the pre-eminence over the whole of them, to whom they look up as the father of one and the whole family.

' A son of Christian was the first born on the island, now about twenty-five years of age, named Thursday October Christian ; the elder Christian fell a sacrifice to the jealousy of an Otaheitan man, within three or four years after their arrival on the island. The mutineers were accompanied thither by six Otaheitan men and twelve women ; the former were all swept away by desperate contentions between them and the Englishmen, and five of the latter died at different periods, leaving at present only one man (Adams) and seven women of the original settlers.

' The island must undoubtedly be that called Pitcairn, although erroneously laid down in the charts. We had the altitude of the meridian sun close to it, which gave us 25° 4′ S. latitude, and 130° 25′ W. longitude, by the chronometers of the Briton and Tagus.

' It produces in abundance yams, plantains,

hogs, goats, and fowls; but the coast affords no shelter for a ship or vessel of any description; neither could a ship water there without great difficulty.

' I cannot, however, refrain from offering my opinion, that it is well worthy the attention of our laudable religious societies, particularly that for propagating the Christian religion, the whole of the inhabitants speaking the Otaheitan tongue as well as the English.

' During the whole of the time they have been on the island, only one ship has ever communicated with them, which took place about six years since, and this was the American ship Topaz, of Boston, Mayhew Folger, master.

' The island is completely iron-bound with rocky shores, and the landing in boats must be at all times difficult, although the island may be safely approached within a short distance by a ship.   (Signed)   ' T. STAINES.'

Such was the first official account received of this little colony. As some further particulars of a society so singular, in all respects, were highly desirable, Captain Pipon, on being applied to, had the kindness to draw up the following narrative, which has all the freshness and attraction of a first communication with a new people.

Captain Pipon takes a more extended view, in his private letter*, of the condition of this little society. He observes, that when they first saw the island, the latitude, made by the Tagus, was

* With which the Editor, at his request, was favoured at the time.

24° 40′ S. and longitude 130° 24′ W., the ships being then distant from it five or six leagues; and, as in none of the charts in their possession was any land laid down in or near this meridian, they were extremely puzzled to make out what island it could possibly be; for Pitcairn's Island, being the only one known in the neighbourhood, was represented to be in longitude 133° 24′ W.* If this new discovery, as they supposed it to be, awakened their curiosity, it was still more excited when they ran in for the land the next morning, on perceiving a few huts, neatly built, amidst plantations laid out apparently with something like order and regularity; and these appearances confirmed them more than ever that it could not be Pitcairn's Island, because that was described by navigators to be uninhabited. Presently they observed a few natives coming down a steep de-

* The only authority that then existed for laying down this island was that of Captain Carteret, who first saw it in 1767. ' It is so high,' he says, 'that we saw it at the distance of more than fifteen leagues, and it having been discovered by a young gentleman, son to Major Pitcairn of the marines, who was unfortunately lost in the Aurora, we called it *Pitcairn's Island.*' He makes it in lat. 25° 2′ S. and long. 133° 30′ W., no less than *three degrees* out of its true longitude! *Three minutes* would *now* be thought a considerable error:—such are the superior advantages conferred by lunar observations and improvements in chronometers.

Pitcairn's Island has been supposed to be the ' *Encarnaçion*' of Quiros, by whom it is stated to be in lat. 24° 30′, and one thousand leagues from the coast of Peru; but as he describes it as ' a low, sandy island, almost level with the sea, having a few trees on it,' we must look for ' *Encarnaçion*' somewhere else; and *Ducies* Island, nearly in that latitude, very low, and within 5° of longitude from Pitcairn's Island, answers precisely to it.

scent with their canoes on their shoulders; and in a few minutes perceived one of those little vessels darting through a heavy surf, and paddling off towards the ships ; but their astonishment was extreme when, on coming alongside, they were hailed in the English language with ' Won't you heave us a rope now?'

The first young man that sprung, with extraordinary alacrity, up the side, and stood before them on the deck, said, in reply to the question, ' Who are you?'—that his name was Thursday October Christian, son of the late Fletcher Christian, by an Otaheitan mother; that he was the first born on the island, and that he was so called because he was brought into the world on a Thursday in October. Singularly strange as all this was to Sir Thomas Staines and Captain Pipon, this youth soon satisfied them that he was no other than the person he represented himself to be, and that he was fully acquainted with the whole history of the Bounty ; and, in short, that the island before them was the retreat of the mutineers of that ship. Young Christian was, at this time, about twenty-four years of age, a fine tall youth, full six feet high, with dark, almost black, hair, and a countenance open and extremely interesting. As he wore no clothes except a piece of cloth round his loins, and a straw hat, ornamented with black cock's-feathers, his fine figure and well-shaped muscular limbs were displayed to great advantage, and attracted general admiration. His body was much tanned by exposure to the weather, and his countenance had a brownish cast,

U

unmixed however with that tinge of red so common among the natives of the Pacific islands.

' Added to a great share of good humour, we were glad to trace,' says Captain Pipon, ' in his benevolent countenance, all the features of an honest English face.' He told them he was married to a woman much older than himself, one of those that accompanied his father from Otaheite. The ingenuous manner in which he answered all questions put to him, and his whole deportment, created a lively interest among the officers of the ship, who, while they admired, could not but regard him with feelings of tenderness and compassion; his manner, too, of speaking English was exceedingly pleasing, and correct both in grammar and pronunciation. His companion was a fine handsome youth of seventeen or eighteen years of age, of the name of George Young, son of Young the midshipman.

If the astonishment of the two captains was great on making, as they thought, this first and extraordinary discovery of a people who had been so long forgotten, and in hearing the offspring of these offenders speaking their language correctly, their surprise and interest were still more highly excited when, on Sir Thomas Staines taking the two youths below, and setting before them something to eat, they both rose up, and one of them, placing his hands together in a posture of devotion, pronounced, distinctly and with emphasis, in a pleasing tone of voice, the words, ' For what we are going to receive the Lord make us truly thankful.'

The youths were themselves greatly surprised at the sight of so many novel objects—the size of the ship—of the guns, and everything around them.   Observing a cow, they were at first somewhat alarmed, and expressed a doubt whether it was a huge goat or a horned hog, these being the only two species of quadrupeds they had ever seen.   A little dog amused them much.   'Oh! what a pretty little thing it is!' exclaimed Young. ' I know it is a dog, for I have heard of such an animal.'

These young men informed the two captains of many singular events that had taken place among the first settlers, but referred them for further particulars to an old man on shore, whose name, they said, was John Adams, the only surviving Englishman that came away in the Bounty, at which time he was called Alexander Smith.

This information induced the two captains to go on shore, desirous of learning correctly from this old man the fate, not only of Christian, but of the rest of his deluded accomplices, who had adhered to his fortunes.   The landing they found to be difficult, and not wholly free from danger; but, with the assistance of their two able conductors, they passed the surf among many rocks, and reached the shore without any other inconvenience than a complete wetting.   Old Adams, having ascertained that the two officers alone had landed, and without arms, concluded they had no intention to take him prisoner, and ventured to come down to the beach, from whence he conducted them to his house.   He was accompanied by his wife, a very old woman, and nearly blind.   It seems they

were both at first considerably alarmed; the sight
of the king's uniform, after so many years, having
no doubt brought fresh to the recollection of
Adams the scene that occurred in the Bounty, in
which he bore so conspicuous a part. Sir Thomas
Staines, however, to set his mind at ease, assured
him, that so far from having come to the island
with any intention to take him away, they were
not even aware that such a person as himself
existed. Captain Pipon observes, ' that although
in the eye of the law they could only consider him
in the light of a criminal of the deepest dye, yet
that it would have been an act of the greatest
cruelty and inhumanity to have taken him away
from his little family, who, in such a case, would
have been left to experience the greatest misery
and distress, and ultimately, in all probability,
would have perished of want.

Adams, however, pretended that he had no great
share in the mutiny: said that he was sick in bed
when it broke out, and was afterwards compelled
to take a musket in his hand; and expressed his
readiness to go in one of the ships to England, and
seemed rather desirous to do so. On this being
made known to the members of the little society, a
scene of considerable distress was witnessed; his
daughter, a fine young woman, threw her arms
about his neck, entreating him not to think of
leaving them and all his little children to perish.
All the women burst into tears, and the young men
stood motionless and absorbed in grief; but on
their being assured that he should, on no account,
be molested, ' it is impossible,' says Captain Pipon,
' to describe the universal joy that these poor

people manifested, and the gratitude they expressed for the kindness and consideration shewn to them.'

They now learned from Adams that Fletcher Christian, on finding no good anchorage close to the island, and the Bounty being too weakly manned again to intrust themselves in her at sea, determined to run her into a small creek against the cliff, in order the more conveniently to get out of her such articles as might be of use, or necessary, for forming an establishment on the island, and to land the hogs, goats, and poultry, which they had brought from Otaheité; and having ac-. complished this point he ordered her to be set on fire, with the view, probably, of preventing any escape from the island, and also to remove an object that, if seen, might excite the curiosity of some passing vessel, and thus be the means of discovering his retreat. His plan succeeded, and by Adams's account, everything went on smoothly for a short time; but it was clear enough that this misguided and ill-fated young man was never happy after the rash and criminal step he had taken; that he was always sullen and morose; and committed so many acts of wanton oppression, as very soon incurred the hatred and detestation of his companions in crime, over whom he practised that same overbearing conduct, of which he accused his commander Bligh. The object he had in view when he last left Otaheité had now been accomplished; he had discovered an uninhabited island out of the common track of ships, and established himself and his associates; so far there was a chance that he had escaped all pursuit ; but there was no escaping from

> ' Those rods of scorpions and those whips of steel
> Which conscience shakes.'

The fate of this misguided young man, brought on by his ill-treatment both of his associates and the Indians he had carried off with him, was such as might be expected—he was shot by an Otaheitán while digging in his field, about eleven months after they had settled on the island, and his death was only the commencement of feuds and assassinations, which ended in the total destruction of the whole party, except Adams and Young. By the account of the former, the settlers from this time became divided into two parties, and their grievances and quarrels proceeded to such a height, that each took every opportunity of putting the other to death. Old John Adams was himself shot through the neck, but the ball having entered the fleshy part only, he was enabled to make his escape, and avoid the fury of his assailants. The immediate cause of Christian's murder was his having forcibly seized on the wife of one of the Otaheité men, which so exasperated the rest, that they not only sought the life of the offender, but of others also, who might, as they thought, be disposed to pursue the same course.

This interesting little colony was now found to contain about forty-six persons, mostly grown-up young people, with a few infants. The young men all born on the island were finely formed, athletic and handsome—their countenances open and pleasing, indicating much benevolence and goodness of heart, but the young women particularly were objects of attraction, being tall, robust, and beautifully formed, their faces beaming with smiles, and indicating unruffled good humour; while their manners and demeanour exhibited a degree of modesty and bashfulness, that would have done honour to the most virtuous and enlightened people on earth. Their teeth are described as beautifully white, like the finest ivory, and perfectly regular, without a single exception; and all of them, both male and female, had the marked expression of English features, though not exactly the clear red and white, that distinguish English skins, theirs being the colour of what we call brunette. Captain Pipon thinks that from such a race of people, consisting of fine young men and handsome well-formed women, there may be expected to arise hereafter, in this little colony, a race of people possessing in a high degree the physical qualifications of great strength, united with symmetry of form and regularity of feature.

But their personal qualifications, attractive as they were, excited less admiration than the account which Adams gave of their virtuous conduct. He assured his visiters that not one instance of debauchery or immoral conduct had occurred among these young people, since their settlement on the island; nor did he ever hear, or believe, that any one instance had occurred of a young woman having suffered indecent liberties to be taken with her. Their native modesty, assisted by the precepts of religion and morality, instilled into their young minds by John Adams, had hitherto preserved these interesting people from every kind of debauchery. The young women told Captain Pipon, with great simplicity, that they were not married, and that their father, as they called Adams, had told them it was right they should wait with patience till they had acquired sufficient property to bring up a young family, before they thought of marrying; and that they always followed his advice because they knew it to be good.

It appeared that, from the time when Adams was left alone on the island, the sole survivor of all the males that had landed from the Bounty, European and Otaheitan, the greatest harmony had prevailed in their little society; they all declared that no serious quarrels ever occurred among them, though a few hasty words might now and then be uttered, but, to make use of their own expression, they were only quarrels of the mouth. Adams assured his visiters that they were all strictly honest in all their dealings, lending or exchanging their various articles of live-stock or produce with each other, in the most friendly manner; and if any little dispute occurred, he never found any difficulty to rectify the mistake or misunderstanding that might have caused it, to the satisfaction of both parties. In their general intercourse they speak the English language commonly; and even the old Otaheitan women have picked up a good deal of this language. The young people, both male and female, speak it with a pleasing accent, and their voices are extremely harmonious.

The little village of Pitcairn is described as forming a pretty square; the house of John

Adams, with its out-houses, occupying the upper corner, near a large banian tree, and that of Thursday October Christian the lower corner opposite to it. The centre space is a fine open lawn, where the poultry wander, and is fenced round so as to prevent the intrusion of the hogs and goats. It was obviously visible, from the manner in which the grounds were laid out, and the plantations formed that, in this little establishment, the labour and ingenuity of European hands had been employed. In their houses they have a good deal of decent furniture, consisting of beds and bedsteads, with coverings. They have also tables and large chests for their clothing; and their linen is made from the bark of a certain tree, and the manufacture of it is the employment of the elderly portion of the women. The bark is first soaked, then beaten with square pieces of wood, of the breadth of one's hand, hollowed out into grooves, and the labour is continued until it is brought to the breadth required, in the same manner as the process is conducted in Otaheité.

The younger part of the females are obliged to attend, with old Adams and their brothers, to the culture of the land, and Captain Pipon thinks this may be one reason why this old director of the work does not countenance too early marriages, for, as he very properly observed, when once they become mothers, they are less capable of hard labour, being obliged to attend to their children; and judging from appearance, ' one may conclude,' says the Captain, ' they would be prolific;' that ' he did not see how it could be otherwise, considering the regularity of their lives,

their simple and excellent though abstemious mode
of living, their meals consisting chiefly of a vegetable diet, with now and then good pork and occasionally fish.'

The young girls, although they have only the
example of their Otaheitan mothers to follow in
their dress, are modestly clothed, having generally a piece of cloth of their own manufacture,
reaching from the waist to the knees, and a
mantle, or something of that nature, thrown
loosely over the shoulders, and hanging sometimes as low as the ancles : this mantle, however,
is frequently thrown aside, being used rather as a
shelter for their bodies from the heat of the sun,
or the severity of the weather, than for the sake
of attaching any idea of modesty to the upper part
of the person being uncovered ; and it is not
possible, he says, to behold finer forms than are
exhibited by this partial exposure.   Captain Pipon
observes, ' it was pleasing to see the good taste and
quickness with which they form little shades or
parasols of green leaves, to place over the head or
bonnets, to keep the sun from their eyes. A young
girl made one of these in my presence, with such
neatness and alacrity, as to satisfy me that a
fashionable dress-maker of London would be delighted with the simplicity and elegant taste of
these untaught females.'   The same young girl,
he says, accompanied them to the boat, carrying
on her shoulders, as a present, a large basket of
yams, ' over such roads and down such precipices,
as were scarcely passable by any creatures except
goats, and over which we could scarcely scramble
with the help of our hands.   Yet with this load

on her shoulders, she skipped from rock to rock like a young roe.'

' But,' says Captain Pipon, ' what delighted us most, was the conviction which John Adams had impressed on the minds of these young people, of the propriety and necessity of returning thanks to the Almighty for the many blessings they enjoy. They never omit saying grace before and after meals, and never think of touching food without asking a blessing from Him who gave it. The Lord's Prayer and the Creed they repeat morning and evening.'

Captain Pipon imagines the island to be about six miles long, and perhaps three or four miles broad, covered with wood; the soil apparently very rich, and the variety of products great and valuable, but much labour would seem to be required to clear away the woods. The dimensions here given, however, are much greater than they have subsequently been found to be.

The visiters having supplied these poor people with some tools, kettles, and other articles, such as the high surf would allow them, with the assistance of the natives, to land, but to no great extent, the two officers again passed through the surf, with the same assistance, and took leave of these interesting people—satisfied that the island is so well fortified by nature, as to oppose an invincible barrier to an invading enemy; that there was no spot apparently where a boat could land with safety, and perhaps not more than one where it could land at all; an everlasting swell of the ocean, rolling in on every side, is dashed into foam against its rocky and iron-bound shores.

Such were the first details that were received respecting this young settlement. It may here be remarked that, at the time when Folger visited the island, Alexander Smith went by his proper name, and that he had changed it to John Adams in the intermediate time between his visit and that of Sir Thomas Staines; but it does not appear, in any of the accounts which have been given of this interesting little colony, when or for what reason he assumed the latter name. It could not be with any view to concealment, for he freely communicated his history to Folger, and equally so to every subsequent visiter.

The interesting account of Captains Sir Thomas Staines and Pipon, in 1814, produced as little effect on the government as that of Folger; and nothing more was heard of Adams and his family for twelve years nearly, when, in 1825, Captain Beechey, in the Blossom, bound on a voyage of discovery, paid a visit to Pitcairn's Island. Some whale-fishing ship, however, had touched there in the intermediate time, and left on the island a person of the name of John Buffet. ' In this man,' says Captain Beechey, ' they have very fortunately found an able and willing schoolmaster; he had belonged to a ship which visited the island, and was so infatuated with the behaviour of the people, being himself naturally of a devout and serious turn of mind, that he resolved to remain among them; and, in addition to the instruction of the children, has taken upon himself the duty of clergyman, and is the oracle of the community.'

On the approach of the Blossom towards the island, a boat was observed, under all sail, hasten-

ing towards the ship, which they considered to be
the boat of some whaler, but were soon agreeably
undeceived by the singular appearance of her
crew, which consisted of old Adams and many of
the young men belonging to the island. They did
not venture at once to lay hold of the ship till they
had first inquired if they might come on board,
and on permission being granted, they sprung up
the side and shook every officer by the hand with
undisguised feelings of gratification.

The activity of the young men, ten in number,
outstripped that of old Adams, who was in his
sixty-fifth year, and somewhat corpulent. He
was dressed in a sailor's shirt and trowsers, and a
low-crowned hat, which he held in his hand until
desired to put it on. He still retained his sailor's
manners, doffing his hat and smoothing down his
bald forehead whenever he was addressed by the
officers of the Blossom.

The young men were tall, robust, and healthy,
with good-natured countenances, and a simplicity
of manner, and a fear of doing something that
might be wrong, which at once prevented the
possibility of giving offence. Their dresses were
whimsical enough; some had long coats without
trowsers, and others trowsers without coats, and
others again waistcoats without either. None of
them had either shoes or stockings, and there
were only two hats among them, ' neither of
which,' Captain Beechey says, ' seemed likely to
hang long together.'

Captain Beechey procured from Adams a narrative of the whole transaction of the mutiny, which
however is incorrect in many parts; and also a

history of the broils and disputes which led to the violent death of all these misguided men, (with the exception of Young and Adams,) who accompanied Christian in the Bounty to Pitcairn's Island.

It may be recollected that the Bounty was carried away from Otaheite by nine of the mutineers. Their names were

1. FLETCHER CHRISTIAN, Acting Lieutenant.
2. EDWARD YOUNG, Midshipman.
3. ALEXANDER SMITH (*alias* JOHN ADAMS), Seaman.
4. WILLIAM M'KOY
5. MATTHEW QUINTAL
6. JOHN WILLIAMS   } Seamen.
7. ISAAC MARTIN
8. JOHN MILLS, Gunner's Mate.
9. WILLIAM BROWN, Botanist's Assistant.

They brought with them six men and twelve women, natives of Tabouai and Otaheite. The first step after their arrival was to divide the whole island into nine equal portions, to the exclusion of those poor people whom they had seduced to accompany them, and some of whom are stated to have been carried off against their inclination. At first they were considered as the friends of the white men, but very soon became their slaves. They assisted in the cultivation of the soil, in building houses, and in fetching wood and water, without murmuring or complaining; and things went on peaceably and prosperously for about two years, when Williams, who had lost his wife about a month after their arrival, by a fall from a rock while collecting bird's eggs, became dissatisfied, and insisted on having another wife, or threatened to leave the island in one of the Bounty's boats. Being useful as an armourer, the Europeans were

unwilling to part with him, and he, still persisting
in his unreasonable demand, had the injustice to
compel one of the Otaheitans to give up his wife
to him.

By this act of flagrant oppression his countrymen made common cause with their injured companion, and laid a plan for the extermination of
the Europeans; but the women gave a hint of
what was going forward in a song, the burden
of which was, ' Why does black man sharpen
axe ?—to kill white man.' The plot being thus
discovered, the husband who had his wife taken
from him, and another whom Christian had shot
at (though, it is stated, with powder only), fled
into the woods, and were treacherously murdered
by their countrymen, on the promise of pardon
for the perpetration of this foul deed.

Tranquillity being thus restored, matters went on
tolerably well for a year or two longer; but the
oppression and ill-treatment which the Otaheitans
received, more particularly from Quintal and
M'Koy, the most active and determined of the
mutineers, drove them to the formation of another
plot for the destruction of their oppressors, which
but too successfully succeeded. A day was fixed
for attacking and putting to death all the Englishmen while at work in their respective plantations.
Williams was the first man that was shot. They
next proceeded to Christian, who was working at
his yam-plot, and shot him. Mills, confiding in
the fidelity of his Otaheitan friend, stood his
ground, and was murdered by him and another.
Martin and Brown were separately attacked and
slain, one with a maul, the other with a musket.

Adams was wounded in the shoulder, but succeeded in making terms with the Otaheitans; and
was conducted by them to Christian's house, where
he was kindly treated.   Young, who was a great
favourite of the women, was secreted by them
during the attack, and afterwards carried to Christian's house.   M'Koy and Quintal, the worst of
the gang, escaped to the mountains.   ' Here,'
says Captain Beechey, ' this day of bloodshed
ended, leaving only four Englishmen alive out of
nine.   It was a day of emancipation to the blacks,
who were now masters of the island, and of hu-
miliation and retribution to the whites.'

The men of colour now began to quarrel about
choosing the women whose European husbands
had been murdered ; the result of which was the
destruction of the whole of the former, some fall-
ing by the hands of the women, and one of them by
Young, who it would seem coolly and deliberately
shot him.   Adams now proceeded into the mountains to communicate the fatal intelligence to the
two Europeans, M'Koy and Quintal, and to solicit their return to the village.   All these events
are stated to have happened so early as October,
1793.

From this time to 1798, the remnant of the
colonists would appear to have gone on quietly
with the exception of some quarrels these four
men had with the women, and the latter among
themselves ; ten of them were still remaining, who
lived promiscuously with the men, frequently
changing their abode from one house to another.
Young, being a man of some education, kept a
kind of journal, but it is a document of very little

interest, containing scarcely anything more than the ordinary occupations of the settlers, the loan or exchange of provisions, the dates when the sows farrowed, the number of fish caught, &c., and it begins only at the time when Adams and he were sole masters of the island; and the truth, therefore, of all that has been told rests solely on the degree of credit that is due to Adams.

M'Koy, it appears, had formerly been employed in a Scotch distillery, and being much addicted to ardent spirits, set about making experiments on the *tee-root* (*dracæna terminalis*), and at length unfortunately succeeded in producing an intoxicating liquor. This success induced his companion Quintal to turn his kettle into a still. The consequence was, that these two men were in a constant state of drunkenness, particularly M'Koy, on whom, it seems, it had the effect of producing fits of delirium; and in one of these he threw himself from a cliff and was killed on the spot. Captain Beechey says, ' the melancholy fate of this man created so forcible an impression on the remaining few, that they resolved never again to touch spirits; and Adams has, I believe, to this day kept his vow.'

Some time in the following year, that is, about 1799, ' we learned from Adams,' says Captain Beechey, ' that Quintal lost his wife by a fall from the cliff, while in search of bird's eggs ; that he grew discontented, and, though there were several disposable women on the island, and ' he had already experienced the fatal effects of a similar demand, nothing would satisfy him but the wife of one of his companions. Of course neither of them

x

felt inclined to accede to this unreasonable demand; and he sought an opportunity of putting
them both to death. He was fortunately foiled
in his first attempt, but swore openly he would
speedily repeat it. Adams and Young having no
doubt he would follow up his intention, and fearing he might be more successful in the next attempt, came to the resolution that, as their own
lives were not safe while he was in existence, they
were justified in putting him to death, which they
did by felling him, as they would an ox, with a
hatchet.

' Such was the melancholy fate of seven of the
leading mutineers, who escaped from justice only
to add murder to their former crimes ;' and such,
it may be added, was the polluted source, thus
stained with the guilt of mutiny, piracy, and murder, from which the present simple and innocent
race of islanders has proceeded ; and what is most
of all extraordinary, the very man, from whom
they have received their moral and religious instruction, is one who was among the first and
foremost in the mutiny, and deeply implicated in
all the deplorable consequences that were the
results of it.   This man and Young were now the
sole survivors out of the fifteen males that had
landed upon the island. Young, as has been stated,
was a man of some education, and of a serious
turn of mind, and, as Beechey says, it would have
been wonderful, after the many dreadful scenes at
which they had assisted, if the solitude and tranquillity that ensued had not disposed them to repentance.   They had a Bible and a Prayer Book,
which were found in the Bounty, and they read

the Church Service regularly every Sunday. They now resolved to have morning and evening family prayers, and to instruct the children, who amounted to nineteen, many of them between the ages of seven and nine years. Young, however, was not long suffered to survive his repentance. An asthmatic complaint terminated his existence about a year after the death of Quintal; and Adams was now left the sole survivor of the guilty and misguided mutineers of the Bounty. It is remarkable that the name of Young should never once occur in any shape as connected with the mutiny, except in the evidence of Lieutenant Hayward, who includes his name in a mass of others. He neither appears among the armed nor the unarmed; he is not stated to be among those who were on deck, and was probably therefore one of those who were confined below. Bligh, nevertheless, has not omitted to give him a character. ' Young was an able and stout seaman ; he, however, always proved a worthless wretch.'

If the sincere repentance of Adams, and the most successful exertions to train up the rising generation in piety and virtue, can be considered as expiating in some degree his former offences, this survivor is fully entitled to every indulgence that frail humanity so often requires, and which indeed has been extended to him, by all the officers of the .navy who have visited the island, and witnessed the simple manners, and the settled habits of morality and piety which prevail in this happy and well-regulated society. They have all strongly felt that the merits and redeeming qualities of the latter years of his life have so far atoned for his former guilt, that he ought not to be molested, but rather encouraged, in his meritorious efforts, if not for his own sake, at least for that of the innocent young people dependent on him.

Still it ought never to be forgotten that he was one of the first and most daring in the atrocious act of mutiny and piracy, and that, had he remained in Otaheité, and been taken home in the Pandora, nothing could have saved him from an ignominious death. His pretending to say that he was in his cot, and that he was forced to take arms, may perhaps be palliated under his peculiar circumstances, wishing to stand as fair before his countrymen as his case would admit—but it is not strictly true; for he was the third upon deck armed, and stood sentry over Bligh with a loaded musket and fixed bayonet. The story he told to Beechey respecting the advice stated to have been given by Mr. Stewart to Christian, ' to take possession of the ship,' is, as has been shown, wholly false ; but here his memory may have failed him. If any such advice was given, it is much more likely to have proceeded from Young. He also told two different stories with regard to the conduct of Christian. To Sir Thomas Staines and Captain Pipon, he represented this ill-fated young man as never happy, after the rash and criminal step he had taken, and that he was always sullen and morose, and committed so many acts of cruelty, as to incur the hatred and detestation of his associates in crime. Whereas he told Captain Beechey, that Christian was always cheerful ; that his example was of the greatest service in exciting

his companions to labour ; that he was naturally
of a happy, ingenuous disposition, and won the
good opinion and respect of all who served under
him : which cannot be better exemplified, he says,
than by his maintaining, under circumstances of
great perplexity, the respect and regard of all who
were associated with him, up to the hour of his
death ; and that, even at the present moment,
Adams, in speaking of him, never omits to say
Mr. Christian. Why indeed should he? Christian was a gentleman by birth, and an officer in
his Majesty's service, and was of course always
so addressed. But why was he murdered within
two years (one account says nine months) after
the party reached the island? Captain Beechey has
answered the question—for oppression and ill-
treatment of the Otaheitans*.

* As the manner of Christian's death has been differently
reported to each different visiter, by Adams, the only evidence in existence, with the exception of three or four Otaheitan women, and a few infants, some singular circumstances may here be mentioned that happened at home,
just at the time of Folger's visit, and which might render
his death on Pitcairn's island almost a matter of doubt.
About the years 1808 and 1809, a very general opinion
was prevalent in the neighbourhood of the lakes of Cum-
berland and Westmorland, that Christian was in that part
of the country, and made frequent private visits to an aunt
who was living there. Being the near relative of Mr.
Christian Curwen, long member of Parliament for Carlisle,
and himself a native, he was well known in the neighbourhood. This, however, might be passed over as mere gossip,
had not another circumstance happened just about the
same time, for the truth of which the Editor does not hesitate to avouch.
In Fore-Street, Plymouth Dock, Captain Heywood found
himself one day walking behind a man, whose shape had so

That Christian, so far from being cheerful,
was, on the contrary, always uneasy in his mind
about his own safety, is proved by his having
selected a cave at the extremity of the high
ridge of craggy hills that runs across the island,
as his intended place of refuge, in the event
of any ship of war discovering the retreat of
the mutineers, in which cave he resolved to sell
his life as dearly as he could. In this recess he
always kept a store of provisions, and near it
erected a small hut, well concealed by trees, which
served the purpose of a watch-house. ' So difficult,' says Captain Beechey, ' was the approach
to this cave, that even if a party were successful
in crossing the ridge, he might have bid defiance,
as long as his ammunition lasted, to any force.'

much the appearance of Christian's, that he involuntarily
quickened his pace. Both were walking very fast, and the
rapid steps behind him having roused the stranger's attention, he suddenly turned his face, looked at Heywood,
and immediately ran off. But the face was as much like
Christian's as the back, and Heywood, exceedingly excited,
ran also. Both ran as fast as they were able, but the
stranger had the advantage, and, after making several
short turns, disappeared.

That Christian should be in England, Heywood considered as highly improbable, though not out of the scope of
possibility ; for at this time no account of him whatsoever had
been received since they parted at Otaheité ; at any rate
the resemblance, the agitation, and the efforts of the
stranger to elude him, were circumstances too strong not to
make a deep impression on his mind. At the moment, his
first thought was to set about making some further enqui-
ries, but on recollection of the pain and trouble such a discovery must occasion him, he considered it more prudent to
let the matter drop ; but the circumstance was frequently
called to his memory for the remainder of his life.

The reflection alone of his having sent adrift, to perish on the wide ocean, for he could entertain no other idea, no less than nineteen persons, all of whom, one only excepted, were innocent of any offence towards him, must have constantly haunted his mind, and left him little disposed to be happy and cheerful.

The truth is, as appears in Morrison's journal, that during the short time they remained at Ta-bouai, and till the separation of the mutineers at Otaheité, when sixteen forsook him, and eight only, of the very worst, accompanied him in quest of some retreat, he acted the part of a tyrant to a much greater extent than the man who, he says, drove him to the act of mutiny. After giving an account of the manner of his death, Captain Beechey says, ' Thus fell a man who, from being the reputed ringleader of the mutiny, has obtained an unenviable celebrity, and whose crime may perhaps be considered as, in some degree, palliated by the tyranny which led to its commission.' It is to be hoped, such an act as he was guilty of will never be so considered.

If mutiny could be supposed to admit of palliation, a fatal blow would be struck not only at the discipline, but at the very existence, of the navy; any relaxation in bringing to condign punishment persons guilty of mutiny, would weaken and ultimately destroy the efficiency of this great and powerful machine. Nor, indeed, is it at all necessary that the punishment for mutiny should admit of any palliation. Whenever an act of tyranny, or an unnecessary degree of severity, is exercised by a commanding officer, let the fact only be proved, and he is certain to be visited with all the rigour that the degree of his oppressive conduct will warrant. Had Christian but waited patiently the arrival of the Bounty in England, and the alleged conduct of Bligh towards his officers and crew had been proved, he would, unquestionably, have been dismissed from his Majesty's service.

With regard to Adams, though his subsequent conduct was highly meritorious, and to him alone it might be said is owing the present happy state of the little community on Pitcairn's Island, his crime like that of Christian's can never be considered as wiped away. Sir Thomas Staines, the first British officer who called at the island, it may well be supposed, had to struggle, on this trying occasion, between duty and feeling. It was his imperative duty to have seized and brought him a prisoner to England, where he must have been tried, and would no doubt have been convicted of a crime for which several of his less active accomplices had suffered the penalty of death; though he might, and probably would, from length of time and circumstances in his favour, have received the king's pardon. Perhaps, however, on the whole, it was fortunate, that in balancing, as it is known this gallant officer did, between the sense of duty and the sense of feeling, the latter prevailed, and justice yielded to mercy. Had a Bligh or an Edwards been placed in his situation, it is to be feared that, judging from their former conduct, passion in the one, and frigidity in the other, would most likely have consigned the criminal to captivity in irons, and the innocent and helpless family, solely dependent on him, to misery and destruction—and yet, in so doing, they would not have deviated from their strict line of duty,—*Dîs aliter visum.*

The Blossom was the first ship of war that John Adams had been on board of since the mutiny; and, as Captain Beechey observes, his mind would naturally revert to scenes that could not fail to produce a temporary embarrassment, but no apprehension for his safety appeared to form any part of his thoughts; and as every person endeavoured to set his mind at rest, he soon found himself at ease and at home. It was several hours before the ship approached the shore, and the boats put off before she came to an anchor.

On account of the rocks and formidable breakers, the party who went on shore were landed by the young men, two at a time, in their whale boat. ' The difficulty of landing,' says Captain Beechey, ' was more than repaid by the friendly reception we met with on the beach from Hannah Young, a very interesting young woman, the daughter of Adams. In her eagerness to greet her father, she had outrun her female companions, for whose delay she thought it necessary, in the first place, to apologize, by saying they had all been over the hill in company with John Buffet to look at the ship, and were not yet returned. It appeared that John Buffet, who was a seafaring man, had ascertained that the ship was a man of war, and, without knowing exactly why, became so alarmed for the safety of Adams, that he either could not or would not answer any of

the interrogatories which were put to him. This
mysterious silence set all the party in tears, as they
feared he had discovered something adverse to
their patriarch. At length his obduracy yielded
to their entreaties; but before he explained the
cause of his conduct, the boats were seen to put
off from the ship, and Hannah immediately
hurried to the beach to kiss the old man's cheek,
which she did with a fervency demonstrative of
the warmest affection. Her apology for her companions was rendered unnecessary by their appearance on the steep and circuitous path down
the mountain, who, as they arrived on the beach,
successively welcomed us to their island, with a
simplicity and sincerity which left no doubt of the
truth of their professions.'

The whole group simultaneously expressed a
wish that the visiters would stay with them several
days; and on their signifying a desire to get to the
village before dark and to pitch the observatory,
every article and instrument found a bearer,
along a steep path which led to the village, concealed by groupes of cocoa-nut trees; the females bearing their burthens over the most difficult parts without inconvenience. The village
consisted of five houses, on a cleared piece of
ground sloping toward the sea. While the men
assisted in pitching the tent, the women employed
themselves in preparing the supper. The mode
of cooking was precisely that of Otaheité, by
heated stones in a hole made in the ground. At
young Christian's, the table was spread with
plates, knives and forks. John Buffet said grace
in an emphatic manner, and this is repeated every

time a fresh guest sits down while the meal is going on. So strict are they in this respect, that it is not deemed proper to touch a bit of bread without saying grace before and after it. ' On one occasion,' says Captain Beechey, ' I had engaged Adams in conversation, and he incautiously took the first mouthful without having said grace; but before he had swallowed it, he recollected himself, and feeling as if he had committed a crime, immediately put away what he had in his mouth, and commenced his prayer.' Their rooms and table are lighted up by torches made of *doodoe* nuts (*aleurites triloba*), strung upon the fibres of a palm-leaf, which form a good substitute for candles.

It is remarkable enough, that although the female part of the society is highly respected, yet, in one instance, a distinction is kept up, which in civilized countries would be deemed degrading. It is that which is rigidly observed in all the South Sea Islands, and indeed throughout almost the whole eastern world, that no woman shall eat in the presence of her husband ; and though this distinction between man and wife is not carried quite so far in Pitcairn's Island, it is observed to the extent of excluding all women from table, when there is a deficiency of seats. It seems they defended the custom on the ground that man was made before woman, and is entitled, therefore, to be first served—a conclusion, observes Beechey, ' that deprived us of the company of the women at table, during the whole of our stay at the island. Far, however, from considering themselves neglected, they very good-naturedly

chatted with us behind our seats, and flapped
away the flies, and by a gentle tap, accidentally or
playfully delivered, reminded us occasionally of
the honour that was done us.' The women, when
the men had finished, sat down to what remained.

The beds were next prepared. A mattress
composed of palm-leaves was covered with native
cloth made of the paper mulberry-tree, in the
same manner as in Otaheité; the sheets were of
the same material; and it appeared, from their
crackling, that they were quite new from the loom,
or rather the beater. The whole arrangement is
stated to have been comfortable, and inviting to repose; one interruption only disturbed their first
sleep; this was the melody of the evening hymn,
which, after the lights were put out, was chanted by
the whole family in the middle of the room. At
early dawn they were also awaked by their morning
hymn and the family devotion; after which the
islanders all set out to their several occupations.
Some of the women had taken the linen of their
visiters to wash; others were preparing for the
next meal; and others were employed in the manufacture of cloth.

The innocence and simplicity of these interesting young creatures are strongly exemplified in
the following description. ' By our bedside had
already been placed some ripe fruits; and our hats
were crowned with chaplets of the fresh blossom
of the *nono* or flower-tree (*Morinda citrifolia*),
which the women had gathered in the freshness
of the morning dew. On looking round the
apartment, though it contained several beds, we
found no partition, curtain, or screens; they had

Drawn & Etched by

I. Wale? Q.ⁿ S.^{tt} ay.

Residence of John Adams, Pitcairns Island.

From a Sketch by Lieut.^t Smith, of H.M.S. Blossom.

Published by John Murray, Albemarle Street, 1831.

not yet been considered necessary. So far, indeed, from concealment being thought of, when
we were about to get up, the women, anxious to
shew their attention, assembled to wish us good
morning, and to inquire in what way they could
best contribute to our comforts, and to present us
with some little gift, which the produce of the
island afforded. Many persons would have felt
awkward at rising and dressing before so many
pretty black-eyed damsels, assembled in the centre
of a spacious room; but by a little habit we over-
came this embarrassment, and from the benefit
of their services in fetching water as we required
it, and in substituting clean linen for such as we
pulled off.'

Their cottages are spacious, and strongly built
of wood, in an oblong form, and thatched with the
leaves of the palm-tree bent round the stem of a
branch from the same, and laced horizontally to
rafters, so placed as to give a proper pitch to the
roof. An upper story is appropriated to sleeping,
and has four beds, one in each angle of the room,
and large enough for three or four persons to
sleep on. The lower is the eating room, having
a broad table with several stools placed round it.
The lower room communicates with the upper, by
a stout ladder in the centre. Immediately round
the village are small enclosures for fattening pigs,
goats, and poultry; and beyond them are the cultivated grounds producing the banana, plantain,
melon, yam, taro, sweet potatoes, *tee*-tree, cloth-
plant, with other useful roots, fruits, and a variety
of shrubs. Every cottage has its out-house for
making cloth, its baking-place, its pig-sty, and its
poultry-house.

During the stay of the strangers on the island,
they dined sometimes with one person, and sometimes with another, their meals being always the
same, and consisting of baked pig, yams, and
taro, and sometimes sweet potatoes.   Goats are
numerous on the island, but neither their,flesh nor
their milk is relished by the natives.   Yams con-
stitute their principal food, either boiled, baked, or
mixed with cocoa-nut, made into cakes, and eaten
with molasses extracted from the tee-root.   Taro-
root is no bad substitute for bread ; and bananas,
plantains and *appoi*, are wholesome and nutritive
fruits.   The common beverage is water, but they
make tea from the tee-plant, flavoured with ginger,
and sweetened with the juice of the sugar-cane.
They but seldom kill a pig, living mostly on fruit
and vegetables.   With this simple diet, early rising,
and taking a great deal of exercise, they are subject to few diseases ; and Captain Beechey says,
' they are certainly a finer and more athletic race
than is usually found among the families of mankind.'

The young children are punctual in their attendance at school, and are instructed by John
Buffet in reading, writing, and arithmetic ; to
which are added, precepts of religion and morality, drawn chiefly from the Bible and Prayer
Book; than which, fortunately, they possess no
others that might mystify and perplex their un-
derstandings on religious subjects.   They seldom
indulge in jokes or other kinds of levity ; and
Beechey says, they are so accustomed to take
what is said in its literal meaning, that irony
was always considered a falsehood in spite of

explanation ; and that they could not see the
propriety of uttering what was not strictly true,
for any purpose whatever. The Sabbath is wholly
devoted to the church service, to prayer, reading,
and serious meditation ; no work of any kind is
done on that day, not even cooking, which is prepared on the preceding evening.

' I attended,' says Beechey, ' their church on
this day, and found the service well conducted ;
the prayers were read by Adams, and the lessons
by Buffet, the service being preceded by hymns.
The greatest devotion was apparent in every individual ; and in the children there was a seriousness
unknown in the younger part of our communities
at home. In the course of the Litany, they prayed
for their sovereign and all the royal family, with
much apparent loyalty and sincerity. Some family prayers, which were thought appropriate to
their own particular case, were added to the usual
service ; and Adams, fearful of leaving out any
essential part, read in addition all those prayers
which are intended only as substitutes for others.
A sermon followed, which was very well delivered
by Buffet ; and lest any part of it should be forgotten or escape attention, it was read three times.
The whole concluded with hymns, which were first
sung by the grown people, and afterwards by the
children. The service thus performed was very
long ; but the neat and cleanly appearance of the
congregation, the devotion that animated every
countenance, and the innocence and simplicity of
the little children, prevented the attendance from
becoming wearisome. In about half an hour
afterwards we again assembled to prayers, and at

sunset service was repeated; so that, with their
morning and evening prayers, they may be said
to have church five times on a Sunday.'

Perhaps it will be thought by some that they
carry their seriousness too far, and that the
younger people are not allowed a sufficient quantity of recreation. The exercise and amusement
of dancing, once so much resorted to in most
of the islands of the Pacific, is here almost excluded. With great difficulty and much entreaty,
the visiters prevailed on three grown-up ladies to
stand up to perform the Otaheitan dance, which
they consented to with a reluctance that showed
it was done only to oblige them. It was little
more than a shuffling of the feet, sliding past each
other, and snapping their fingers. They did not
long continue this diversion, considering it as too
great a levity, and only the three before-men-
tioned ladies could be prevailed on to exhibit their
skill. They appeared to have little taste for music
either instrumental or vocal. Adams, when on
board the Blossom for two or three days, made
no difficulty of joining in the dance and was remarkably cheerful, but on no occasion neglected
his usual devotions. Captain Beechey has no
doubt of the sincerity of his piety. He slept in
the same cabin, but would never get into his cot
until the captain was in bed, and supposed to be
asleep, when, in a retired corner of the cabin, he
fell on his knees and performed his devotions;
and he was always up first in the morning for the
same purpose.

This good old man told Beechey one day,
that it would add much to his happiness if he

would read the marriage ceremony to him and
his wife, as he could not bear the idea of living
with her without its being done, when a proper
opportunity should offer, as was now the case.
Though Adams was aged, and the old woman had
been blind and bedridden for several years,
Beechey says he made such a point of it, that it
would have been cruel to refuse him. They were
accordingly, the following day, duly united, and
the event noted in a register by John Buffet.
The marriages that take place among the young
people are, however, performed by Adams, who
makes use of a ring for such occasions, which has
united every couple on the island since its first
settlement; the regulated age under which no
man is allowed to marry is twenty, and that of the
woman eighteen. The restrictions with regard to
relationship are the same as with us, and are
strictly put in force when parties are about to
marry. Adams also officiates at christenings.

Captain Beechey observes, that these amiable
people rigidly adhere to their word and promise,
even in cases where the most scrupulous among
Europeans might think themselves justified in
some relaxation of them. Thus, George Adams,
in his early days, had fallen in love with Polly
Young, a girl somewhat older than himself; but
Polly, for some reason or other, had incautiously
declared, she *never would* give her hand to George
Adams; who, however, still hoped she would one
day relent, and of course was unremitting in his
endeavours to please her; nor was he mistaken;
his constancy and his handsome form, which
George took every opportunity of displaying

Y

before her, softened Polly's heart, and she would willingly have given him her hand. But the vow of her youth was not to be got over, and the love-sick couple languished on from day to day, victims to the folly of early resolutions. This weighty case was referred to the British officers, who decided that it would be much better to marry than to continue unhappy in consequence of a hasty resolution made before the judgment was matured; but Polly's scruples still remained, and those who gave their decision left them unmarried. Captain Beechey, however, has recently received a letter, stating that George Adams and Polly Young had joined hands and were happy; but the same letter announced the death of John Adams, which took place in March, 1829.

The demise of this old patriarch is the most serious loss that could have befallen this infant colony. The perfect harmony and contentment in which they appear to live together, the innocence and simplicity of their manners, their conjugal and parental affection, their moral, religious, and virtuous conduct, and their exemption from any serious vice, are all to be ascribed to the exemplary conduct and instructions of old John Adams; and it is gratifying to know, that five years after the visit of the Blossom, and one year subsequent to Adams's death, the little colony continued to enjoy the same uninterrupted state of harmony and contentment as before.

In consequence of a representation, made by Captain Beechey when there, of the distressed state of this little society, with regard to the want of certain necessary articles, his Majesty's government sent out to Valparaiso, to be conveyed from thence for their use, a proportion for sixty persons of the following articles : sailors' blue jackets and trowsers, flannel waistcoats, pairs of stockings and shoes, women's dresses, spades, mattocks, shovels, pickaxes, trowels, rakes; all of which were taken in his Majesty's ship Seringapatam, commanded by Captain the Hon. William Waldegrave, who arrived there in March, 1830.

The ship had scarcely anchored when George Young was alongside in his canoe, which he guided by a paddle ; and soon after Thursday October Christian, in a jolly-boat, with several others, who, having come on board, were invited to breakfast, and one of them said grace as usual both before and after it. The captain, the chaplain, and some other officers accompanied these natives on shore, and having reached the summit of the first level or plain, which is surrounded by a grove or skreen of cocoa-nut trees, they found the wives and mothers assembled to receive them. ' I have brought you a clergyman,' says the captain. ' God bless you,' issued from every mouth; ' but is he come to stay with us ? '—' No.' ' You bad man, why not ? '—' I cannot spare him, he is the chaplain of my ship ; but I have brought you clothes and other articles, which King George has sent you.' ' But,' says Kitty Quintal, ' we want food for our souls.'

' Our reception,' says Captain Waldegrave, ' was most cordial, particularly that of Mr. Watson, the chaplain ; and the meeting of the wives and husbands most affecting, exchanging expressions of joy that could not have been exceeded had they just returned from a long absence. The men sprang up to the trees, throwing down cocoa-nuts, the husks of which were torn off by others with their teeth, and offering us the milk. As soon as we had rested ourselves, they took us to their cottages, where we dined and slept.'

Captain Waldegrave says it was highly gratifying to observe their native simplicity of manners, apparently without guile: their hospitality was unbounded, their cottages being open to all, and all were welcome to such food as they possessed; pigs and fowls were immediately killed and dressed, and when the guests were seated, one of the islanders, in the attitude of prayer, and his eyes raised towards heaven, repeated a simple grace for the present food they were about to partake of, beseeching, at the same time, spiritual nourishment; at the end of which each responded *amen.* On the arrival of any one during the repast, they all paused until the new guest had said grace.

At night they all assembled in one of the cottages to hear the afternoon church service performed by Mr. Watson, and Captain Waldegrave describes it as a most striking scene. The place chosen was the bed-room of one of the double cottages, or one with an upper story. The ascent was by a broad ladder from the lower room through a trap-door. The clergyman took his station between two beds, with a lamp burning close behind him. In the bed on his right were three infants sound asleep; at the foot of that on his left were three men sitting. On each side and in front were the men, some wearing only the

simple mara, displaying their gigantic figures;
others in jackets and trowsers, their necks and
feet bare; behind stood the women, in their mo-
dest home-made cloth dresses, which entirely covered the form, leaving only the head and feet
bare. The girls wore, in addition, a sheet knotted in the manner of a Roman senator's *toga*,
thrown over the right shoulder and under the left
arm. When the general confession commenced,
they all knelt down facing the clergyman, with
their hands raised to the breast in the attitude of
prayer, slowly and distinctly repeating the confession after the clergyman. They prayed for the
King of England, whom they consider as their
sovereign. A sermon followed from a text which
Captain Waldegrave thinks was most happily
chosen : ' Fear not, little flock, for it is your
Father's good pleasure to give you the kingdom.'
At the conclusion of the service they requested
permission to sing their parting hymn, when the
whole congregation, in good time, sang ' Depart
in peace.'

Captain Waldegrave, like all former visiters,
bears testimony to the kind disposition and active
benevolence of these simple islanders. The children, he says, are fond and obedient, the parents
affectionate and kind towards their children. None
of the party ever heard a harsh word made use of
by one towards another. They never slander or
speak ill of one another. If any question was asked
as to the character or conduct of a particular individual, the answer would probably be something
of this kind, ' If it could do any good, I would
answer you ; but as it cannot, it would be wrong to

tell tales;' or if the question applied to one who
had committed a fault, they would say, ' It would
be wrong to tell my neighbour's shame.' The
kind and benevolent feeling of these amiable
people is extended to the surviving widows of the
Otaheite men who were slain on the island, and
who would be left in a helpless and destitute state,
were it not for the humane consideration of the
younger part of the society, by whom they are
supported and regarded with every mark of attention.

The women are clothed in white cloth made
from the paper mulberry, the dress extending from
the shoulders to the feet, in double folds, and so
loose as entirely to conceal the shape of the person.   The mothers, while nursing, carry the infant within their dress ; as the child advances in
growth it sits across the hip of the parent with its
little hands clinging to the shoulder, while the
mother's arm passing round it keeps it in safety.
The men and boys, except on Sunday, when they
appear in English dresses, generally wear only
the *mara,* or waist-cloth, which, passing over the
hips, and between the legs, is knotted behind;
the climate is in fact too hot for cumbersome clothing.   The women, when working, use only a pet-
ticoat, with a jacket.

The men are stated to be from five feet eight
inches to six feet high, of great muscular strength
and excellent figures. ' We did not see,' says
Captain Waldegrave, ' one cripple or defective
person, except one boy, whom, in the most good-
humoured way, and laughing heartily, they brought
to me, observing, "You ought to be brothers, you

have each lost the right eye." I acknowledged
the connexion, and no doubt for the future he
will be called the Captain.'

Captain Beechey has given a more detailed account of the physical qualities of the Pitcairn
Islanders. He says they are tall, robust, and
healthy; their average height five feet ten inches;
the tallest man measured six feet and one quarter
of an inch, and the shortest of the adults five feet
nine inches and one-eighth ; their limbs well pro-
portioned, round and straight ; their feet turning
a little inwards. A boy of eight years measured
four feet and one inch ; another of nine years, four
feet three inches. Their simple food and early
habits of exercise give them a muscular power
and activity not often surpassed. It is recorded
on the island that George Young and Edward
Quintal have each carried, at one time, a kedge
anchor, two sledge hammers, and an armourer's
anvil, weighing together upwards of six hundred
pounds; and that Quintal once carried a boat
twenty-eight feet in length. In the water they
are almost as much at home as on land, and can
remain almost a whole day in the sea. They frequently swim round their little island, the circuit
of which is at the least seven miles ; and the
women are nearly as expert swimmers as the men.

The female descendants of the Otaheité women
are almost as muscular as the males, and taller
than the generality of the sex. Polly Young, who
is not the tallest on the island, measured five feet
nine inches and a half. The features of both men
and women are regular and well-formed ; eyes
bright and generally hazel, though in a few in-

stances blue ; the eyebrows thin and rarely meeting ; the nose a little flattened, and being rather
extended at the nostrils, partakes of the Otaheitan
character, as do the lips, which are broad and
strongly sulcated; their ears moderately large,
and the lobes are invariably united with the cheek;
they are generally perforated, when young, for the
reception of flowers, a very common custom
among the natives of the South Sea Islands; hair
black, sometimes curling, sometimes straight;
teeth regular and white. On the whole they are
a well-looking people.

Captain Beechey says, the women have all
learned the art of midwifery ; that parturition generally takes place during the night-time ; that
the duration of labour is seldom longer than five
hours, and has not yet in any case proved fatal;
but there is no instance of twins, nor of a single
miscarriage, except from accident. Infants are
generally bathed three times a day in cold water,
and are sometimes not weaned for three or four
years; but when that does takes place, they are
fed upon ' popoe,' made of ripe plantains and
boiled taro-root rubbed into a paste. Mr. Collie,
the surgeon of the Blossom, remarks that nothing
is more extraordinary, in the history of the island,
than the uniform good health of the children ; the
teething is easily got over, they have no bowel
complaints, and are exempt from those conta-
gious diseases which affect children in large communities. He offered to vaccinate the children as
well as all the grown persons ; but they deemed
the risk of infection of small-pox to be too small
to render that operation necessary.

As a proof how very much simple diet and constant exercise tend to the healthful state of the body, the skin of these people, though in such robust health, compared with that of the Europeans, always felt cold, and their pulses always considerably lower. The doctor examined several of them: in the forenoon he found George Young's only sixty; three others, in the afternoon, after dinner, were sixty-eight, seventy-two, and seventy-six, while those of the officers who stood the heat of the climate best were above eighty.

It is impossible not to feel a deep interest in the welfare of this little society, and at the same time an apprehension that something may happen to disturb that harmony and destroy that simplicity of manners which have hitherto characterized it. It is to be feared, indeed, that the seeds of discord are already sown. It appears from Captain Waldegrave's statement, that no less than three Englishmen have found their way into this happy society. One of them, John Buffet, mentioned by Beechey, is a harmless man, and, as it has been stated, of great use to the islanders in his capacity of clergyman and schoolmaster; he is also a clever and useful mechanic, as a shipwright and joiner, and is much beloved by the community. Two others have since been left on the island, one of them, by name John Evans, son of a coach-maker in the employ of Long of St. Martin's Lane, who has married a daughter of John Adams, through whom he possesses and cultivates a certain portion of land; the third is George Hunn Nobbs, who calls himself pastor, registrar, and schoolmaster, thus infringing on the privileges of John

Buffet; and being a person of superior talents, and
of exceeding great impudence, has deprived Buffet of a great number of his scholars; and hence
a sufficient cause exists of division and dissension
among the members of the little society, which
were never known before.   Buffet and Evans
support themselves by their industry, but this
Nobbs not only claims exemption from labour as
being their pastor, but also as being entitled to a
maintenance at the expense of the community.
He has married a daughter of Charles, and grand-
daughter to the late Fletcher, Christian, whose
descendants, as captain of the gang, might be
induced to claim superiority, and which, probably,
might be allowed by general consent, had they
but possessed a moderate share of talent; but it is
stated that Thursday October and Charles Christian, the sons of the chief mutineer, are ignorant,
uneducated men.   The only chance for the continuance of peace is the general dislike in which
this Nobbs is held, and the gradual intellectual
improvement of the rising generation*.

It seems that Adams on his death-bed called all
the heads of families together, and urged them to
appoint a chief;—this, however, they have not

* This Nobbs is probably one of those half-witted persons who fancy they have received a *call* to preach nonsense—some cobler escaped from his stall, or tailor from
his shopboard. Kitty Quintal's cant phrase—' we want
food for our souls,' and praying at meals for ' spiritual nourishment,' smack not a little of the jargon of the inferior
caste of evangelicals. Whoever this pastoral drone may be,
it is but too evident that the preservation of the innocence,
simplicity, and happiness of these amiable people, is intimately connected with his speedy removal from the island.

done, which makes it the more to be apprehended that Nobbs, by his superior talent or cunning, will force himself upon them into that situation. Captain Waldegrave thinks, however, that Edward Quintal, who possesses the best understanding of any on the island, will in time arrive at that honour; his only book is the Bible, but it is quite astonishing, he observes, what a fund of knowledge he has derived from it. His wife, too, is stated to be a woman of excellent understanding; and their eldest boy, William, has been so carefully educated, that he excels greatly all the others. The descendants of Young are also said to be persons generally of promising abilities.

How the patriarch Adams contrived to instil into the minds of these people the true principles of religion and morality is quite surprising. He was able to read, but only learnt to write in his latter days; and having accomplished this point, he made a scheme of laws by which he succeeded to govern his little community in the way we have seen. The celebration of marriage and baptism were strictly observed, according to the rites of the Church of England, but he never ventured on confirmation and the sacrament of the Lord's Supper. He taught the children the Church catechism, the ten commandments, the Lord's prayer, and the Creed, and he satisfied himself, that in these were comprized all the Christian duties. By the instrumentality of these precepts, drawn from the book of Common Prayer and the Bible*, he was enabled, after the slaughter

* Well may Adams have sought for rules for his little society in a book, which contains the foundation of the civil

of all his associates, to rear up all the children in the principles and precepts of Christianity, in purity of morals, and in a simplicity of manners, that have surprised and delighted every stranger that has visited the island.

Captain Waldegrave says they are so strongly attached to those beautiful prayers that are found in the liturgy of the Church of England, that there is no danger of a dissenting minister being received among them. It is to be hoped this may be the case; but it may be asked, will they escape from the snares of George Hunn Nobbs? It would seem, indeed, that this man has already thrust upon them what he calls a code of laws, in which he enumerates crimes, such as murder and adultery, unknown and unheard of among these simple people since the time that Adams was sole legislator and patriarch. The punishment of adultery, to give a specimen of Nobbs's legislation, is whipping for the first offence to both parties, and

and religious policy of two-thirds of the human race,—in that wonderful book, into whose inspired pages the afflicted never seek for consolation in vain. Millions of examples attest this truth. ' There is no incident in Robinson Crusoe,' observes a writer in a critical journal, ' told in language more natural and affecting, than Robert Knox's accidental discovery of a Bible, in the midst of the Candian dominions of Ceylon. His previous despondency from the death of his father, his only friend and companion, whose grave he had but just dug with his own hands, " being now," as he says, " left desolate, sick, and in captivity,"—his agitation, joy, and even terror, on meeting with a book he had for such a length of time not seen, nor hoped to see—his anxiety lest he should fail to procure it—and the comfort, when procured, which it afforded him in his affliction—all are told in such a strain of true piety and genuine simplicity. as cannot fail to interest and affect every reader of sensibility.'

marriage within three months; for the second, if
the parties refuse to marry, the penalties are, forfeiture of lands, property, and banishment from
the island. Offenders are to be tried before three
elders, who pronounce sentence. It is quite clear
this silly person does not understand what is
meant by adultery. As to the tenure of land, it
is fortunately provided for previous to his arrival
on the island. The whole island, it seems, was
partitioned out by Adams among the families of
the original settlers, so that a foreigner cannot
obtain any, except by purchase or marriage. Captain Waldegrave reckons, that eleven-twelfths are
uncultivated, and that population is increasing so
rapidly, that in the course of a century the island
will be fully peopled, and that the limit may be
taken at one thousand souls.

The rate at which population is likely to increase may, perhaps, be determined by political
economists from the following data.

In 1790 the island was first settled by fifteen
men and twelve women, making a total of twenty-
seven. Of these were remaining in 1800, one
man and five women, with nineteen children, the
eldest nine years of age, making in the whole
twenty-five. In 1808, Mr. Folger makes the
population amount to thirty-five, being an increase
of ten in eight years. In 1814, six years afterwards, Sir Thomas Staines states the *adult* population at forty, which must be a mistake, as fourteen years before, nineteen of the twenty-five
then existing were children. In 1825, Captain
Beechey states the whole population at sixty-six,
of whom thirty-six were males, and thirty females.

And in 1830, Captain Waldegrave makes it amount to seventy-nine ; being an increase of thirteen in five years, or twenty per cent., which is a less rapid increase than might be expected ; but there can be little doubt it will go on with an accelerated ratio, provided the means of subsistence should not fail them.

Captain Waldegrave's assumption, that this island is sufficiently large for the maintenance of one thousand souls, is grounded on incorrect data ; it does not follow, that because one-twelfth of the island will maintain eighty persons, the whole must support nine hundred and sixty persons. The island is not more than four square miles, or two thousand five hundred and sixty acres ; and as a ridge of rocky hills runs from north to south, having two peaks exceeding one thousand feet in height, it is more than probable that not one half of it is capable of cultivation. It would seem, indeed, from several ancient morais being discovered among these hills ; some stone axes or hatchets of compact basaltic lava, very hard and capable of a fine polish ; four stone images, about six feet high, placed on a platform, not unlike those on Easter Island, one of which has been preserved, and is the rude representation of the human figure to the hips, hewn out of a piece of red lava :—these remains would seem to indicate a former population, that had found it expedient to abandon the island from its insufficiency to support it. Captain Beechey observes, that 'from these images and the large piles of stones, on heights to which they must have been dragged with great labour, it may be concluded that the island was inhabited for a considerable time; and from bones being found, always buried under these piles, and never upon the surface, we may presume that those who survived, quitted the island in their canoes to seek an asylum elsewhere.'

It appears from Beechey, that Adams had contemplated the prospect of an increasing population with the limited means of supporting it, and requested that he would communicate with the British Government upon the subject, which he says he did, and that, through the interference of the Admiralty and Colonial Office, means have been taken for removing them to any place they may choose for themselves. It is to be hoped, however, that no such interference will take place; for half a century, at least, there is no danger of any want of food. The attempt, however, was made through the means of a Mr. Nott, a missionary of Otaheite, who, being on a visit to this country, was authorized, on his return, to make arrangements for their removal to Otaheite, if they wished it, and if Pomarré, the king of the island, should not object to receive them; and he carried a letter to this chief from Lord Bathurst, acquainting him with the intention of the British Government, and expressing the hope that he would be induced to receive under his protection a people whose moral and religious character had created so lively an interest in their favour; but it fortunately happened that this missionary passed the island without stopping. A Mr. Joshua Hill subsequently proposed their removal to New South Wales, but his vessel was considered too small for the purpose.

Two years after this, as difficulties had occurred to prevent the above-mentioned intentions from being carried into effect, Sir George Murray deemed it desirable that no time should be lost in affording such assistance to these islanders as might, at all events, render their present abode as comfortable as circumstances would allow, *until* arrangements could be made for their future disposal, either in one of the Society Islands, as originally proposed, or at one of our settlements on New Holland. The assistance here alluded to has been afforded, as above mentioned, by his Majesty's ship Seringapatam.

It is sincerely to be hoped that such removal will be no longer thought of. No complaint was made, no apprehension of want expressed to Captain Waldegrave, who left them contented and happy; and Captain Beechey, since his return, has received a letter from John Buffet, who informs him of a notification made by Nott the missionary at Otaheite, that the king was willing to receive them, and that measures would be taken for their removal; but, he adds, the people are so much attached to, and satisfied with, their native island, as not to have a wish to leave it. The breaking up of this happy, innocent, and simple-minded little society, by some summary process, and consigning them to those sinks of infamy on New Holland or Van Diemen's Land, or to mix them up with the dram-drinkers, the psalm-singers, and the languid and lazy Otaheitans, would, in either case, be a subject of deep regret to all who take an interest in their welfare; and to themselves would be the inevitable loss of all those amiable qualities which have obtained for them the kind and generous sympathy of their countrymen at home. We have a person who acts as consul at Otaheite, and it is to be hoped he will receive instructions, on no account to sanction, but on the contrary to interdict, any measure that may be attempted on the part of the missionaries for their removal;—perhaps, however, as money would be required for such a purpose, they may be considered safe from that quarter.

The time must come when they will emigrate on their own accord. When the hive is full, they will send out their swarms. Captain Beechey tells us that the reading of some books of voyages and travels, belonging to Bligh and left in the Bounty, had created a desire in some of them to leave it; but that family ties and an ardent affection for each other, and for their native soil, had always interposed, on the few occasions that offered, to prevent individuals going away singly. George Adams, however, who had failed when the Blossom was there to soften the heart of Polly Young, and had no wife to detain him, was very anxious to embark in that ship, that he might see something of the world beyond the narrow limits of his own little island; and Beechey would have taken him, had not his mother wept bitterly at the idea of parting from him, and wished to impose terms touching his return to the island, that could not be acceded to.

Pitcairn Island lies at the south-eastern extremity of a chain of islands, which, including the Society and Friendly Islands, exceed a hundred in number, many of them wholly uninhabited, and the

z

rest but thinly peopled, all speaking the same or
nearly the same language, which is also spoken
by the natives of Pitcairn Island; and all of the
two groupes are richly clothed with the spontaneous products of nature fit for the use of man.
To all these they will have, when necessity
prompts them, easy means of access. No large
vessels are required for an emigration of this
kind; the frailest barks and single canoes have
been driven hundreds of miles over the Pacific.
The Pitcairners have already proceeded from the
simple canoe to row-boats, and the progress from
this to small decked vessels is simple and natural.
They may thus at some future period, which is not
at all improbable, be the means of spreading
Christianity and consequently civilization throughout the numerous groupes of islands in the Southern Pacific; whereas to remove them, as has been
imprudently suggested, would be to devote them
at once to misery and destruction.

That there is no deficiency in the number and
variety of plants, producing food and clothing for
the use of man, will appear from the following
list, which is far from being complete:

INDIGENOUS.

Cocos nucifera	Cocoa-nut.
Musa Paradisiaca . . .	Plantains.
Musa sapientum . . .	Bananas.
Dioscorea sativum . . .	Yams.
Convolvulus batatas . .	Sweet potatoes.
Arum esculentum . . .	Taro root.
Arum costatum	Yappa.
Broussonetia papyrifera .	Cloth-tree.
Dracœna terminalis . . .	*Tee*-plant.
Aleurites triloba	Doodoe.

Morinda citrifolia . . .	Nono.
———————— . . .	Toonena, a large tim-. ber tree.
Ficus indica	Banyan-tree.
Morus Chinensis. . . .	Mulberry.
Pandanus odoratissimus ?	

And a great number of other indigenous plants, some of which are useful and others ornamental.

INTRODUCED.

Artocarpus incisa . . .	Bread-fruit.
Cucurbita citrullus . . .	Water-melons.
Cucurbita pepo	Pumpkins.
Solanum esculentum . .	Potatoes.
Nicotiana tabaccum . . .	Tobacco.
Citrus lemoneum. . . .	Lemon.
——— *aurantium* . . .	Orange.

Besides these they have European peas, beans, and onions; sugar-canes, ginger, pepper, and turmeric. In fact, situated as the island is, in a temperate climate just without the tropic, and enjoying abundance of rain, there is scarcely any vegetable, with the exception of a few of the equinoxial plants, that may not be cultivated here. The zea mays, or Indian corn, would be infinitely useful both for themselves, their poultry, and their pigs.

As a great part of the island is at present covered with trees, which would necessarily give way to an extended cultivation, and as trees attract rain, Captain Waldegrave seems to think that when these are removed showers will be less frequent; but there is little fear of this being the case; the central 'ridge, with points that exceed eleven hundred feet in height, will more effectually attract and condense the clouds than any

z 2

quantity of trees growing at a less elevation; and
there can be little doubt that plenty of water will
be found by digging at the foot of the hills or
close to the sea-coast.

The climate appears to be unexceptionable. During the sixteen days of December (the height of
summer) that the Blossom remained there, the
range of the thermometer on the island, from nine
in the morning till three in the afternoon, was
from 76° to 80°; on board ship from 74° to 76°;
from whence Captain Beechey places the mean
temperature during that time at 76½. In winter
he says the south-westerly winds blow very cold,
and even snow has been known to fall.

Not one visiter to this happy island has taken
leave of its amiable inhabitants without a feeling
of regret. Captain Beechey says, ' When we
were about to take leave, our friends assembled
to express their regret at our departure. All
brought some little present for our acceptance,
which they wished us to keep in remembrance of
them; after which they accompanied us to the
beach, where we took our leave of the female part
of the inhabitants. Adams and the young men
pushed off in their own boat to the ship, determined to accompany us to sea, as far as they
could with safety. They continued on board, unwilling to leave us, until we were a considerable
distance from land, when they shook each of us
feelingly by the hand, and, amidst expressions of
the deepest concern at our departure, wished us a
prosperous voyage, and hoped that we might one
day meet again. As soon as they were clear of
the ship, they all stood up in their boat, and gave

us three hearty cheers, which were as heartily returned. As the weather became foggy, the barge towed them towards the shore, and we took a final leave of them, unconscious, until the moment of separation, of the warm interest their situation and good conduct had created in us.'

Happy, thrice happy people! May no improper intruders thrust themselves into your peaceful and contented society! May that Providence which has hitherto protected you, still continue to pour down those blessings upon you, of which you appear to be so truly sensible, and for which you are justly thankful! May it throw round the shores of your enviable little Eden, ' cherubim and a flaming sword,' to guard its approaches from those who would endanger your peace; and above all, shield you from those who would perplex and confuse your unsophisticated minds, by mysterious doctrines which they do not themselves comprehend! Remain stedfast to the faith, which your late father and benefactor has instilled into your minds, culled from the precepts of your Bible, and be content for the present to observe those simple rules for your religious and moral conduct, which he has taught you, and which he drew pure and undefiled from that sacred source; and be assured that, so long as you shall adhere to the line of conduct you have hitherto pursued, and be contented with your present lot, your happiness is secure; but once admit ignorant or false teachers among you, and from that period you may date the commencement of misfortunes and misery!

CONCLUSION.

MANY useful and salutary lessons of conduct may be drawn from this eventful history, more especially by officers of the navy, both old and young, as well as by those subordinate to them. In the first place, it most strongly points out the dreadful consequences that are almost certain to ensue from a state of insubordination and mutiny on board a ship of war ; and the equally certain fate that, at one time or other, awaits all those who have the misfortune to be concerned in a transaction of this revolting nature. In the present instance, the dreadful retribution which overtook them, and which was evinced in a most extraordinary manner, affords an awful and instructive lesson to seamen, by which they may learn, that although the guilty may be secured for a time in evading the punishment due to the offended laws of society, yet they must not hope to escape the pursuit of Divine vengeance. It will be recollected that the number of persons who remained in the Bounty, after her piratical seizure, and of course charged with the crime of mutiny, was twenty-five ; that these subsequently separated into two parties, sixteen having landed at Otaheite, and afterwards taken from thence in the Pandora, as prisoners, and nine having gone with the Bounty to Pitcairn's Island.

Of the sixteen taken in the Pandora :—

1. Mr. PETER HEYWOOD, midshipman, was sentenced to death, but pardoned.
2. JAMES MORRISON, boatswain's mate,   do.   do.
3. WILLIAM MUSPRATT, commander's steward, do.   do.
4. THOS. BURKITT, seaman,
5. JOHN MILLWARD, do. } condemned and executed.
6. THOS. ELLISON, do.
7. JOSEPH COLEMAN, armourer,
8. CHARLES NORMAN, carpenter's mate, } tried   and   ac-
9. THOS. M'INTOSH, carpenter's crew, } quitted.
10. MICHAEL BYRNE, seaman,
11. Mr. GEORGE STEWART, midshipman, } drowned in irons
12. JOHN SUMNER, seaman, } when the Pan-
13. RICHARD SKINNER, seaman, } dora was
14. HENRY HILLBRANT, cooper. } wrecked.
15. CHAS. CHURCHILL, master-at-arms, murdered by Matthew Thompson.
16. MATTHEW THOMPSON, seaman, murdered by Churchill's friends in Otaheité.

Of the nine who landed on Pitcairn's Island :—

1. Mr. FLETCHER CHRISTIAN, acting-lieut.
2. JOHN WILLIAMS, seaman, } were murdered
3. ISAAC MARTIN, do. } by the Ota-
4. JOHN MILLS, gunner's mate, } heitans.
5. WILLM. BROWN, botanist's assistant,
6. MATTHEW QUINTAL, seaman, put to death by Young and Adams in self-defence.
7. WILLIAM M'KOY, seaman, became insane, and killed by throwing himself from a rock.
8. Mr. EDWARD YOUNG, midshipman, died of asthma.
9. ALEX. SMITH, *alias* John Adams, seaman, died in 1829.

Young officers of the navy, as well as the common seamen, may also derive some useful lessons from the events of this history. They will see the melancholy results of affording the least encouragement for seamen to depart from their strict line of duty, and to relax in that obedience to the orders of superiors, by which alone the discipline of the service can be preserved; they will learn how dangerous it is to show themselves careless and indifferent in executing those orders, by thus setting a bad example to the men. It ought also to enforce on their minds, how necessary it is to avoid even the appearance of acting in any way that can be considered as repugnant to, or subversive of, the rules and regulations of the service; and most particularly to guard against any conduct that may have the appearance of lowering the authority of their superiors, either by their words or actions.

No doubt can remain on the minds of unprejudiced persons, or such as are capable of weighing evidence, that the two young midshipmen, Stewart and Heywood, were perfectly innocent of any share in the transaction in question; and yet, because they happened to be left in the ship, not only contrary to their wish and intention, but kept down below by force, the one lost his life, by being drowned in chains, and the other was condemned to die, and only escaped from suffering the last penalty of the law by a recommendation to the royal mercy. The only point in which these two officers failed, was, that they did not at once demand permission to accompany their commander, while they were allowed to remain on deck and had the opportunity of doing so. The manly conduct of young Heywood, throughout his long and unmerited sufferings, affords an example of firmness, fortitude, and resignation to the divine will, that is above all praise; in fact, nothing short of conscious innocence could have supported him in the severe trials he had to undergo.

The melancholy effects which tyrannical conduct, harsh and opprobrious language, ungovernable passion, and a worrying and harassing temper, on the part of naval commanders, seldom fail to produce on the minds of those who are subject to their capricious and arbitrary command, are strongly exemplified in the cause and consequences of the mutiny in the Bounty, as described in the course of this history. Conduct of this kind, by making the inferior officers of a ship discontented and unhappy, has the dangerous tendency, as in the case of Christian, to incite the crew to partake in their discontent, and be ready to assist in any plan to get rid of the tyrant. We may see in it, also, how very little credit a commander is likely to gain, either with the service or the public at large, when the duties of a ship are carried on, as they would appear to have been in the Pandora, in a cold, phlegmatic, and unfeeling manner, and with an indifference to the comfort of all around him,—subjecting offenders of whatever description to unnecessary restraint, and a severity of punishment, which, though strictly within the letter of the law, contributes in no way to the ends of discipline or of justice.

The conduct of Bligh, however mistaken he may have been in his mode of carrying on the duties of the ship, was most exemplary throughout the long and perilous voyage he performed in an open boat, on the wide ocean, with the most scanty supply of provisions and water, and in the worst weather. The result of such meritorious

conduct holds out every encouragement to both
officers and men, by showing them that, by firmness and perseverance, and the adoption of well-
digested measures, steadily pursued in spite of
opposition, the most hopeless undertaking, to all
appearance, may be successfully accomplished.

And lastly—The fate that has attended almost
every one of those concerned in the mutiny and
piracy of his Majesty's ship Bounty ought to
operate as a warning to, and make a deep impression on the minds of, our brave seamen, not to
suffer themselves to be led astray from the straight-
forward line of their duty, either by order or persuasion of some hot-brained, thoughtless, or designing person, whether their superior or equal,
but to remain faithful, under all circumstances, to
their commanding officer, as any mutinous proceedings or disobedience of his orders are sure to be
visited upon them in the long run, either by loss of
life, or by a forfeiture of that liberal provision
which the British government has bestowed on its
seamen for long and faithful services.

P.S. Just as this last sheet came from the
press, the editor has noticed, with a feeling of
deep and sincere regret, a paragraph in the news-
papers, said to be extracted from an American
paper, stating that a vessel sent to Pitcairn's
Island by the missionaries of Otaheité has carried off the whole of the settlers to the latter
island. If this be true—and the mention of the

name of Nott gives a colour to the transaction
—the ' cherubim' must have slept, the ' flaming
sword' have been sheathed, and another Eden
has been lost : and, what is worse than all, that
native simplicity of manners, that purity of morals, and that singleness of heart, which so peculiarly distinguished this little interesting society,
are all lost. They will now be dispersed among
the missionary stations as humble dependents,
where Kitty Quintal and the rest of them may
get ' food for their souls,' such as it is, in exchange for the substantial blessings they enjoyed
on Pitcairn's Island.

ADDITIONAL NOTE.

IN reference to the subject of extraordinary passages made in open boats on the wide ocean, and the note thereon at page 121, the following may be added as another instance, the most painfully interesting, and the most calamitous, perhaps, ever recorded. It was related to Mr. Bennet, a gentleman deputed by the Missionary Society of London, together with the Rev. Daniel Tyerman, to visit their several stations in the South Sea Islands, by Captain George Pollard, the unfortunate sufferer, whom these gentlemen met with at Raiatea, then a passenger in an American vessel, having a second time lost his ship near the Sandwich Islands. The narrative is extracted from 'The Journal of Voyages and Travels,' just published, of the two gentlemen above-mentioned, and is as follows:—

' My first shipwreck was in open sea, on the 20th of November, 1820, near the equator, about 118° W. long. The vessel, a South Sea whaler, was called the Essex. On that day, as we were on the look out for sperm whales, and had actually struck two, which the boats' crews were following to secure, I perceived a very large one—it might be eighty or ninety feet long—rushing with great swiftness through the water, right towards the ship. We hoped that she would turn aside, and dive under, when she perceived such a baulk in her way. But no! the animal came full force against

our stern-post : had any quarter less firm been
struck, the vessel must have been burst ; as it was,
every plank and timber trembled, throughout her
whole bulk.

' The whale, as though hurt by a severe and
unexpected concussion, shook its enormous head,
and sheered off to so considerable a distance that
for some time we had lost sight of her from the starboard quarter ; of which we were very glad, hoping
that the worst was over. Nearly an hour afterwards, we saw the same fish—we had no doubt of
this, from her size, and the direction in which she
came—making again towards us. We were at
once aware of our danger, but escape was impossible. She dashed her head this time against the
ship's side, and so broke it in that the vessel filled
rapidly, and soon became water-logged. At the
second shock, expecting her to go down, we
lowered our three boats with the utmost expedition, and all hands, twenty in the whole, got into
them—seven, and seven, and six. In a little
while, as she did not sink, we ventured on board
again, and, by scuttling the deck, were enabled
to get out some biscuit, beef, water, rum, two sex-
tants, a quadrant, and three compasses. These,
together with some rigging, a few muskets, powder, &c., we brought away ; and, dividing the
stores among our three small crews, rigged the
boats as well as we could ; there being a compass
for each, and a sextant for two, and a quadrant
for one, but neither sextant nor quadrant for the
third*. Then, instead of pushing away for some

* If there were *three* instruments and *three* boats, there
must have been *one* for *each*, for the quadrant was just as
good as a sextant.—ED.

port, so amazed and bewildered were we that we continued sitting in our places gazing upon the ship, as though she had been an object of the tenderest affection. Our eyes could not leave her, till, at the end of many hours, she gave a slight reel, then down she sank. No words can tell our feelings. We looked at each other—we looked at the place where she had so lately been afloat —and we did not cease to look, till the terrible conviction of our abandoned and perilous situation roused us to exertion, if deliverance were yet possible.

' We now consulted about the course which it might be best to take—westward to India, eastward to South America, or south-westward to the Society Isles. We knew that we were at no great distance from Tahiti, but were so ignorant of the state and temper of the inhabitants, that we feared we should be devoured by cannibals, if we cast ourselves on their mercy. It was determined, therefore, to make for South America, which we computed to be more than two thousand miles distant. Accordingly we steered eastward, and though for several days harassed with squalls, we contrived to keep together. It was not long before we found that one of the boats had started a plank, which was no wonder, for whale-boats are all clinker-built, and very slight, being made of half-inch plank only, before planing. To remedy this alarming defect we all turned to, and having emptied the damaged boat into the two others, we raised her side as well as we could, and succeeded in restoring the plank at the bottom. Through this accident, some of our biscuit had become injured by the salt-water.

This was equally divided among the several boats' crews. Food and water, meanwhile, with our utmost economy, rapidly failed. Our strength was exhausted, not by abstinence only, but by the labours which we were obliged to employ to keep our little vessels afloat amidst the storms which repeatedly assailed us. One night we were parted in rough weather; but though the next day we fell in with one of our companion-boats, we never saw or heard any more of the other, which probably perished at sea, being without either sextant or quadrant *.

'When we were reduced to the last pinch, and out of everything, having been more than three weeks abroad, we were cheered with the sight of a low, uninhabited island, which we reached in hope, but were bitterly disappointed. There were some barren bushes and many rocks on this forlorn spot. The only provisions that we could procure were a few birds and their eggs: this supply was soon reduced; the sea-fowls appeared to have been frightened away, and their nests were left empty after we had once or twice plundered them. What distressed us most was the utter want of fresh water; we could not find a drop anywhere, till, at the extreme verge of ebb tide, a small spring was discovered in the sand; but even that was too scanty to afford us sufficient to quench our thirst before it was covered by the waves at their turn.

'There being no prospect but that of starvation here, we determined to put to sea again. Three

* The mistake is here again repeated; it would be absurd to suppose that one boat had both quadrant and sextant.

of our comrades, however, chose to remain, and
we pledged ourselves to send a vessel to bring
them off, if we ourselves should ever escape to a
Christian port. With a very small morsel of biscuit for each, and a little water, we again ventured
out on the wide ocean. In the course of a few
days our provisions were consumed. Two men
died; we had no other alternative than to live
upon their remains. These we roasted to dryness
by means of fires kindled on the ballast-sand at
the bottom of the boats *. When this supply was
spent, what could we do? We looked at each
other with horrid thoughts in our minds, but we
held our tongues. I am sure that we loved one
another as brothers all the time; and yet our
looks told plainly what must be done. We cast
lots, and the fatal one fell on my poor cabin-boy.
I started forward instantly, and cried out, "My
lad, my lad, *if you don't like your lot*, I'll shoot
the first man that touches you." The poor ema-
ciated boy hesitated a moment or two; then,
quietly laying his head down upon the gunnel of
the boat, he said, "*I like it as well as any
other.*" He was soon despatched, and nothing
of him left. I think, then, another man died
of himself, and him, too, we ate. But I can
tell you no more—my head is on fire at the recollection; I hardly know what I say. I forgot
to say that we had parted company with the second boat before now. After some more days of
horror and despair, when some were lying down
at the bottom of the boat not able to rise, and

* It is not explained with what kind of fuel they performed this distressing operation.

scarcely one of us could move a limb, a vessel
hove in sight. We were taken on board, and
treated with extreme kindness. The second lost
boat was also picked up at sea, and the survivors
saved. A ship afterwards sailed in search of our
companions on the desolate island, and brought
them away.'

Captain Pollard closed his dreary narrative
with saying, in a tone of despondency never to be
forgotten by him who heard it, ' After a time I
found my way to the United States, to which I
belonged, and got another ship. That, too, I
have lost by a second wreck off the Sandwich
Islands, and now I am utterly ruined. No owner
will ever trust me with a whaler again, for all will
say I am an *unlucky* man.'

The following account respecting the three men
that were left on the uninhabited island, is given
in a note of the same work, and said to be extracted from a religious tract, No. 579, issued by
the Society in Paternoster-row.

' On the 26th of December the boats left the
island : this was, indeed, a trying moment to all :
they separated with mutual prayers and good
wishes, seventeen* venturing to sea with almost
certain death before them, while three remained
on a rocky isle, destitute of water, and affording hardly anything to support life. The prospects of these three poor men were gloomy :
they again tried to dig a well, but without suc-

* Here, again, is another mistake; the number must
have been *eleven* at most, one of the boats having parted
before the others reached the island.—ED.

2 A

cess, and all hope seemed at an end, when
providentially they were relieved by a shower
of rain.   They were thus delivered from the
immediate apprehension of perishing by thirst.
Their next care was to procure food, and their
difficulties herein were also very great ; their
principal resource was small birds, about the size
of a blackbird, which they caught while at roost.
Every night they climbed the trees in search of
them, and obtained, by severe exertions, a scanty
supply, hardly enough to support life.   Some of
the trees bore a small berry which gave them a
little relief, but these they found only in small
quantities.   Shell-fish they searched for in vain ;
and although from the rocks they saw at times a
number of sharks, and also other sorts of fish,
they were unable to catch any, as they had no
fishing tackle.   Once they saw several turtles, and
succeeded in taking five, but they were then without water : at those times they had little inclination to eat, and before one of them was quite
finished the others were become unfit for food.
    ' Their sufferings from want of water were the
most severe, their only supply being from what
remained in holes among the rocks after the
showers which fell at intervals ; and sometimes
they were five or six days without any ; on these
occasions they were compelled to suck the blood
of the birds they caught, which allayed their thirst
in some degree ; but they did so very unwil-
lingly, as they found themselves much disordered
thereby.
    ' Among the rocks were several caves formed
by nature, which afforded shelter from the wind

and rain. In one of these caves they found eight human skeletons, in all probability the remains of some poor mariners who had been shipwrecked on the isle, and perished for want of food and water. They were side by side, as if they had laid down and died together! This sight deeply affected the mate and his companions; their case was similar, and they had every reason to expect ere long the same end: for many times they lay down at night, with their tongues swollen and their lips parched with thirst, scarcely hoping to see the morning sun; and it is impossible to form an idea of their feelings when the morning dawned, and they found their prayers had been heard and answered by a providential supply of rain.

' In this state they continued till the 5th of April following. On the morning of that day they were in the woods as usual, searching for food and water, as well as their weakness permitted, when their attention was aroused by a sound which they thought was distant thunder; but looking towards the sea, they saw a ship in the offing, which had just fired a gun. Their joy at this sight may be more easily imagined than described; they immediately fell on their knees, and thanked God for his goodness, in thus sending deliverance when least expected; then, hastening to the shore, they saw a boat coming towards them. As the boat could not approach the shore without great danger, the mate, being a good swimmer, and stronger than his companions, plunged into the sea, and providentially escaped a watery grave at the moment when deliverance was at hand. His companions crawled out further on the rocks, and, by the great exertions of the crew, were taken into the boat, and soon found themselves on board the Surrey, commanded by Captain Raine, by whom they were treated in the kindest manner, and their health and strength were speedily restored.'

Mr. Montgomery, the editor, observes, ' there is some incongruity in these two narratives, which more minute particulars might reconcile.' We have noticed them. Mr. Bennet received the account verbally, and may be mistaken in some points, but there is little doubt of its being substantially correct.

This melancholy history supplies an additional and complete answer to Bligh's doubts of men feeding on each other to preserve existence.

THE END.